WHO LOSES IN THE DOWNTURN? ECONOMIC CRISIS, EMPLOYMENT AND INCOME DISTRIBUTION

RESEARCH IN LABOR ECONOMICS

Series Editor: Solomon W. Polachek

IZA Co-Editor: Konstantinos Tatsiramos

Volume 23: Accounting for Worker Well-Being
Edited by Solomon W. Polachek

Volume 24: The Economics of Immigration and Social Diversity
Edited by Solomon W. Polachek, Carmel Chiswick and Hillel Rapoport

Volume 25: Micro-Simulation in Action
Edited by Olivier Bargain

Volume 26: Aspects of Worker Well-Being
Edited by Solomon W. Polachek and Olivier Bargain

Volume 27: Immigration: Trends, Consequences and Prospects For The United States
Edited by Barry R. Chiswick

Volume 28: Work Earnings and Other Aspects of the Employement Relation
Edited by Solomon W. Polachek and Konstantinos Tatsiramos

Volume 29: Ethnicity and Labor Market Outcomes

Volume 30: Jobs, Training, and Worker Well-Being
Edited by Solomon W. Polachek and Konstantinos Tatsiramos

RESEARCH IN LABOR ECONOMICS   VOLUME 32

WHO LOSES IN THE DOWNTURN? ECONOMIC CRISIS, EMPLOYMENT AND INCOME DISTRIBUTION

EDITED BY

HERWIG IMMERVOLL

*Organisation for Economic Co-operation and Development
(OECD), Paris, France and IZA, Bonn, Germany*

ANDREAS PEICHL

IZA, Bonn, Germany

KONSTANTINOS TATSIRAMOS

IZA, Bonn, Germany

IZA

Emerald

United Kingdom – North America – Japan
India – Malaysia – China

Emerald Group Publishing Limited
Howard House, Wagon Lane, Bingley BD16 1WA, UK

First edition 2011

Copyright © 2011 Emerald Group Publishing Limited

Reprints and permission service
Contact: booksandseries@emeraldinsight.com

No part of this book may be reproduced, stored in a retrieval system, transmitted in any
form or by any means electronic, mechanical, photocopying, recording or otherwise
without either the prior written permission of the publisher or a licence permitting
restricted copying issued in the UK by The Copyright Licensing Agency and in the USA
by The Copyright Clearance Center. No responsibility is accepted for the accuracy of
information contained in the text, illustrations or advertisements. The opinions expressed in
these chapters are not necessarily those of the Editor or the publisher.

British Library Cataloguing in Publication Data
A catalogue record for this book is available from the British Library

ISBN: 978-0-85724-749-0
ISSN: 0147-9121 (Series)

Emerald Group Publishing
Limited, Howard House,
Environmental Management
System has been certified by
ISOQAR to ISO 14001:2004
standards

Awarded in recognition of
Emerald's production
department's adherence to
quality systems and processes
when preparing scholarly
journals for print

INVESTOR IN PEOPLE

CONTENTS

LIST OF CONTRIBUTORS   *vii*

PREFACE   *ix*

RECENT TRENDS IN INCOME INEQUALITY:
LABOR, WEALTH AND MORE COMPLETE
MEASURES OF INCOME
    Timothy M. Smeeding and Jeffrey P. Thompson   *1*

CONSUMPTION AND INCOME POVERTY OVER
THE BUSINESS CYCLE
    Bruce D. Meyer and James X. Sullivan   *51*

PATTERNS OF EMPLOYMENT DISADVANTAGE
IN A RECESSION
    Richard Berthoud and Lina Cardona Sosa   *83*

JOB FLOWS, DEMOGRAPHICS, AND THE
GREAT RECESSION
    Eva Sierminska and Yelena Takhtamanova   *115*

THE IMPACT OF THE GREAT RECESSION ON THE
ITALIAN LABOUR MARKET
    Francesco D'Amuri   *155*

REVERSED ROLES? WAGE AND EMPLOYMENT
EFFECTS OF THE CURRENT CRISIS
    Lutz Bellmann and Hans-Dieter Gerner   *181*

THE ECONOMIC CRISIS, PUBLIC SECTOR PAY AND
THE INCOME DISTRIBUTION
    Tim Callan, Brian Nolan and John Walsh   *207*

AUTOMATIC STABILIZERS, ECONOMIC CRISIS AND
INCOME DISTRIBUTION IN EUROPE
   Mathias Dolls, Clemens Fuest and Andreas Peichl   227

ECONOMIC DOWNTURN AND STRESS TESTING
EUROPEAN WELFARE SYSTEMS
   Francesco Figari, Andrea Salvatori and Holly   257
   Sutherland

LIST OF CONTRIBUTORS

Lutz Bellmann	University of Erlangen-Nuremberg, Erlangen, Germany
Richard Berthoud	Institute for Social and Economic Research (ISER), University of Essex, Essex, UK
Tim Callan	Economic and Social Research Institute (ESRI), Dublin, Ireland
Lina Cardona Sosa	Department of Economics, University of Essex, Essex, UK
Francesco D'Amuri	Bank of Italy, Italy; Institute for Social and Economic Research (ISER), University of Essex, Essex, UK
Mathias Dolls	University of Cologne, Cologne, Germany
Francesco Figari	Institute for Social and Economic Research (ISER), University of Essex, Essex, UK; University of Insubria, Italy
Clemens Fuest	Centre for Business Taxation, University of Oxford, Oxford, UK
Hans-Dieter Gerner	Institute for Employment Research (IAB), Nuremberg, Germany
Bruce D. Meyer	Harris School of Public Policy Studies, University of Chicago, Chicago, IL, USA
Brian Nolan	School of Applied Social Science, University College Dublin, Dublin, Ireland
Andreas Peichl	Institute for the Study of Labor (IZA), Bonn, Germany

Andrea Salvatori	Institute for Social and Economic Research (ISER), University of Essex, Essex, UK
Eva Sierminska	CEPS/INSTEAD Research Institute, Luxembourg, Luxembourg; DIW Berlin, Germany
Timothy M. Smeeding	Institute for Research on Poverty, Robert M. La Follette School of Public Affairs, University of Wisconsin Madison, WI, USA
James X. Sullivan	Department of Economics, University of Notre Dame, Notre Dame, IN, USA
Holly Sutherland	Institute for Social and Economic Research (ISER), University of Essex, Essex, UK
Yelena Takhtamanova	Federal Reverse Bank of San Francisco, San Francisco, CA, USA
Jeffrey P. Thompson	Political Economy Research Institute, University of Massachusetts Amherst, MA, USA
John Walsh	Economic and Social Research Institute (ESRI), Dublin, Ireland

PREFACE

Macroeconomic shocks such as the recent global economic crisis can have far-reaching effects on the levels and the distribution of resources at the individual and the household levels. A recession associated with a labor market downturn and turbulent property and financial markets gives rise to significant and widespread losses for workers and households. Identifying the likely pattern of losses is, however, not straightforward. This is especially the case at the outset of a severe recession, when up-to-date information about current household circumstances is patchy, and economic conditions are subject to rapid change.

For instance, in most cases, the data needed for detailed distributional analyses are two years or more out-of-date. This is a big drawback in periods characterized by volatile markets and quickly changing policy settings. Although it is possible to make informed guesses about the groups that are likely to be hardest hit, more detailed distributional studies are largely backward-looking and, as such, not directly useful for informing crisis response policies.

The lack of detailed knowledge about the incidence of losses hampers the identification of effective and timely policy responses that seek to alleviate adverse effects on households. There can also be a risk that, without regular assessments of the likely incidence of job and earnings losses, distributional concerns might carry insufficient weight in the debate about crisis-response measures.

This volume contains new results on how the economic downturn affects employment and the distribution of well-being. It contains nine original research papers that were presented at the IZA/OECD Workshop "Economic Crisis, Rising Unemployment and Policy Responses: What Does It Mean for the Income Distribution?" in Paris in February 2010. The different chapters shed light on what drives the distributional impact of severe labor market downturns in Europe and the United States.[1] The chapters offer insights into issues such as how consumption and income poverty change over the business cycle, how wages, employment, and incomes are affected by the crisis, which demographic groups are most vulnerable in the recession, and how well existing welfare provisions protect the newly unemployed.

Several of the chapters give illustrations of forward-looking simulation methods, providing scenarios of distributional outcomes before detailed data on actual household experiences become available.

In many countries, including the United States, the recent recessionary period follows a well-documented medium-term trend toward a more unequal income distribution.[2] In these cases, an important question is whether the recent downturn will exacerbate long-running trends toward higher inequality. In Chapter 1, Timothy Smeeding and Jeffrey Thompson use an extraordinarily comprehensive income concept to trace inequality trends over the 1989–2007 period. Their measure of "more complete income" (MCI) extends the standard disposable-income concept by adding incomes that accrue from the ownership of different types of wealth (stocks, bonds, mutual funds, home-equity, residential real estate, and business assets). Notably, the analysis seeks to include unrealized capital gains, which are particularly sizable among high-income groups. Using different sources of the most recent aggregate and micro-data, the authors then project MCI components to 2009 to investigate how changes in overall income, and its components, may have driven distributional outcomes during the "Great Recession." The findings illustrate that *overall* measured inequality need not necessarily go up during recessions, even if there are large losses for some of the poorest income groups. MCI-based income inequality appears to have peaked in 2007, with some measures of inequality declining at the top of the MCI distribution and significant losses of real-estate owners in the middle of the distribution (capital shares, which are an important driver of incomes at the top, have declined back to 2004 levels following the economic crisis, after increasing from 1989 to 2007). However, despite a projected decline from the 2007 peak, results suggest that overall income inequality in the United States in 2009 remains much higher than at most points during the past 20 years.

In Chapter 2, Bruce Meyer and James Sullivan zoom in on US trends at the bottom of the distribution and how they are associated with macroeconomic conditions. Past movements of poverty measures over the business cycle are of particular interest because they provide clues about the challenges facing households and policymakers in the current downturn. On a more fundamental level, the strength of the relationship between poverty and economic growth is at the very heart of controversies about the effectiveness of alternative antipoverty strategies. If growth and employment are associated with substantial poverty reduction, then this strengthens the case for pursuing growth-friendly policies, whereas policies that inhibit growth would be costly not only on aggregate, but for poor households in particular. Using income and consumption data from 1960 to 2008, Meyer and Sullivan employ different concepts of income and consumption poverty, which go beyond official US "pretax" poverty measures, and enable them to provide an unusually rich account of the situation of economically vulnerable households. They find that a 1 percentage point increase in unemployment is associated with an increase in the after-tax income poverty rate of 0.9–1.1 percentage points, and an increase in the consumption poverty rate of 0.3–1.2 percentage points. If extrapolated to the recent downturn, these estimates would indicate a very large possible increase in poverty. However, the results in this chapter also show that, in the United States, the relationship between economic conditions and poverty has been highly unstable over the past 50 years. This raises some doubts about the usefulness of extrapolating results from previous downturns and underlines the need to analyze the current downturn more specifically.

Chapter 3 explicitly takes up the question to what extent experiences of different population groups in previous recessions are useful for estimating how they are likely to fare in the current downturn. Using household survey data for the United Kingdom covering a 32-year period, Richard Berthoud and Lina Cardona Sosa ask whether the effects observed in earlier business cycles are likely to be repeated in the current crisis. The authors analyze the impact of cyclical factors on overall employment patterns and the extent to which different population groups are affected. Importantly, the multivariate logistic regression analysis considers changes in both unemployment and labor market inactivity and therefore captures withdrawals from the labor force resulting from the increase in the number of discouraged workers that are associated with extended periods of slack labor markets. A key question is whether groups that are already disadvantaged are especially susceptible to job loss in a downturn. The authors then use recent data to test how far the experience of previous business cycles is being repeated in the current recession. In terms of the incidence of employment reductions, the predicted patterns are consistent with observed ones for a number of groups: men, younger people, and those with low qualifications are all shown to have been more sensitive to cyclical trends in the demand for labor in past recessions as well as in the most recent one. However, patterns observed for ethnic minorities in earlier periods are not repeated, and the regional concentration of employment losses is different as well. Interestingly, the results also suggest that there is not necessarily a "vicious cycle of disadvantage," in the sense that those already facing labor market disadvantage would be most likely to face additional problems when jobs are scarce. For instance, findings by gender, age, and disability status indicate that, while the extent of disadvantage differs substantially between groups, existing disadvantage appears to be stable across business cycles.

Chapter 4 by Eva Sierminska and Yelena Takhtamanova also examines the severity of this recession compared to previous ones. However, it goes beyond an analysis of static employment status by looking at worker flows into and out of unemployment and, hence, throwing light on the drivers of increasing joblessness. The authors employ the US Current Population Survey spanning over six decades to measure transitions into and out of unemployment for different groups, showing the extent to which job losses and job finding rates differ by age, gender, and race. During the recent downturn, up until the end of 2009, men are found to have faced higher job separation probabilities as well as lower job finding probabilities than women. Across all groups, job-finding probabilities in the United States during the most recent recession exhibited their biggest ever drop from peak to trough. In addition, job separation probabilities showed one of the largest increases in the postwar period. The recent increases in unemployment rates are driven to a larger extent by the lack of hiring (low outflows). But flows into unemployment are nonetheless very important for understanding unemployment rate dynamics. In particular, the authors find that inflows into unemployment are not as acyclical as part of the literature suggests.

Like the previous chapter for the US, Francesco D'Amuri shows in Chapter 5 that the recession significantly reduced hirings and increased lay-offs also in Italy. Employing the same methodological framework and using data from the Italian Labor Force Survey to estimate transition equation into and out of unemployment, he finds that the recession had a negative impact both on job finding and on job separation probabilities. As may be expected in the highly segmented Italian labor market, the latter is found to differ substantially by type of contract. Employees on fixed-term contracts experienced the biggest increases in separation rates, whereas employees on open-ended contracts appeared to be largely immune to higher unemploy-ment risks. As Italian workers on fixed-term contracts are very often not eligible for unemployment benefits, this pattern raises concerns about the income protection for job losers. D'Amuri then uses the estimated transition probabilities to simulate the likely evolution of the distribution of labor *earnings* in 2010 by means of multiple stochastic imputations, taking into account the flow into and out of unemployment for different groups of workers. On the basis of the predicted changes in the composition of the labor force, and the increase in unemployment, the results indicate rising earnings inequality. However, this change appears to be driven almost entirely by the increasing number of unemployed. Despite a large number of transitions into and out of employment, the author does not find evidence for changing with-group inequality among the employed (probably because most of the transitions concern lower paid workers on fixed-term contracts).

Although movements into and out of employment are important drivers of overall earnings inequality, recessions also affect the earnings of those who manage to keep their jobs (or move from one job to another). Chapter 6 by Lutz Bellmann and Hans-Dieter Gerner analyzes the balance of employment and earnings changes in Germany. Unlike in Anglo-Saxon and Southern European countries, the economic crisis in Germany has resulted in unusually and, to many, surprisingly small movements in overall employment rates. Instead, many firms sought to retain workers and reduce labor costs by adjusting the earnings of existing employees. As, also in contrast to other countries, the effects of the crisis were largely restricted to export-oriented industries, such adjustments were particularly important in those sectors. A particular question concerns wage levels as one possible driver of earnings adjustments: did wage reductions among high-skilled workers counteract the precrisis trend in Germany toward increasing earnings inequality? Using detailed establishment-level data for the private sector, the authors find that although aggregate employment was stable, establishments affected by the economic crisis *did* in fact reduce employment levels significantly. Furthermore, the results indicate that the economic crisis was associated with declining wages. However, wages appear not to have been a primary adjustment channel in establishments that could easily reduce labor costs by reducing working hours (e.g., those operating working-time accounts). In sum, the authors find no evidence of a reversal of relative wage trends as a result of the crisis. Instead, it appears that the low-skilled have faced more sizable losses than better-qualified groups of workers.

The economic crisis not only impacts on private sector pay but can also put extreme pressure on public spending as fiscal deficits soar. In Chapter 7, Tim Callan, Brian Nolan, and John Walsh analyze the consequences for the income distribution of cutting public-sector pay using a microsimulation model for Ireland. In Ireland, labor costs in the public sector constitute one of the most important elements of public expenditure. As is well known, Ireland has also faced a particularly severe fiscal crisis and ballooning fiscal deficits. Next to tax-benefit reforms, innovative measures have already been implemented to claw back pay from public-sector workers. In addition to redistribution policies, public-sector pay and employment are the most direct levers for governments to change household income, with potentially sizable consequences for the overall distribution of incomes. The authors analyze three rounds of tax-benefit policy responses, as well as the subsequent public-sector pay cuts. The results provide some useful pointers for other countries facing the challenge of reducing large fiscal deficits. Tax-benefit policy changes announced in three budgets in 2009 and 2010 are found to result in large income losses for the bottom income decile, while they are mainly inequality-reducing for all income groups above the bottom 10%. On top of these changes, public-sector pay cuts have reduced the pay of many of the affected workers by several percentage points, and by significantly more than 10% for some high-earning public-sector employees. Interestingly, the adjustment burden has not been shared with retired public-sector workers, whose pension entitlements were protected. The central finding regarding these pay cuts is that they reduced inequality, both because public employees are predomi-nantly located in the middle and upper parts of the income distribution and because pay reductions were progressive, with much higher cuts for better-paid individuals. The authors suggest that, with the precrisis public-sector pay premia now reversed into public-sector penalties, there are limits to the scope for further pay cuts along similar lines.

A crucial determinant of the immediate budgetary implications of a recession, as well as of household income losses, is the design of tax-benefit policies. In Chapter 8, Mathias Dolls, Clemens Fuest, and Andreas Peichl analyze to what extent tax benefit systems in 19 different EU countries provide protection for households at different income levels. The authors use the multicountry microsimulation model EUROMOD to investigate the responsiveness of household taxes and benefits to two stylized shocks on market income and employment. They ask what part of the shock is absorbed by public policies automatically, that is, how much automatic stabilization is provided by different tax benefit systems. Although this is not a forecasting exercise, the approach provides forward-looking scenarios to understand potential distributional implications of the crisis. Dolls, Fuest, and Peichl show that the extent to which households are protected differs across income levels and countries. A key finding is that a proportional income shock leads to a reduction in inequality whereas distributional implications of asymmetric unemployment shocks crucially depend on who is most affected by rising unemployment. Using subgroup decompositions, the authors show that different countries place unequal weights on the income insurance provided for different groups. In particular, there is little stabilization for low-income groups in Eastern and Southern Europe whereas the opposite is true for the majority of Nordic and continental European countries. A principal reason is the rather low coverage of out-of-work benefits in the former group of countries.

The final chapter by Francesco Figari, Andrea Salvatori, and Holly Sutherland undertakes an in-depth analysis of the role of social protection systems, and especially unemployment benefits, as a means of income insurance for the newly unemployed. Their "stress test" of welfare states focuses on five EU countries and, like the previous chapter, also uses the EUROMOD tax-benefit model. The chapter provides evidence on the differing degrees of resilience of household incomes of the newly unemployed. This variation is not only due to different tax-benefit policies but also due to the household context of the unemployed person. The highest degree of income insurance is provided in countries with contribution-financed unemployment benefits. However, the major source of income protection is not provided by the government but by other household members with earnings. Unsurprisingly, if no other household incomes are present, household incomes fall much lower as a proportion of precrisis income. This highlights the importance of facilitating households' shock-adjustment capabilities, for example, by strengthening female employment. Furthermore, the authors show the correlation of the degree of income insurance with the resulting effect on government budgets. In particular, costs per unemployed person rises with precrisis income level. Interestingly, it is not benefit expenditures, but the income taxes and social contributions lost through unemployment, which are the main drivers of overall budgetary costs.

Income and labor-market micro-data covering the entire recession period will soon become available. With these data, it will be possible to analyze the distributional consequences of the crisis in more detail than is possible at the outset of a recession. Together with the early evidence in this volume, ex-post analysis of later and more comprehensive information on households' crisis experiences will allow assessing the strengths and weaknesses of the different forward-looking approaches presented here. The aim of such validation exercises should be to further refine the methods available for providing timely advice on the effectiveness of different policy responses to the next downturn.

As with past volumes, we aimed to focus on important policy and methodological issues and to maintain the highest levels of scholarship. We encourage readers who have prepared manuscripts that meet these stringent standards to submit them to *Research in Labor Economics* (RLE) through the IZA website (http://www.iza.org/rle) for possible inclusion in future volumes. We thank all referees for insightful editorial advice in preparing this volume.

NOTES

1. The views expressed are entirely those of the authors. In particular, they do not represent the official opinions of the OECD or of individual member countries.

2. OECD, 2008, *Growing Unequal? Income Distribution and Poverty in OECD Countries*, OECD Publishing, Paris.

Herwig Immervoll
Andreas Peichl
Konstantinos Tatsiramos
Editors

RECENT TRENDS IN INCOME INEQUALITY: LABOR, WEALTH AND MORE COMPLETE MEASURES OF INCOME

Timothy M. Smeeding and Jeffrey P. Thompson

ABSTRACT

The impact of the "Great Recession" on inequality is unclear. Because the crises in the housing and stock markets and mass job loss affect incomes across the entire distribution, the overall impact on inequality is difficult to determine. Early speculation using a variety of narrow measures of earnings, income, and consumption yield contradictory results. In this chapter, we develop new estimates of income inequality based on "more complete income" (MCI), which augments standard income measures with those that are accrued from the ownership of wealth. We use the 1989–2007 Surveys of Consumer Finances, and also construct MCI measures for 2009 based on projections of assets, income, and earnings.

We investigate the level and trend in MCI inequality and compare it to other estimates of overall and "high incomes" in the literature. Compared to standard measures of income, MCI suggests higher levels of inequality and slightly larger increases in inequality over time. Several MCI-based inequality measures peaked in 2007 at their highest levels in 20 years.

Who Loses in the Downturn? Economic Crisis, Employment and Income Distribution
Research in Labor Economics, Volume 32, 1–50
Copyright © 2011 by Emerald Group Publishing Limited
All rights of reproduction in any form reserved
ISSN: 0147-9121/doi:10.1108/S0147-9121(2011)0000032004

The combined impact of the Great Recession on the housing, stock, and labor markets after 2007 has reduced some measures of income inequality at the top of the MCI distribution. Despite declining from the 2007 peak, however, inequality remains as high as levels experienced earlier in the decade, and much higher than most points over the last 20 years. In the middle of the income distribution, the declines in income from wealth after 2007 were the result of diminished value of residential real estate; at the top of the distribution, declines in the value of business assets had the greatest impact.

We also assess the level and trend in the functional distribution of income between capital and labor, and find a rising share of income accruing to real capital or wealth from 1989 to 2007. The recent economic crisis has diminished the capital share back to levels from 2004. Contrary to the findings of other researchers, we find that the labor share of income among high-income groups declined between 1992 and 2007.

Keywords: income and wealth distribution; capital and labor Shares; great recession

JEL Classification: D31; D33

1. INTRODUCTION

This chapter is an attempt to capture the effects of secular and cyclical forces on the inequality of income across Americans who are suffering through the "Great Recession," and the period of slow employment growth and housing market stagnation that has followed. A full accounting of inequality in this period will have to wait years, as impacts of the recession and its aftermath are still unfolding, and the necessary data will not be available until late 2011. The most current micro data that can be used to analyze income distribution are from calendar year (CY) 2009 (Current Population Survey [CPS] income or poverty), or CY 2007 (Survey of Consumer Finances [SCF] wealth).

Based on currently available data, however, we do know quite a lot about some of the economic hardships resulting from the recession. The economy lost jobs every month between December 2007 and October 2009 – four months after the official end of the Great Recession – 8.3 million jobs in all, and unemployment rose from 5.0 to 10.1 percent (NBER, 2010). The incidence of job loss has been particularly severe among young workers, and those with lower levels of education. Total employment declined by less than 5 percent, but among teens it declined by 20 percent and among those with high school degrees or less it declined by 7 percent (Engemann & Wall, 2009). Poverty rose in 2009, and forecasts based on available employment and food stamp data indicate it was likely even higher in 2010 (Census, 2010; Monea & Sawhill, 2009).

Expected changes in the distribution of income in 2009, 2010, and beyond, though, are not as clear. Past recessions (excepting the Great Depression of the 1930s) tended to hurt people at the bottom of the distribution to a greater extent than people at the top (Atkinson, 2009). These effects are and were tempered by the safety net, and are driven by the loss of labor market earnings, which recovers when employment recovers. However, a major aspect of the recent recession has been the drop in property income values, financial assets, and home prices, as well as employment losses. Because all parts of the income distribution have suffered losses of income and wealth, the impacts on the overall distribution are more difficult to determine.

Preliminary analysis and speculation over shifts in the distribution suggests a range of potential outcomes. There is some evidence that the collapse in the stock and housing markets has produced declining CEO pay, lower dividends, and reduced Wall Street bonuses, which could cause the income gap to shrink "at the expense of the wealthy" (Davis & Frank, 2009; Leonhardt & Fabrikant, 2009). Looking at the data on consumption, some researchers have found evidence of declining inequality between 2006 and 2009 (Meyer & Sullivan, 2010; Heathcote, Perri, & Violante, 2010a, 2010b). Much of that decline is attributable to a notable drop in consumption at the top of the distribution, partially reversed in 2009 as the Obama ARRA plan boosted durables spending and the stock market recovery took hold (Parker & Vissing, 2009; Petev, Pistaferri, & Saporta, 2010). Overall consumption still fell in 2008 and 2009 combined, but the change in inequality is less certain once we look at the 2009 and early 2010 data.

Early indicators from some standard income inequality measures from the Census Bureau, however, suggest that high-income shares, as well as Gini and Theil indices, rose between 2007 and 2009 (Census, 2010). The major losses in income, in proportional terms, were experienced by the 80th and 10th percentiles, with relatively smaller losses for the 90th percentile (Smeeding & Thompson, 2010). These findings are fully consistent with those of Krueger, Perri, Pistaferri, and Violante (2010) and Heathcote et al. (2010a, 2010b), who also find earnings and disposable income inequality rising secularly in rich countries, and also in recessions, including this recession (Heathcote et al., 2010b), and especially for bottom income units. Because of top-coding in the CPS, though, these data can tell us little about what is going on at the very top of the distribution.

Data with broad measures of income, and that also contain detailed information for households at the very top of the distribution, are not yet available to give an updated understanding of inequality. The Congressional Budget Office "tax burden" series, for example, is only available up through 2007 (CBO, 2010). Similarly, the SCF as well as the IRS tax data used in analysis of high incomes are only available through 2008 (Smeeding & Thompson, 2010; Piketty & Saez, 2006; Saez, 2010). But, as Burkhauser, Feng, Jenkins, and Larrimore (2009) show – using non-top-coded Census Income data – most of the change in income inequality over the past decade has been among the rich. However, even these data exclude the vast majority of capital income – the issue to which we now turn.

In the remainder of this chapter, we will, first, briefly review some of the different approaches to analyzing trends in income distribution; second, describe our method for calculating a "more complete" measure of income (MCI); third, compare levels and trends – for recent years and across the last couple of decades – for inequality using MCI and other standard income measures; fourth, describe the impact of using MCI on the trends in capital versus labor shares; and finally, discuss some potentially policy implications of these trends.

The MCI income concept incorporates a broader range of the resources available to households than the definition of income in the typical survey, and, as such, is a better representation of economic "well-being." Motivated by the classic Haig–Simons income, MCI is intended to reflect the possibility to consume, and is also arguably a better representation of well-being than actual measured consumption. Estimated with data from the SCF, MCI results in higher income across the distribution, but especially at the top end. We also find a greater trend toward income concentration at the top of the distribution using MCI than do other analysts. A number of standard measures of inequality using MCI peaked in 2007, after rising relatively steadily since 1989, including the Gini index, the 99/50 ratio, and the income shares of top 1 percent and next 4 percent. Nearly all of the increase in inequality is the result of large gains at the very top of the distribution, with little evidence of rising inequality at the bottom of the distribution. The Great Recession appears to have halted, temporarily at least, the trend toward greater inequality. Any declines, however, have so far been modest, leaving inequality as high as any point before the 2007 peak.

We also assess the level and trend in the functional distribution of income between capital and labor. We find that if properly measured, the labor share is closer to 55 percent of total income rather than the 75 percent that is sometimes claimed. The results using MCI suggest that, contrary to the findings of Piketty and Saez (2003, 2006), the capital share of income at the top of the income distribution has risen in recent decades (as also found cross nationally by Glyn, 2009). By 2007, income from capital accounted for more than half of MCI among the top few percentiles of the income distribution.

2. APPROACHES TO UNDERSTANDING INEQUALITY AND THE DISTRIBUTION OF INCOME

For some time there has been widespread concern about growing inequality in the distribution of household income in the United States. The U.S. Census Bureau shows the Gini index of household income rose from .40 to .47 between 1967 and 2009, and that the ratio of incomes of households at the 90th and 10th percentiles of the income distribution rose from 9.2 to 11.4 over the same period. And while there is a general consensus among researchers that income inequality has increased in the United States and much of the rest of the world (Brandolini & Smeeding, 2009), there is less agreement over how much it has increased, or whether income is even the most important factor in understanding inequality, let alone the causes of the increase.

Labor economists have shown that inequality in hourly wages increased considerably over the same period (Autor, Katz, & Kearney, 2008). With earnings representing the single largest portion of household income, some argue that trends in earnings inequality are the key factor behind inequality in the U.S. income distribution.[1] A number of recent provocative studies highlight the role of extremely high earnings among "superstars," CEOs, athletes, rock stars, and celebrities (Kaplan & Rauh, 2010; Walker, 2005; Gordon & Dew-Becker, 2005), but these papers are only able to identify about 25–30 percent of even the highest-income earners.

And, labor income in the form of wages had declined to 50.2 percent of national income by the third quarter of 2006 – a 50-year low as a share of national income (Aron-Dine & Shapiro, 2006; Bureau of Economic Analysis, 2010; Goldfarb & Leonard, 2005). Even after adding together labor income (even including supplements or employee benefits) and corporate profits, which peaked at 13.7 percent of total national income in the third quarter of 2006 after rising for three decades, there is still more than a fifth of the nation's economic pie missing. Other uncounted components of national income such as net interest, proprietor's income, and rental incomes are largely missing from micro data-based income distribution calculations (see Table 1).

Meyer and Sullivan (2010) argue that levels of income inequality are not as great as suggested by the Census Bureau, and that the emphasis on income itself is misplaced. With appropriate adjustments for household size, taxes, and transfers, Meyer and Sullivan (2010) show that the 90/10 ratio was 5.3 in 2008, up from 4.1 in 1979. More important, they argue that consumption is a better proxy for well-being or even permanent income than the income measures used in most of the inequality research (also see Slesnick, 1994, 2001).[2] Consumption inequality has showed no trends toward greater inequality in recent decades, and has – as mentioned above – declined in the last few years.

Consumption is a strong predictor of different measures of hardship (Meyer & Sullivan, 2003), but it is deficient in some important respects as a

Table 1. Relation of Gross Domestic Product, Gross National Product, and National Income – Including Those Accounted for in this chapter (Italics) [Quarters Seasonally Adjusted at Annual Rates].

	2006-III (Billions of Dollars)	Share (%)	2009-IV (Billions of Dollars)	Share (%)
National income	12,093		12,466	
Compensation of employees	7,484	61.9	7,773	62.4
Wage and salary accruals	*6,075*	*50.2*	*6,266*	*50.3*
Supplements to wages and salaries	*1,409*	*11.6*	*1,507*	*12.1*
Proprietors' income with inventory valuation and capital consumption adjustments	*1,131*	*9.4*	*1,060*	*8.5*
Rental income of persons with capital consumption adjustment	*140*	*1.2*	*287*	*2.3*
Corporate profits with inventory valuation and capital consumption adjustments	*1,655*	*13.7*	*1,468*	*11.8*
Net interest and miscellaneous payments	*662*	*5.5*	*783*	*6.3*
Taxes on production and imports less subsidies	992	8.2	1,034	8.3
Business current transfer payments	84	0.7	128	1.0
Current surplus of government enterprises	−5	0.0	−7	−0.1

Source: BEA NIPA Table 1.12, Available at www.bea.gov

Note: *We account for supplements to wages and salaries only in so far as they appear as part of defined contribution pension plans. Health care and other employer subsidies are not counted.*

measure of well-being. As Dickens' famous line suggests, it might be better to treat the debt-financed consumption of low-income households whose consumption far exceeds their income instead as a measure of hardship:

> Annual income twenty pounds, annual expenditure nineteen six, result happiness. Annual income twenty pounds, annual expenditure twenty pound ought and six, result misery.
>
> – David Copperfield

And by focusing on the 90th percentile of the distribution, much of the consumption-oriented research misses what is going on at the very top of distribution.

Several analysts have suggested that most, if not all, of the gains in incomes from rapid expansion of productivity in the 1990 and early 2000s accrued to the richest 1–5 percent of Americans (Gordon & Dew-Becker, 2005; Piketty & Saez, 2003, 2006).[3] This result is supported by the analysis of top-coded Census Income data by Burkhauser et al. (2009). The long-term analysis by Atkinson, Piketty, and Saez (2009) shows that since the early 1970s income growth among the top 5 percent (particularly the top 1 percent) has far outpaced the rest of the nation.

Even in micro data that accurately reflect affluent households (Piketty & Saez, 2006; CBO, 2010), however, the annual income measures only include the flow realized from wealth (capital) in any one year.[4] In addition, the higher one goes in the income or earnings distribution, the more likely one is to find high rates of turnover in top *incomes* from year to year. Indeed, advocates of high American income mobility point out that the top 1 percent of income earners have 70 percent turnover rates year-to-year (Cox & Alm, 1999).

This problem is exacerbated by the fact that powerful income recipients can choose the form and timeframe in which their compensation is paid, e.g., for tax reasons (Auten & Carroll, 1999; Gruber & Saez, 2002). For instance, the two founders of Google, in a widely reported press story, took $1 each in earnings in 2005. Of course, each one also exercised less highly taxed stock options, which left them with $1.0 billion or more in "asset incomes" in that year (Ackerman, 2006). Whether for reasons of tax and estate planning, or simple accumulation, the large majority of the gains from wealth are not realized annually.[5]

The question we address in this chapter is how to add this income to household distributional micro data, and determine to whom did this property or capital income accrue? The key to pulling these disparate sources and trends in economic well-being together is a more full accounting of annual income from wealth, whether realized or not. Indeed, we believe that much of what has been interpreted as "consumption from wealth" is not drawing down wealth stocks at all, but comes from spending out of accretions to wealth (see Love & Smith, 2007, for older households; and Sierminska & Takhtamanova, 2006, for an international comparison). Similarly, the declines in U.S. savings rates over many years, leading up to the recession, were largely composed of spending from accumulated assets, especially owned homes and other appreciating assets. While the run-up in home values and dividends received through 2007 fueled consumer spending (e.g., Baker, Nagel, & Wurgler, 2006), steep declines in housing values since have diminished consumption due to a decrease in wealth stocks (Glick & Lansing, 2010) and the savings rate has risen. Clearly, wealth increasingly matters for consumption as well as for income.

The idea of accounting for income from wealth as well as income from earnings and other sources is not new (see Weisbrod & Hansen, 1968; Taussig, 1973), and has been used recently by Wolff and Zacharias (2006a, 2006b) and Haveman, Holden, Wolfe, and Sherlund (2006) in some fashion, to study inequality trends in the 1980s and 1990s.[6] Nevertheless, it is clearly time for a reappraisal given recent seismic changes in overall labor and capital income flows.

3. INCOME THEORY AND METHODOLOGY

There are many definitions of personal (macro) and household (micro) income from both "sources" and "uses" perspectives. According to the most popular theoretical measure of income, the Haig–Simons (H-S) income definition, income (I) is equal to consumption (C) and the change in net worth (ΔNW) realized over the income accounting period. So defined, H-S income is a measure of potential consumption or the amount one could consume without changing one's total net worth (one's stock of assets or debts). Thus, according to a "uses" of income definition:

$$I = C + \Delta NW \tag{1}$$

From the functional or "sources" side of income, we can arrive at the same measure by adding together income from earnings (E, including self-employment income), income from capital (KI, including capital gains plus other income from wealth), plus net transfers (NT, which include those received minus those paid, whether private or public in nature), resulting in the following definition:

$$I = E + KI + NT \tag{2}$$

If we ignore NT for now, and divide self-employment income into income from labor and capital, we are left with the macroeconomists' functional distribution of income.

The key element that is included above but largely missing in most estimates of both micro and macro estimates of income distribution is the distribution of income from capital. Despite long-standing interest in labor and capital "factor shares," macroeconomists (e.g., Goldfarb & Leonard, 2005; Guscina, 2006) and microeconomists who study distribution are both seemingly content with using data where only a small fraction of income from capital is measured. Interest, rent, and dividends received are reported in most micro data-based income definitions such as the one used by the Census Bureau. Capital gains and losses (KG, including those from realized stock options) and royalties are counted in other income definitions such as that used by the CBO (2010) and by Federal Reserve Bank in the SCF income distribution measure.[7]

However, the large majority of capital income (KI) accrues to persons but is never realized (and is therefore not counted in any given year). This includes imputed rental flows for owner-occupied housing, business savings in the form of corporate and noncorporate retained earnings, and unrealized capital gains. Much of this income stays with the firm that utilizes capital and is not realized by the owners of these assets (except as it is reflected the value of their enterprise, either self-owned or as shares of corporate stock).

Thus, we define "more complete income" (or MCI) as follows. We retain earnings and net transfers (*E* and NT), and maintain that portion of capital income (KI) received as capital gains and royalties (KG). But we then subtract *reported* interest, rent, and dividends (IRD) while adding back in an *imputed* return to all forms of net worth, or "imputed capital income" (IKI). Thus, we impute interest, rent, and dividends to owners of assets and forego the amounts actually reported by respondents.[8] This produces

$$MCI = E + NT + (KG - IRD + IKI) \tag{3}$$

Indeed the following more complete definition of capital income (KI) comes close to measuring the concept of "ΔNW" that intrigued both Haig and Simons:

$$KI = KG - IRD + IKI \tag{4}$$

MCI is an incomplete concept of income as we are unable to measure such items as employer benefits, pension fund accruals not counted as personal wealth such as defined benefit pension plans (though pension flows for elders are counted as transfers received), or unrealized stock options and other promised contractual benefits ("golden parachutes") that are not yet exercised or received.[9]

3.1. Developing MCI Estimates with the SCF

We calculate MCI using the SCF, a national representative triennial survey that includes an oversample of wealthy households that are under-represented in most standard surveys. The SCF contains high-quality, detailed information on household assets as well as income.[10] There are 16 broad asset classes, including stocks, bonds, mutual funds, home equity, residential real estate, and business assets, as well as six broad classes of debt. The data include an income definition (SCF income) that is broader than the standard Census money income definition. SCF income includes wages, self-employment and business income (SEBI), taxable and tax-exempt interest, dividends, realized capital gains, food stamps and other support programs provided by the government, pension income and withdrawals from retirement accounts, Social Security income, alimony and other support payments, and miscellaneous sources of income.[11]

Income net wealth (income less capital) is calculated by subtracting realized income from capital from the SCF income definition. Gains from the sale of an asset (capital gains), however, are retained in the income measure.[12] After removing income from capital from SCF income, flows to assets are imputed for the full range of assets measured in the SCF data. In calculating the implicit return on various assets, we employ two techniques: first we apply "short-run" (3-year) average rates of return to 22 specific asset/debt types in each of our eight income years, and then also "long-run" (30-year) average returns over the entire period.[13] These long-run rates allow us to separate more permanent long-run returns from more volatile short-run changes, and to assess more smooth trends in income from assets. They also allow us to test the sensitivity of our results to various assumed rates of return.

Separate rates of return were calculated for stocks, bonds, and housing assets, based, respectively, on the Dow Jones Industrial Average, 10-year U.S. Treasury Notes, and the House Price Index of the Federal Housing Finance Agency (FHFA). In addition, flows to assets are calculated gross of the inflation rate (CPI-U), while some flows are based on the average of two different types of return (the average of the return to stocks and bonds, for example). The actual rates used to impute these flows are included in Tables A1 and A2. The complete details on the construction of MCI, including how taxes are calculated for the various components of MCI so that we can create pre-tax as well as after-tax inequality measures, are provided in the Technical Appendix.[14]

The following additive series of combined capital income flows are added to income, net of reported interest, rent, and dividends, in the following order:

- *"plus finance"* adds imputed flows to directly held stocks, stock mutual funds, combination mutual funds, bonds, other bond mutual funds, savings bonds, government bond mutual funds, and tax-free bond mutual funds, as well as "other managed assets," such as trusts and annuities to *"income less capital"*;
- *"plus retire"* adds flows to "quasi-liquid retirement accounts," such as IRA/Keoghs and account-type pensions to *"plus finance"*;
- *"plus home"* adds flows to owner-occupied home equity to *"plus retire"*;
- *"plus other investments"* adds flows to investment real estate equity, transaction accounts, certificates of deposit (CDs), and the cash value of whole life insurance to *"plus home"*;
- *"plus business"* adds flows to other business assets and vehicles – only vehicles worth more than $50,000 – to *"plus other investments"*;
- *MCI* subtracts flows to non-real-estate debt, including credit card debt, installment loans, and other debt from *"plus business"* – after replacing observations, where "plus business" value incomes were below SCF income with the SCF income value.

Separate estimates for each of these income concepts are created using both long-run (30-year) averages and short-run (3-year) time-specific rates. The long-run rates are based on the average annual return between 1977 and 2007, with the same long-run rate applied to each year of SCF data – 1989, 1992, 1995, 1998, 2001, 2004, 2007, and projections of the data into 2009.

We also explore an alternative treatment of the vehicle assets, computing a service flow to vehicle ownership, following Slesnick (1994).[15] We consider how modifying treatment of this asset that is particularly important for middle- and low-income households influences levels and trends in inequality. For SCF income, MCI, and all of its components, we calculate a variety of standard distributional measures, including the Gini Index, ratios of key income percentiles (including, for example, the 99/50, 90/50, and the 10/50), in addition to income shares held by the top 1, 5, and 10 percent of the distribution.

3.2. Projecting SCF into 2009

The next round of the SCF (the eventual SCF 2010) will reflect economic conditions in 2009, but will not be available until mid-2011. Since the economy entered into a deep recession after 2007, heavily impacting earnings as well as stock markets and housing values, the portrait of inequality in the most recently available data cannot be expected to reflect current conditions. In order to present estimates of inequality that reflect the impacts of the "Great Recession," we have projected the data from 2007 SCF into 2009. These projections are based on income data from the BEA National Income and Product Accounts, asset data from the Federal Reserve Board Flow of Funds data, and earnings data from the CPS.

The income and asset categories used to calculate MCI are adjusted according to the percent change observed in these same categories between the last two quarters of 2007 and 2009. The changes by income and asset category, and the detailed source of each are displayed in Table A3. Changes over this period for the stock market reflect not just the decline in the total market capitalization that started at the end of 2007, but some of the rebound in market value since the first quarter of 2009. Changes in annual earnings are allowed to vary by education and industry class, reflecting – at least in part – how the labor markets of different demographic groups have been impacted by the Great Recession, as described by Engemann and Wall (2009).[16] The earnings measures in the SCF are adjusted based on the changes in total weekly earnings between the first 11 months of 2007 and 2009. The change in earnings is calculated for 20 separate industry–education cells, and reflects the combined impact of changes in employment, hours, and wages (Table A4).[17] Not adjusted for inflation, total earnings declined for most workers with less than a college degree. Total earnings of workers with a high school diploma or more education rose between 2007 and 2009, but at a rate less than inflation. Total earnings increased for workers with a college degree in all six industry groups, but less than inflation in three of those.

Fewer sets of results are calculated for the 2009 projected incomes. Partly this is a result of not being able to apply short-run rates to data that are themselves projected using changes in assets and income categories that are themselves functions of short-run rates of return. But, it is also the case since some of the tables and figures in the chapter are driven by the demographic composition of the population, which is not modified in the projection to 2009.

4. RESULTS

We begin by tracing how the addition of unrealized capital income changes the distribution of income, in both tables and figures. Then we look at after-tax income and finally examine levels and trends in various income percentiles and the share of final income that is either from wealth (capital) or labor. We also briefly explore the demographic profile of high-MCI households.

4.1. From SCF Income to MCI

We begin with Table 2 and Fig. 1, where we apply the long-run rates of return to various asset types and chart the way in which this process changes mean and median income in 2006–2007, as well as the 99th, 95th, 90th, and 10th percentiles (and the Gini inequality measure). As the figures reviewed in Table 1 suggest, capital income makes a great deal of difference to correctly measured income in the United States. Subtracting some capital income from SCF gross income ("less capital") reduces the mean and median, but as we successively add wealth-related income components in Table 2, both measures change dramatically. Moving from SCF income to MCI, mean income rises by 31 percent and the median by 16 percent. The biggest changes come from stocks, imputed rent on owned homes, and business assets. Owned homes ("plus home") affect large changes in both mean and median as housing is the quintessential "middle class asset" and is the only capital income flow that significantly boosts the median. Stocks and bonds ("plus finance") and business assets ("plus business") have larger affects on the mean due to the skewed distribution of returns accruing mostly to high-MCI units. Indeed, the 99th, 95th, and 90th percentiles rise by 49, 41, and 32 percent, respectively, in 2007 dollars from SCF to MCI. In contrast, the 10th percentile increases only by 17 percent across these same measures. When we take into account the changes in the medians, the relative inequality measures, the 99/50, 95/50, and 90/50 ratios still rise by 28, 21, and 13 percent, respectively. The 10/50 ratio is the same in SCF income and MCI. The correction of negatives and the subtraction of debts, reflected in the difference between "plus business" and MCI, seem to have little effect on the overall results.

Table 2.   SCF (2006–2007) – Full Income Definition Summary Statistics
– Original Rankings and Long-Run Rates of Return.

	SCF income	Less capital	Plus finance	Plus retire	Plus home	Plus oth invest	Plus business	MCI	Change	
									SCF to MCI	As percentage of SCF
Mean	84,144	73,058	79,292	84,763	92,876	98,868	108,677	110,147	26,003	31
Median (P50)	47,305	43,808	46,157	47,444	51,997	54,488	55,768	55,014	7,709	16
P90	140,887	128,546	135,571	148,855	163,986	175,709	184,423	185,892	45,005	32
P95	206,702	185,106	200,588	218,850	241,284	259,486	287,293	290,835	84,133	41
P10	12,340	11,369	12,340	12,340	13,839	14,397	14,407	14,397	2,057	17
P99	693,121	516,327	611,309	669,215	728,744	822,229	1,011,830	1,031,528	338,407	49
90/10	11.4	11.3	11.0	12.1	11.8	12.2	12.8	12.9	1.5	13
90/50	3.0	2.9	2.9	3.1	3.2	3.2	3.3	3.4	0.4	13
10/50	0.26	0.26	0.27	0.26	0.27	0.26	0.26	0.26	0.00	0
95/50	4.4	4.2	4.3	4.6	4.6	4.8	5.2	5.3	0.9	21
99/50	14.7	11.8	13.2	14.1	14.0	15.1	18.1	18.8	4.1	28
99/90	4.9	4.0	4.5	4.5	4.4	4.7	5.5	5.5	0.6	13
Gini	0.572	0.539	0.559	0.569	0.562	0.572	0.599	0.608	0.04	6

Notes:

SCF income — Fed default gross household income definition, includes wages, self-employment and business income, taxable and tax-exempt interest, dividends, realized capital gains, food stamps and other support programs provided by the government, pension income and withdrawals from retirement accounts, Social Security income, alimony and other support payments, and miscellaneous sources of income.

Less capital — SCF income less income from wealth (interest, dividends, rent, royalties, and income from trusts and nontaxable investments, including bonds, as well as some self-employment income).

Plus finance — + imputed flows to stocks, bonds, annuities, and trusts.

Plus retire — + imputed flows to quasi-liquid retirement accounts (401(k), IRA, etc.).

Plus home — + imputed flow to primary residence.

Plus oth invest — + imputed flow to other residences and investment real estate, transaction accounts, CDs, and whole life insurance.

Plus business — + imputed flow to other assets and businesses + imputed flow to vehicle wealth.

MCI — − imputed interest flow for remaining debt (after adjusting for negative incomes).

In numerical terms, households at the 10th percentile of MCI have incomes of $14,397 (Table 2) and net assets of $23,112 (Table A6). Income from wealth increases SCF income by only $2,057 at the 10th percentile. This is in contrast with MCI and net worth values of $185,892 and $864,138

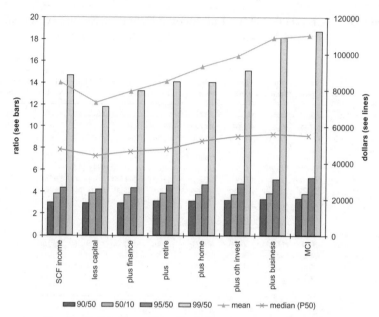

Fig. 1. Full-Income 2006–2007 SCF – Long-Run Returns.

at the 90th percentile, where capital income is $45,005 in 2007. At the median MCI level of $55,014, a household has a net worth of $152,491 and a gain of $7,709. However, at the 99th percentile of MCI, where MCI is $1,031,528, net worth is over $6.5 million and SCF incomes in 2007 are increased by $338,000 in moving to MCI. Table 3 does the same with short-run rates of return, with very similar results because short-run returns in 2006–2007 are very close to the long-run rates.

The dramatic nature and extent of these changes are easier seen in Fig. 1. The mean and median values on the right side show steady increases, especially for "plus home" at the median where the appreciation of owned homes leads to a jump from one plateau to another. In contrast, the mean income rises steadily with big jumps as noted above and smaller changes at other definitional points. The 95th and 90th percentiles also rise relative to the median. The increases are most dramatic at the very top of the distribution where the bars show that the 99/50 ratio starts below 15 for SCF income and rises to almost 19 for MCI, with the jump mostly due to business assets and "other investments." Hence gains from income from wealth accrue largely to the very top of the income distribution, even after

Table 3. SCF (2006–2007) – Full Income Definition Summary Statistics – Original Rankings and Short-Run Rates of Return.

	SCF income	Less capital	Plus finance	Plus retire	Plus home	Plus oth invest	Plus business	MCI	Change SCF to MCI	As percentage of SCF
Mean	84,144	73,058	79,475	85,181	94,645	100,908	111,131	112,384	28,240	34
Median (P50)	47,305	43,808	46,214	47,602	53,070	55,196	56,858	55,917	8,612	18
P90	140,887	128,546	135,625	149,259	167,868	179,678	189,333	189,740	48,854	35
P95	206,702	185,106	200,865	218,977	245,110	265,998	294,841	295,743	89,041	43
P10	12,340	11,369	12,340	12,340	14,234	14,402	14,503	14,398	2,058	17
P99	693,121	516,327	613,923	679,215	754,758	842,751	1,040,259	1,062,867	369,746	53
90/10	11.4	11.3	11.0	12.1	11.8	12.5	13.1	13.2	1.8	15
90/50	3.0	2.9	2.9	3.1	3.2	3.3	3.3	3.4	0.4	14
10/50	0.26	0.26	0.27	0.26	0.27	0.26	0.26	0.26	0.00	−1
95/50	4.4	4.2	4.3	4.6	4.6	4.8	5.2	5.3	0.9	21
99/50	14.7	11.8	13.3	14.3	14.2	15.3	18.3	19.0	4.4	30
99/90	4.9	4.0	4.5	4.6	4.5	4.7	5.5	5.6	0.7	14
Gini	0.572	0.540	0.560	0.570	0.563	0.573	0.601	0.610	0.04	7

Notes: See *Notes* in Table 2 for details.

we re-rank incomes with each successive component of wealth (or finally, debt), and compare incomes to the median household.[18]

Table 4 shows the impacts of moving to MCI in the 2009 projected income – using long-run rates. The SCF incomes are very similar to levels from 2007, slightly lower at the mean and median and at the 99th, 95th, and 90th percentiles, but slightly higher at the 10th percentile. MCI incomes, however, are considerably lower for most groups in 2009. Moving from SCF income to MCI raises the mean and median by 27 and 15 percent, respectively, compared to 31 percent and 16 percent in 2007. Adding in the imputed flows to equity in owner-occupied residential real estate ("plus home") has very little impact on income at either the mean or the median, reflecting the huge national losses in housing values. Moving to MCI raised the 99th percentile by 43 percent in 2009, but 49 percent in 2007.

4.2. Including Taxes

The after-tax changes, using 2007 SCF data, are summarized in Table 5. We employ the NBER TAXSIM model to estimate taxes, given existing, and

Table 4. SCF (2009 Projection) – Full Income Definition Summary Statistics – Original Rankings and Long-Run Rates of Return.

	SCF income	Less capital	Plus finance	Plus retire	Plus home	Plus oth invest	Plus business	MCI	Change	
									SCF to MCI	As percentage of SCF
Mean	82,298	71,322	78,891	83,597	88,381	94,396	102,221	104,303	22,005	27
Median (P50)	46,293	43,275	45,027	46,564	49,709	52,499	53,980	53,366	7,072	15
P90	138,860	129,558	136,123	146,651	157,373	167,196	173,378	175,040	36,179	26
P95	206,047	181,699	195,087	214,132	224,616	249,409	268,612	272,497	66,451	32
P10	13,484	12,898	13,042	13,042	14,228	14,592	14,884	14,768	1,284	10
P99	652,315	489,283	629,802	681,997	708,786	778,926	893,783	934,017	281,702	43
90/10	10.3	10.0	10.4	11.2	11.1	11.5	11.6	11.9	1.6	15
90/50	3.0	3.0	3.0	3.1	3.2	3.2	3.2	3.3	0.3	9
10/50	0.29	0.30	0.29	0.28	0.29	0.28	0.28	0.28	−0.01	−5
95/50	4.5	4.2	4.3	4.6	4.5	4.8	5.0	5.1	0.7	15
99/50	14.1	11.3	14.0	14.6	14.3	14.8	16.6	17.5	3.4	24
99/90	4.7	3.8	4.6	4.7	4.5	4.7	5.2	5.3	0.6	14
Gini	0.561	0.527	0.555	0.565	0.560	0.568	0.590	0.600	0.04	7

Notes: See *Notes* in Table 2 for details.

advantaged, rates for taxable property income.[19] Indeed, while including taxes considerably reduces the incomes of high-income households (MCI declines about $120,000 for the 99th percentile after including taxes), the percentage gains from adding wealth are even greater in after-tax terms at the highest-income levels. The 99th percentile of after-tax income rises by 75 percent compared to a 49 percent change for the before tax incomes (Table 2). These results also confirm that after-tax inequality is lower than pre-tax inequality, with the 99/50 ratio for MCI (short-run rates) falling from 18.8 to 16.4 after including taxes. The Gini index of MCI falls from .608 to .579 after taxes.[20]

4.3. Trends in Income Inequality for Key Income Definitions

So far, we have discovered that at any point in time, accounting for income from wealth drastically increases both the level of income and the inequality of income. To see how the trend has evolved over the last 20 years, we calculate similar before tax figures for 1988–1989, 1991–1992, 1994–1995,

1997–1998, 2000–2001, and 2003–2004.[21] We prefer the long-run rates when calculating trends, but figures and tables using short-run rates are available from the authors. Results for these earlier years show much the same pattern as we saw above in 2006–2007 with few changes.[22] The six graphs in Fig. 2 summarize the trend in key income definitions and component comparisons, using long-run rates, over that period. First, MCI is at the top of every set of lines (except the 10/50 ratio where moving from SCF to MCI has little impact).

While SCF and MCI follow similar patterns at the top of the distribution, the gap between MCI and SCF income is especially apparent for the 99/50 and 95/50 ratios and for the pattern of mean incomes. Thus, the trend in inequality is stronger with a more complete (vs. a less complete) income measure. At the bottom, we see that mean and median incomes both rise over the period for each income definition, with stagnant periods during previous recessions (early 1990s and 2001), but outright declines in the Great Recession. The 90/50 ratios show little trend, suggesting most gains over the period are concentrated at the top of the distribution. The dips in the 99/50 ratio in 2003 and again in 2009 reflect the collapse of the stock (and housing in 2009) market in those periods.

Adding imputed flows for financial wealth ("plus finance") to income "less capital" leaves the 99/50 ratio very similar to SCF income. Adding housing wealth ("plus home") produces little change in the 99/50 and 95/50 ratios, but accounts for the bulk of the change at the median (panel F) and a large portion of the change in the mean (panel E). The bulk of the gap between SCF income and MCI in the 99/50 ratio is a result of one of the final elements of MCI, imputed flows to business wealth. The relevance of business wealth shows up in the means (panel E) and the 99/50 ratio (panel A), but not the other trend statistics.[23]

In general, the trends presented in Fig. 2 suggest the effects of adding income from wealth follow a similar pattern of rising inequality as seen in the SCF income as well as other measures of income inequality over this period (e.g., Smeeding, 2005; CBO, 2010). While inequality is higher in any given year for MCI income than SCF income, the 95/50 and 90/50 ratios follow the same upward trend as the SCF income (panels B and C). For the very top of the distribution, however, the inclusion of income from wealth results in a more dramatic rise in inequality (panel A). The 99/50 ratio rises 57 percent between 1988–1989 and 2006–2007 in the SCF income measure, but it increases 64 percent for MCI. Therefore, while Wolff and Zacharias (2006a, 2006b)

Table 5. After-Tax Concepts (2006–2007).

	After-Tax Concepts		Change	
	dpi[a]	MCI less tax	dpi to MCI less tax	As percentage of dpi
Panel A. Short-run rates of return				
Mean	72,089	105,674	33,584	47
Median (P50)	44,409	56,626	12,217	28
P90	120,798	176,554	55,756	46
P95	172,232	277,522	105,290	61
P10	12,372	16,179	3,807	31
P99	520,282	925,758	405,475	78
90/10	9.8	10.9	1.1	12
90/50	2.7	3.1	0.4	15
10/50	0.28	0.29	0.0	3
95/50	3.9	4.9	1.0	26
99/50	11.7	16.3	4.6	40
99/90	4.3	5.2	0.9	22
Gini	0.532	0.5806	0.049	9
Panel B. Long-run rates of return				
Mean	72,089	103,260	31,171	43
Median (P50)	44,409	55,511	11,102	25
P90	120,798	171,887	51,089	42
P95	172,232	271,000	98,768	57
P10	12,372	15,962	3,590	29
P99	520,282	910,311	390,029	75
90/10	9.8	10.8	1.0	10
90/50	2.7	3.1	0.4	14
10/50	0.28	0.29	0.0	3
95/50	3.9	4.9	1.0	26
99/50	11.7	16.4	4.7	40
99/90	4.3	5.3	1.0	23
Gini	0.532	0.579	0.047	9

Notes:

dpi   Income less federal taxes – calculated with TAXSIM.
MCI less tax   MCI less federal taxes – calculated with TAXSIM.
[a]Since dpi does not include any imputed flows to wealth, results are the same for short-run and long-run rates of return.

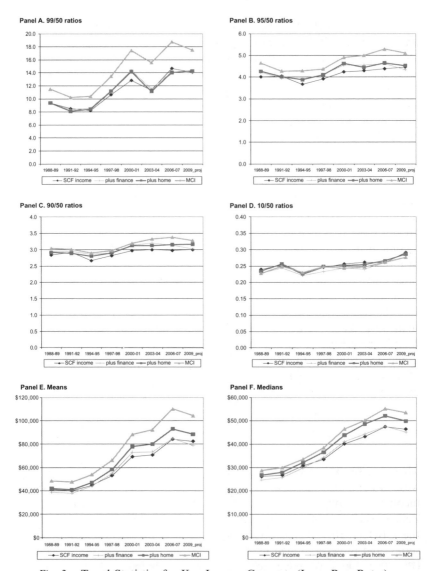

Fig. 2. Trend Statistics for Key Income Concepts (Long-Run Rates).

show that an augmented measure of wealth results in about the same rise in inequality as traditional measures of money income, our approach suggests that inequality appears to rise even higher when we use more complete measures of income.

Projections to 2009 suggest that the run-up in inequality between 1989 and 2007 was halted by the Great Recession. The 99/50 ratio declined from 18.8 in 2007 to 17.5 in 2009 using MCI and by a smaller amount using SCF income. Other MCI-based measures of inequality (Table A5) also declined over this period; the Gini index dropped from .608 to .600. Most of these measures, however, also show that inequality remains at high levels.

4.4. Percentile Growth in Incomes

Fig. 3 (panels A and B) summarizes the 1989 to 2007 growth rates for SCF income and MCI across the entire distribution. The growth in MCI is greater than SCF income for all households above the 40th percentile of the income distribution. Over most of the income distribution, the importance of moving to MCI appears to be roughly constant with the gap in growth rates fluctuating between 10 and 20 percentage points (panel B). At the top of the distribution, however, the gap in growth rates increases dramatically. For the top 3 percent of the income distribution, growth in MCI is more than 30 percent higher than SCF. For the 99th percentile, MCI growth was 35 percentage points faster than SCF income. Hence, the inclusion of income from wealth results in a rising inequality trend, when the measure of inequality contrasts the highest-income households with any other grouping.

4.5. Tends in the Income Share of Top-Income Households

There are several sets of estimated income trends among the rich to which we can compare our results. In Fig. 4, we compare MCI shares of total income using long-run rates to those found in three other studies: the Wolff–Zacharias (WZ, 2006a, 2006b) annuity value measures of income-net worth; the CBO (2010) income after taxes and benefits including capital gains series; and those compiled in the "top income" papers of Piketty and Saez (PS, 2003, 2006). We have plotted the shares, and have calculated the trends and the slopes of each line.

First we note that the top 1 percent shares using MCI are roughly in line with those of PS and WZ (panel A). And, while Reynolds (2007) and Tatom (2007) have criticized the PS numbers because more of high income is not reported for tax reasons, our MCI measure avoids this problem, as we include unrealized and therefore untaxed income from wealth, and our

Panel A. Growth between 1989 and 2007 by percentile of SCF and MCI distribution (long-run rates)

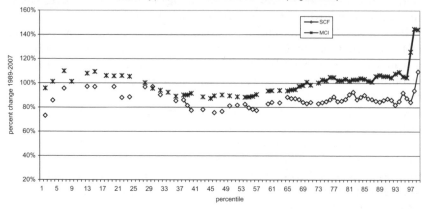

Panel B. Difference in MCI and SCF Growth Rates by percentile

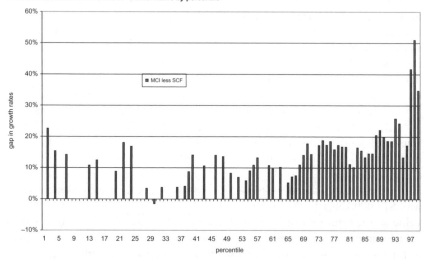

Fig. 3. MCI and SCF Growth Compared.

shares are at least as high if not higher. For the top 1 percent, all lines rise over the period, suggesting an increase in share for either the 1989–2007 or 1989–2001 periods. For the 1989–2001 period, MCI and PS had the steepest slopes for growth in the income share of the top 1 percent, well above the rates of increase in either the CBO or WZ figures. Between 1989 and 2007, though, the MCI slope was close to, but slightly smaller than, the CBO slope, and considerably smaller than the PS slope. To varying degrees, all of the series show a rising share at the very top.

For the next tier of top-income households – the 95th to 99th percentiles of the distribution (panel B) – the PS and CBO series show relatively low growth over the period (1989–2001 or 1989–2007). Using MCI, however, the income share of this group rises considerably, as does the WZ series for 1989–2001. All of the series show slightly declining income shares for the next tier of top-income households – the 90th to 95th percentiles of the distribution (panel C).

Based on the projections for 2009, MCI shows that the top income shares have declined slightly since 2007; the income share of the top 1 percent fell from 22.3 to 21.9 percent between 2007 and 2009, while the share of the next-highest 4 percent declined from 18.5 to 18.0 percent. The most recent IRS tax data analyzed by Piketty and Saez also show a decline in the income share of the top 1 percent between 2007 and 2008, but record a slight uptick in the share of the next 4 percent. The crisis in the financial sector and the decline in business assets appear to have made a small dent in the income share of the highest-income households, but the shares remain higher than every year before 2007.

4.6. Impact of Vehicle Service Flow

The levels and trends in MCI shown in Tables 2–4 and Figs. 1–4 do not impute any flow of income to vehicle assets below $50,000 in value. For low- and middle-income households, however, vehicles are an important asset, and are typically valued well below $50,000. In 2007, median vehicle value was $13,000. Nearly 90 percent of households had vehicle assets, and the value at the 90th percentile was under $41,000. Changing the treatment of vehicles in MCI, by calculating an annual service flow to vehicle ownership following the approach of Slesnick (1994), suggests somewhat higher levels of MCI, particularly for low-income households.[24] On including vehicle service flow, MCI at the 99th percentile was $943,740 in 2009, 1 percent higher than the baseline approach in Table 4. MCI at the 10th percentile, though, was $15,538 with vehicle service flow, 5.2 percent higher than baseline MCI. Including vehicle service flows also modestly changes measures in the level of inequality, but has no appreciable impact on inequality trends. The Gini index of MCI in 2007, for example, falls from .600 to .593 after including vehicle service flow. The trend in the Gini index, though, is not affected (Fig. 5, panel A). Adding vehicle service flow to MCI

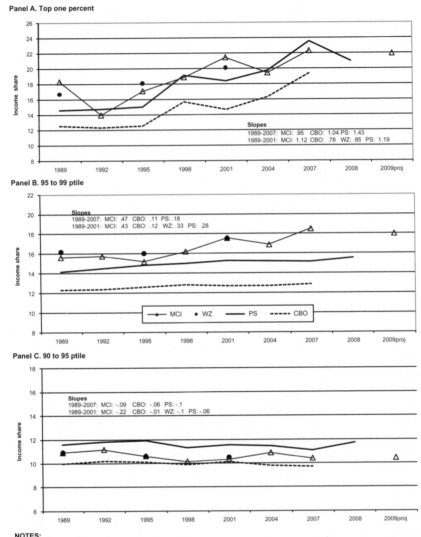

Panel A. Top one percent

Slopes
1989-2007: MCI: .95 CBO: 1.04 PS: 1.43
1989-2001: MCI: 1.12 CBO: .78 WZ: .85 PS: 1.19

Panel B. 95 to 99 ptile

Slopes
1989-2007: MCI: 47 CBO: .11 PS: .18
1989-2001: MCI: 43 CBO: .12 WZ: .33 PS: .28

MCI • WZ —— PS ---- CBO

Panel C. 90 to 95 ptile

Slopes
1989-2007: MCI: -.09 CBO: -.06 PS: -.1
1989-2001: MCI: -.22 CBO: -.01 WZ: -.1 PS: -.06

NOTES:
1. MCI is based on long-run rates of return.
2. CBO uses a measure of "comprehensive income" that includes realized capital gains.
3. WZ is "wealth-adjusted" income from Wolff and Zacharias, May 2006.
4. PS figures include capital gains income.

Fig. 4.   Comparing Income Shares of Top Fractiles (1989–2009) (with Slopes).

results in similar small changes in other inequality measures, including the income share of top 5 percent on households and the 99/50 income ratio, but leaves the overall trends unchanged (Fig. 5, panels B and C).

4.7. Labor versus Capital Income

A more complete accounting for income from wealth as well as from labor produces large changes in the functional income distribution. At the top of Fig. 6 in panel A, we see the SCF traditional micro data-based pattern of household income components. Earned income is 63–70 percent of gross incomes over the period we study. Indeed most authors (e.g., Cowen, 2007; Tatom, 2007) assume that labor income is always about 65–70 percent of total income. Conventional reported income from interest, rent, dividends, and sometimes capital gains is between 10 and 15 percent of SCF income. "Other" (largely public transfer) net income is 9–15 percent of gross income, while income from capital and Self-Employment Business Income (SEBI) are both no more than 10 percent. This is the standard picture with almost all household income micro data sets, but the pattern is considerably different when we consider the MCI distribution (panel B).

Now, because we assess all capital income in MCI, capital income is both higher than in panel A and also growing from 1988–1989 to 2006–2007. The capital share of income in MCI rises from 30 to 40 percent over this period, with a recession induced dip in 1991–1992 and plateau in 2003–2004, before falling back to 37 percent in the Great Recession. Over the same period, the labor share of income falls to 52 percent in 2006–2007, before bouncing back to 55 percent in 2009. "Other" (net transfer) income changes very little.[25] Using short-run rates (not shown) results in very noisy results that fail to show any trend between 1989 and 2007.

These trends, especially using long-run rates, suggest the role of income from wealth is growing stronger in the United States, while labor income is falling in importance. Simply put, income from wealth rises and income from labor falls once we take a more complete view of Haig–Simons income.

4.8. Labor Shares at the Top of the Distribution

Similar to Wolff and Zacharias (2006a, 2006b) we find that our expanded measure of income using the SCF fails to support Piketty and Saez's (2003, 2006)

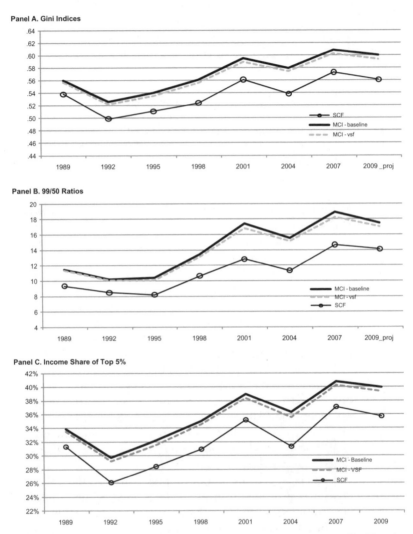

Fig. 5. The Impact of Including Vehicle Service Flow on Inequality Trends.

finding of the rising importance of income from labor. Using federal tax return data, Piketty and Saez document a rising labor share of total money income for high-income households. Using the expanded income definition of MCI, we find that income from wealth represents the largest

Panel A. SCF Gross Income

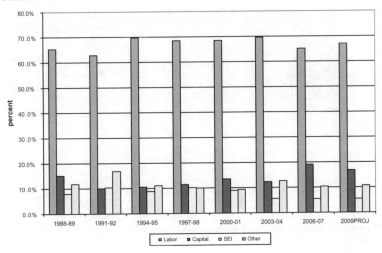

Panel B. MCI (Long-run Rates)

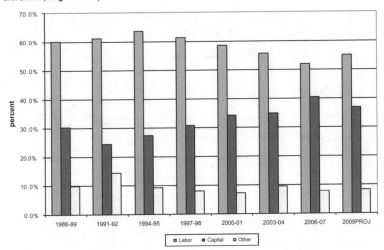

Fig. 6. Labor and Capital Shares – SCF and MCI Gross Income.

share of MCI at the top of the distribution and that the wealth share is rising.[26]

Fig. 7 shows the share composition of MCI over the entire distribution. For the lowest MCI households, labor and capital combined represent less

Panel A. Labor, Capital, and Other Share of MCI by percentile - 2007

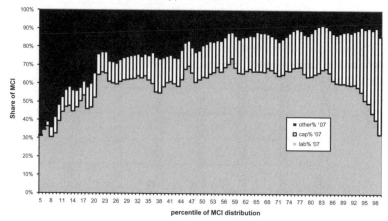

Panel B. Labor and Capital Shares of MCI by percentile - 1989 and 2007

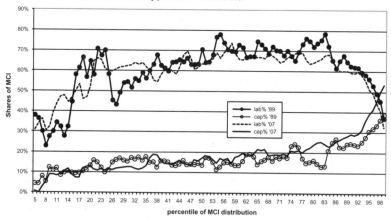

Fig. 7.   Labor and Capital Shares of MCI by Percentiles of MCI Distribution. Smoothed 3 Percentile Average Using Long-Run Rates.

than one third of total MCI in 2007, but for the highest MCI households, capital income alone constitutes more than half of MCI (panel A). The trend comparisons (panel B) suggest that capital income represents the largest portion of MCI for the top few percentiles, and the capital share increased between 1989 and 2007 for the top 5 percentiles. For the top 1 percent of the MCI distribution, the capital share rose from 39 percent of MCI in 1989 to 53 percent by 2007.

The labor share of MCI, conversely, has declined at the top of the distribution. Fig. 8 shows the labor share of income for top-income households using both SCF income (panel A) and MCI (panel B). Using SCF income, the labor share of income for the top 1 percent has risen, though not steadily, since 1989. Using MCI, the labor share declined between 1989 and 2007 for the top 1 percent as well as the next 4 percent, before rising in the "Great Recession."

4.9. Who are the Rich?

The demographic profile of households by MCI class (Table 6) shows that, relative to other households, high-MCI households are older, better educated, more likely to be white and married, more likely to be self-employed or in a

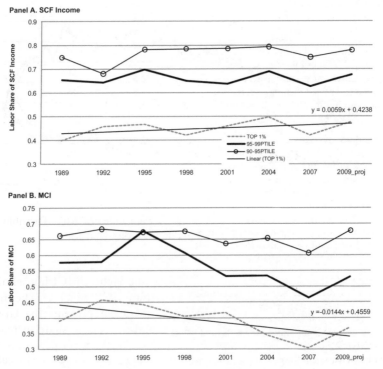

Fig. 8. Labor Share of Income of High-Income Households, by Income Concept.

Table 6. Demographic Profile of Households by MCI Levels – 2007
SCF.

Characteristics of Household Head	Top 10 Percent	Top 5 Percent	Top 1 Percent	All	Bottom 90 Percent
Average age	53.4	55.3	56.6	50.0	49.6
Education status					
Average years of education	15.5	15.8	16.1	13.3	13.0
Share with at least college degree (percent)	76.7	80.2	87.3	35.3	30.2
Household status					
Share of households headed by married couple or partners (percent)	86.9	86.5	91.7	58.8	55.3
Share with any kids (percent)	46.8	44.1	41.5	43.9	43.6
Average number of kids (of those with kids)	1.90	1.91	2.04	1.9	1.9
Race					
Share non-Hispanic white (percent)	86.9	89.7	92.0	70.7	68.7
Share black (percent)	2.7	1.7	1.8	12.6	13.8
Share Hispanic (percent)	2.4	1.7	1.5	9.4	10.3
Share "other" (percent)	8.0	6.9	4.7	7.3	7.2
Working status					
Employed by someone else (percent)	53.3	42.4	37.7	59.9	60.7
Self-employed or partner (percent)	29.6	41.3	45.2	10.5	8.1
Retired/disabled/student (percent)	15.8	15.2	16.2	25.0	26.1
Otherwise not in labor force (percent)	1.3	1.1	0.9	4.6	5.1
Industry					
Agriculture (percent)	1.4	1.4	0.4	3.0	3.2
Mining and Construction (percent)	7.7	7.1	12.3	12.5	13.2
Manufacturing and publishing (percent)	10.5	12.0	9.5	13.8	14.3
Trade, restaurants, and bars (percent)	11.0	10.4	8.6	15.2	15.9
Data, financial, business, repair, and security services (percent)	16.1	19.2	26.1	12.0	11.5
Utility and transport, professional, scientific, technical, travel, cleaning, administrative, health, education, and personal services (percent)	46.5	44.8	41.5	36.3	34.8
Public administration and armed services (percent)	6.8	5.1	1.6	7.1	7.1
Occupations					
Executives, managers, scientists, architects, engineers, lawyers, teachers, counselors and social workers, health care practitioners, technicians and support, entertainment, sports, and media (percent)	75.7	83.4	88.4	39.1	33.6
Technicians, sales, office, and computer operators (percent)	13.1	9.7	9.5	19.5	20.3

Table 6. (*Continued*)

Characteristics of Household Head	Top 10 Percent	Top 5 Percent	Top 1 Percent	All	Bottom 90 Percent
Protective services, food preparation, cleaning and building services, personal care, and armed services (percent)	4.5	3.1	0.0	11.5	12.5
Construction and skilled labor and crafts (percent)	4.0	1.9	1.0	18.2	20.3
Unskilled labor (percent)	2.2	1.3	1.1	10.5	11.8
Farm, fishing, forestry, and animal training and care (percent)	0.5	0.6	0.0	1.3	1.5

partnership, and are disproportionately grouped in managerial and professional occupations. Nearly 92 percent of households in the top 1 percent were headed by non-Hispanic whites and 92 percent were married, compared to nearly 69 percent and 55 percent, respectively, for the bottom 90 percent of households.[27] Age alone is not a terribly good predictor of high wealth as nearly 42 percent of the group in the top 1 percent have children under age 18, little different from the bottom 90 percent of households.

The educational and occupational differences between high-MCI households and the general population are quite striking. Nearly 9 of 10 (87 percent) household heads in the top 1 percent of MCI had at least a college degree compared to 30 percent among the bottom 90 percent. Nearly half (47 percent) of working households in the top 1 percent of MCI had at least some postgraduate education.[28] Hence accumulation of human capital is indirectly linked to income from wealth. More than 88 percent of household heads in the top 1 percent of the MCI distribution were in the managerial and professional occupation class, and 45 percent were self-employed or a partner in a firm, compared to just 34 percent and 8 percent, respectively, for the bottom 90 percent of the distribution. Moreover, nearly half (46 percent) of working households in the top 1 percent were self-employed/partner in a managerial and professional occupation.

High-MCI households are a varied lot in certain respects, but their education–occupation–industry profile suggests a large concentration of managers, business owners, and entrepreneurs. Human capital is important to high MCI, but it appears most successful when combined with employment or investment in partnerships, self-held companies, and high-level management responsibilities. High-MCI households are not especially aged and almost half of high-MCI families still have children under age 18.

A more thorough treatment of demographics, including means, medians, and distributional breakdowns by age, family composition, and ethnicity for SCF income and MCI, as well as a consideration of the influence of population ageing on inequality is included in previous drafts.[29]

5. SUMMARY/DISCUSSION

Augmenting the standard income definition with flows imputed to assets results in greater resources for households across the distribution. MCI exceeds SCF income by 16 percent at the median and 17 percent at the 10th percentile of the distribution (for 2007). Accounting for the flow of services provided by, and opportunity to consume represented by, assets suggests households are better off than if we only consider more narrow definitions of income, but these resources are also exposed to fluctuations in the stock and housing markets as well as the labor market. Median income declined by $1,000 between 2007 and 2009 using SCF income, but by $1,650 using MCI.

Broadening the income concept to incorporate the benefits of wealth and asset ownership also results in even larger gains at the top of the distribution; at the 99th percentile MCI was 49 percent larger than SCF income. At any point in time, income inequality measures are larger using MCI than standard income concepts – the 95/50 ratio in 2007 was 5.3 using MCI compared to 4.4 for SCF income. And the rise in the concentration of income among the top few deciles of the distribution in recent decades appears even greater using this broader income concept – between 1989 and 2007 the 99/50 ratio rose 63 percent (from 11.5 to 17.5) for MCI, but only 57 percent using SCF income.

We have documented these increases in inequality using Gini indexes, ratios of key percentiles (95/50, etc.), and income shares of top-income groups. There are, however, other inequality metrics that have been developed in recent years specifically to address distributional questions at the top of the income distribution, including the "affluence measures" proposed by Peichl, Schaefer, and Scheicher (2010) and the approach to ranking intersecting Lorenz curves developed by Aaberge (2009). These measures will be explored in future work with the MCI concept.

The income trends we are documenting are not simply across the distribution increasingly toward households with very high incomes, but also across sources of income, from labor to capital income. High-income families are not increasingly represented by high earners, as Piketty and Saez (2003, 2006) argue; instead, high earners and other asset-rich households are building up assets and accumulating high-unmeasured incomes from these assets. MCI brings out these patterns in some detail.

Not unlike the Medici period in Italy, this "Richistan" (Frank, 2007) pattern is definitely at work in the early 21st century where flat earnings below the 80th percentile and falling median incomes for the nonelderly have drawn repeated questions about where the nation's productivity gains have gone (Gordon & Dew-Becker, 2005; Mishel, Bernstein, & Allegretto, 2005; Lemieux, MacLeod, & Parent, 2007; Aron-Dine & Shapiro, 2006). The answer is that they went to, and remain in, higher value assets, including higher value corporate assets, proprietor's incomes, net interest, and profits (which drive up stock and bond market returns and the value of business equity).

And, the United States is not alone in this situation, as OECD figures reported by Porter (2006), Glyn (2009), and Guscina (2006) suggest that the labor share of total income has fallen in most rich OECD nations over the 1990–2004 period. Indeed the labor share in Germany and Japan fell by even more than in the United States over this period, while at the same time, the German trend has been increasingly for market incomes to accrue to the highest-income households (Bach, Corneo, & Steiner, 2007). In addition, concentration of wealth is on the rise in Europe as well as in the United States (Atkinson, 2006).

Institutional and economic changes have created a greater emphasis on worldwide "free market" capitalism, high returns to the entrepreneurs – the inventors and creative users of capital (Acemoglu, 2002). These changes have been combined with tax advantages for both capital income and high incomes, and have led to the worsening of the social and political position of labor more generally (Levy & Temin, 2007). All of these factors have contributed to the shift to higher capital versus labor income. Ever greater global trade and further technological change should only intensify these changes (Blinder, 2007; Freeman, 2007). While some claim labor incomes will rise more in the future than will capital incomes due to world population aging (Krueger & Ludwig, 2006), others see high and rising returns to asset holdings for those with productive assets such as pension savings (Poterba, Venti, & Wise, 2007; Love & Smith, 2007). Indeed while human capital and technology are "racing" for higher income shares (Goldin & Katz, 2007), technology and the entrepreneurs who own and deploy such capital are currently winning the race, and are increasingly likely to receive higher rewards in a world of mobile capital and workers (see also Freeman, 2007).

NOTES

1. See Autor, Katz, and Kearney (2006); Katz (2006); Lemieux et al. (2007); Lemieux (2006); and Cowen (2007).

2. Other work by Michelangeli, Peluso, and Trannoy (2009) does not use consumption data as a proxy for lifetime income, but instead develops a method for detecting changes in permanent income concentration when only consumption data are available. In their empirical analysis of the United States, Michelangeli et al. (2009) find some support for rising concentration, but not as great as that suggested when using data for household net worth.

3. Only a few recent analysts doubt there has been a widespread increase in inequality that can be generally attributed to the growth of high incomes (Reynolds, 2007; Tatom, 2007; but see critiqued in Burtless, 2007).

4. Unearned income from transfers, public and private, also accrues but accounts for under 10 percent of incomes.

5. The sporadic realization of growing incomes from wealth in both the personal and corporate sector has led to serious miss-estimates of both individual and corporate income tax revenues at the federal and state level for the past decade, and especially in recent years (e.g., Schwabish, 2006; CBO, 2006a, 2006b; Orszag, 2007).

6. Wolff and Zacharias (2006a, 2006b) and Haveman, Holden, Wolfe, and Romanov (2006, 2007) use an annuity-based measure of inequality that assumes that all persons, including high income–high wealth persons consume all wealth before they die. Such measures imply the need for assumptions on discount rates, life expectancy, and other variables, and they therefore assume no bequest or inter-vivos transfer behaviors and they ignore the observed behavior of the rich (e.g., see Goolsbee, 2007; Carroll, 2000). We prefer a more straightforward estimate of income from wealth using current and long-run rates of return on existing assets. This seems closer to Haig–Simons income in terms of capacity to consume, without the extra baggage entailed with the annuity estimates, which necessarily suggest higher incomes for much older persons, by design.

7. Indeed Pryor (2007) attests to the importance of interest, rent, and dividends in resizing economic inequality using the PSID.

8. Reported interest, rent, and dividends in the CPS are barely more than half the aggregate amount that other data suggest ought to be reported (CBO, 2006b).

9. Assets in defined benefit pensions are problematic both because of the potential not to be collected and because of back loading in benefit determination. We are less worried about the distributional consequences because most such pensions accrue to the top end of the income distribution and therefore do not affect lower incomes. Our analyses also ignore noncash public sector benefits such as those provided by health, education, and the taxes used to pay for them (see Garfinkel, Rainwater, & Smeeding, 2006, on the latter). While these benefits are especially important for low-income persons, they pale in comparison to the levels of imputed income from assets for the large majority of households, especially middle- and high-income units. Hence, while MCI helps us better understand the impact and importance of residual wealth and the way it affects public and private finances and inequality, it does not represent a complete accounting of all flows of income from all sources.

10. The sample size for the surveys conducted in 2006, 2003, and 2001 was approximately 4,500 households, a slight increase over that in previous years.

11. Household weights contained in the SCF data are used in all of the calculations.

12. To the extent that capital gains realized in year X are not consumed, but reinvested and emerge as assets in year $X+1$, retaining capital gains in the income less capital measure introduces the possibility of "double counting" into the MCI concept. In any case, this decision to include or exclude realized capital gains has a negligible effect on the results presented here. And, to the extent that these gains are consumed and not reinvested, excluding them would understate capital incomes.

13. Other analysts have described the limitations of standard measures of income for welfare and inequality analysis, and proposed solutions by supplementing income with wealth, as much as a half-century ago. Weisbrod and Hansen (1968) and Taussig (1973) added the annuity value of net worth to current income to develop measures they respectively called "income-net worth" and "comprehensive income." In more recent work, Wolff and Zacharias (2006a, 2006b) and Goolsbee (2007) use the annuity approach for nonhousing wealth and impute rental income for homeowners. There are a number of additional differences between the approach used in this chapter and the one used by Wolff and Zacharias (WZ). WZ use SCF for 1983–2001, we use data for 1989–2007. WZ do not conduct any after-tax analysis. For their inequality measures, WZ rely primarily on the Gini index and income shares of different percentile groupings (top 10 percent, top 1 percent, etc.) We use Ginis as well, but rely primarily on ratios of key percentiles of the income distribution (99/50, 95/50, 99/90, etc.) because we find that the biggest impact from using the more complete income approach is found at the very highest income levels and does not have as great of an impact in the Gini. In contrast to prior annuity approaches, WZ assign different rates of return to the different asset types that they annuitize. These rates are long-run returns covering 1960–2000, and generally based on federal Flow of Funds data.

14. We take no account of the amounts of income, which might have been shifted from a heavily taxed form, earnings, to another less heavily taxed form, capital gains or dividends, for instance (Lemieux et al., 2007).

15. See also ERS (2010).

16. We also know that the distribution of housing wealth is not equally distributed across the population, but exhibits considerable regional variation (Carson & Dastrup, 2009). Because of the sample size and absence of subnational geographic identifiers, we are only able to project an average change in housing wealth across the entire country.

17. Changes in weeks worked between 2007 and 2009, because of temporary layoffs or furloughs, will not be reflected in our measure of earnings changes.

18. The MCI rich are similar to but not the same as the "high income" units studied by others. For instance, while 79 percent of the same households are counted in the top 1 percent for both SCF income and MCI, 84 percent of the same units are in the top 10 percent. These percents have fallen over the past 18 years as well. In 1989, the overlap was 83 percent in the top centile and 89 percent in the top decile. Hence the top end of the MCI is increasingly divergent from the top end of the "high income" sample. As the value of assets continues to appreciate in the longer run, and

as the fraction of income from capital grows relative to labor, we expect that the top centiles in each distribution will increasingly diverge.

19. For a discussion of the TAXSIM model see Feenberg and Coutts (1993).

20. We do not calculate the effects of "privileged" types of taxable income (capital gains, dividends, and housing sales) on the composition of pre-tax income.

21. Figures illustrating equivalent trends for after-tax income were included in previous draft, and are available from the authors.

22. Data for years before 2007 are contained both in an earlier version of the chapter, available at http://www.irp.wisc.edu/aboutirp/people/affiliates/Smeeding/ 14-INCOME-FROM-WEALTH_6_21_07.pdf, as well as an additional series of data tables: http://www.irp.wisc.edu/aboutirp/people/affiliates/Smeeding/14b-Appendix-tables-available-from-authors-Jun-7-2007.pdf.

23. Equivalent figures using short-run rates show essentially the same patterns.

24. The SCF includes a set of detailed questions about household vehicles, but in the public-use version of the data only includes the value of the vehicle. SCF staff calculates vehicle value based on the age, make, model, and condition of the vehicle. To calculate the vehicle service flow, we multiply the vehicle value by the rate of depreciation plus the rate of depreciation. Also, following Slesnick (1994, 2001), we assume a rate of depreciation of 10 percent.

25. The estimates of labor share exclude the nonpension portion of total nonwage compensation. Adding in employer subsides for health care, the one large and ignored element of compensation, might reduce the trend slightly, but it would not change the qualitative conclusion that the long-term capital share is rising

26. Lemieux et al. (2007) describe how performance-based or incentive-based pay has increasingly driven the income share of the top centime, but these same annual performance pay increases are no doubt also driving accumulated wealth at the tip of the MCI distribution in recent years, but with a one-year or longer lag

27. These relationships include legally married couples and other couples that are "partners."

28. Results in expanded tables available from the authors.

29. Available at http://www.irp.wisc.edu/aboutirp/people/affiliates/Smeeding/ 14-INCOME-FROM-WEALTH_6_21_07.pdf.

30. Three different versions of the SCF data for each year are used. The household income variable and many of the broader asset and income definitions as well as key demographic details are available in the "Extract of the Full Public Data Set" (in Stata) version of the SCF. This version of the data contains the variables used in Federal Reserve *Bulletin* article. Detailed asset classes not included in the extract file were accessed through the "Full Public Data Set" (in Stata). Key variables from the full data set were merged into the extract file. Finally, the full public access version of the data was accessed a second time in SAS. This was done because the SCF tax programs are coded in SAS. Use of the SCF tax programs and NBER's TAXSIM is discussed in more detail below. (All of these versions are available at the SCF web site: www.federalreserve.gov/Pubs/oss/ oss2/scfindex.html.)

31. This adjustment was made on account of households with negative incomes even after imputation of flows to all assets. These households had large trust and royalty income, but experienced negative capital gains income that left them with

relatively low (or zero) SCF income. When the trust and royalty income was subtracted from SCF income, the result was deeply negative income that dwarfed the imputed flow to their assets. This occurred in less than 3 percent of households in the 2003 data. The adjustment has little or no effect on the overall results.

32. The actual long-run rates applied reduced the return to bonds and stocks by roughly 3.0 percentage points to adjust for annual rates of inflation. See Table A1 for details.

33. Tables A1 and A2 include details for the long-run and short-run rates of return applied to each income concept between 1989 and 2007. The year-to-year short-run rates vary by period and asset type (see Table A2).

34. The TAXSIM is available online at http://www.nber.org/~taxsim/.

35. These are fields 9 and 10 of the TAXSIM input file.

36. In addition, these results are also calculated with the imputed flows in MCI classified as "other property income" in TAXSIM. The impacts of this difference are minimal, and only present for 2004 and after.

ACKNOWLEDGMENTS

The opinions and conclusions are solely those of the authors and should not be construed as representing the opinions of our employers. We thank Anthony B. Atkinson, Andrea Brandolini, Gary Burtless, Daniel Feenberg, Robert Haveman, Karen Nordberg, Emanuel Saez, Eugene Smolensky, Robert Pollack, John Nye, Jodi Sandfort, Barbara Torrey, Rosa García Fernández, and Bruce Meyer for comments and suggestions on a previous draft; and also the participants in seminars given at the OECD, The Tobin Project, Washington University, St Louis, Syracuse University, and the MacArthur Network on the Family and the Economy. We thank Kati Foley, Karen Cimilluca, and Mary Santy for data and manuscript preparation.

REFERENCES

Aaberge, R. (2009). Ranking intersecting Lorenz curves. *Social Choice and Welfare, 33*(2), 235–259.

Acemoglu, D. (2002). Technical change, inequality, and the labor market. *Journal of Economic Literature, 40*(1), 7–72.

Ackerman, E. (2006). Google 'Business Founder' No. 1 – 289 million, plus stock option gains. *Mercury News*, May 21, 2006.

Aron-Dine, A., & Shapiro, I. (2006). *Share of national income going to wages and salaries at record low in 2006: Share of income going to corporate profits at record high,* Washington, DC: Center on Budget and Priorities. Revised March 29, 2007. http://www.cbpp.org/8-31-06inc.pdf.

Atkinson, A. B. (2006). *Concentration among the rich*. Research Paper no. 2006/151, December. United Nations University – World Institute for Development Economics Research, Helsinki, Finland.

Atkinson, A. B. (2009). Income inequality in historical and comparative perspective: A graphical overview. In: *Conference on inequality in a time of contraction at Stanford University*, November 2009.

Atkinson, A. B., Piketty, T., & Saez, E. (2009). *Top incomes in the long run of history*. NBER Working Paper no. 15408, October.

Auten, G., & Carroll, R. (1999). The effect of income taxes on household income. *Review of Economics and Statistics, 81*(4), 681–693.

Autor, D., Katz, L. F., & Kearney, M. S. (2008). Trends in U.S. wage inequality: Revising the revisionists. *Review of Economics and Statistics, 90*(2), 300–323.

Autor, D. H., Katz, L. F., & Kearney, M. S. (2006). The polarization of the U.S. labor market. *American Economic Review, 96*(2), 189–194.

Bach, S., Corneo, G., & Steiner, V. (2007). *From bottom to top: The entire distribution of market income in Germany, 1992–2001*. IZA Discussion Papers, 2723, April. Institute for the Study of Labor.

Baker, M., Nagel, S., & Wurgler, J. (2006). *The effect of dividends on consumption*. NBER Working Paper no. 12288, June. National Bureau of Economic Research, Cambridge, MA.

Blinder, A. S. (2007). *How many US jobs might be offshorable*? CEPS Working Paper no. 142, March. Center for Economic Policy Studies, Princeton, NJ.

Brandolini, A., & Smeeding, T. (2009). Income inequality in richer and OECD countries. In: W. Salverda, B. Nolan & T. M. Smeeding (Eds), *Oxford handbook of economic inequality* (pp. 71–100). Oxford, UK: Oxford University Press.

Bureau of Economic Analysis. (2010). *National income and product accounts*, Table 1.12.

Burkhauser, R. V., Feng, S., Jenkins, S., & Larrimore, J. (2009). *Recent trends in top income shares in the USA: Reconciling estimates from March CPS and IRS tax return data*. NBER Working Paper no. 15320. National Bureau of Economic Research, Cambridge, MA.

Burtless, G. (2007). Comments on 'Has US income inequality *really* increased'. Presented at Cato Institute.

Canberra Group. (2001). *Expert group on household income statistics: Final report and recommendations*. Ottawa, Canada: Statistics Canada.

Carroll, C. D. (2000). Why do the rich save so much? In: J. B. Slemrod (Ed.), *Does atlas shrug? The economic consequences of taxing the rich* (pp. 465–484). Cambridge, MA: Harvard University Press.

Carson, R., & Dastrup, S. (2009). *After the fall: An ex post characterization of housing price declines across metropolitan areas*. U.C. San Diego Working Paper, November 23.

Case, K. (2010). A dream house after all. *The New York Times*. September 1.

Congressional Budget Office. (2006a). *How CBO forecasts income*. Congressional Budget Office Background Paper, August. CBO, Washington, DC.

Congressional Budget Office. (2006b). *The treatment of federal receipts and expenditures in the national income and product accounts* (September). Washington, DC: CBO.

Congressional Budget Office. (2010). *Historical effective federal tax rates: 1979 to 2007* (June). Washington, DC: CBO.

Cowen, T. (2007). Why is income inequality in America so pronounced? Consider education. *New York Times*, May 17.

Cox, W. M., & Alm, R. (1999). *Myths of rich & poor: Why we're better off than we think* (1st ed.). New York: Basic Books.

Davis, B., & Frank, R. (2009). Income gap shrinks at the expense of the wealthy. *Wall Street Journal*, September 10.

Economic Research Service. (2010). *Farm household well-being: Comparing consumption- and income-based measures.* US Department of Agriculture Economic Research Report no. ERR-91, February.

Engemann, K., & Wall, H. (2009). *The effects of recessions across demographic groups.* Federal Reserve Bank of St. Louis, Working Paper 2009–052A, October.

Feenberg, D., & Coutts, E. (1993). An introduction to the TAXSIM model. *Journal of Policy Analysis and Management, 12*(1), 189–194.

Frank, R. (2007). *Richistan: A journey through the American wealth boom and the lives of the new rich.* New York: Crown Publishers.

Freeman, R. B. (2007). *America works: Critical thoughts on the exceptional U.S. labor market.* New York: Russell Sage Foundation.

Garfinkel, I., Rainwater, L., & Smeeding, T. M. (2006). A reexamination of welfare state and inequality in rich nations: How in-kind transfers and indirect taxes change the story. *Journal of Policy Analysis and Management, 25*(4), 897–919.

Glick, R., & Lansing, K. (2010). *Global household leverage, house prices, and consumption.* Economic Letter #2010-01, January. Federal Reserve Bank of San Francisco.

Glyn, A. (2009). Functional distribution of income. In: W. Salverda, B. Nolan & T. M. Smeeding (Eds), *Oxford handbook of economic inequality* (pp. 101–125). Oxford, UK: Oxford University Press.

Goldfarb, R. S., & Leonard, T. C. (2005). Inequality of what among whom? Rival conceptions of distribution in the 20th century. In: W. J. Samuels, J. E. Biddle & R. B. Emmett (Eds), *Research in the history of economic thought and methodology* (Vol. 23-A, pp. 75–118). Oxford, UK: Elsevier.

Goldin, C., & Katz, L. F. (2007). *The race between education and technology: The evolution of U.S. educational wage differentials, 1890 to 2005.* NBER Working Paper no. 12984, March. National Bureau of Economic Research, Cambridge, MA.

Goolsbee, A. (2007). Why do the richest people rarely intend to give it all away? *New York Times*, March 1.

Gordon, R. J., & Dew-Becker, I. (2005). Where did the productivity growth go? Inflation dynamics and the distribution of income. *Brookings Papers on Economic Activity* (2), 67–127.

Gruber, J., & Saez, E. (2002). The elasticity of taxable income: Evidence and implications. *Journal of Public Economics, 84*(1), 1–32.

Guscina, A. (2006). *Effects of globalization on labor's share in national income.* IMF Working Paper 06/294, December. International Monetary Fund, Washington, DC.

Haveman, R., Holden, K., Wolfe, B., & Romanov, A. (2007). Assessing the maintenance of savings sufficiency over the first decade of retirement. *International Tax and Public Finance*, August.

Haveman, R., Holden, K., Wolfe, B., & Sherlund, S. (2006). Do newly retired workers in the United States have sufficient resources to maintain well-being? *Economic Inquiry, 44*(2), 249–264.

Heathcote, J., Perri, F., & Violante, G. L. (2010a). Unequal we stand: An empirical analysis if economic inequality in the US, 1967–2006. *Review of Economic Dynamics, 13*(1), 15–51.

Heathcote, J., Perri, F., & Violante, G. L. (2010b). Inequality in times of crisis: Lessons from the past and a first look at the current recession. VoxEU.org, February.

Kaplan, S. N., & Rauh, J. D. (2010). Wall street and main street: What contributes to the rise in the highest incomes? *The Review of Financial Studies, 23*(3), 1004–1050.

Katz, L. (2006). Narrowing, widening, polarizing: The evolution of the U.S. wage structure. Presented at Society of Labor Economists Eleventh Annual Meeting, May, Cambridge, MA.

Krueger, D., & Ludwig, A. (2006). *On the consequences of demographic change for rates of returns to capital, and the distribution of wealth and welfare.* NBER Working Paper no. 12453, August. National Bureau of Economic Research, Cambridge, MA.

Krueger, D., Perri, F., Pistaferri, L., & Violante, G. L. (2010). Cross-sectional facts for macroeconomists. *Review of Economic Dynamics, 13*(1), 1–14.

Lemieux, T. (2006). Increasing residual wage inequality: Composition effects, noisy data, or rising demand for skill? *American Economic Review, 96*(3), 461–498.

Lemieux, T., MacLeod, W. B., & Parent, D. (2007). *Performance pay and wage inequality.* NBER Working Paper no. 13128, May. National Bureau of Economic Research, Cambridge, MA.

Leonhardt, D., & Fabrikant, G. (2009). Rise of the super-rich hits a sobering wall. *New York Times,* August 21.

Levy, F., & Temin, P. (2007). *Inequality and institutions in 20th century America.* NBER Working Paper no. 13106, May. National Bureau of Economic Research, Cambridge, MA.

Love, D., & Smith, P. (2007). Measuring dissaving out of retirement wealth. Available at SSRN: http://ssrn.com/abstract=968431. Accessed on March 2007.

Meyer, B., & Sullivan, J. (2003). Measuring the well-being of the poor using income and consumption. *Journal of Human Resources, 38*(S), 1180–1220.

Meyer, B., & Sullivan, J. (2010). *Consumption and income inequality in the US: 1960–2008.* Working Paper, December 27, 2009.

Michelangeli, A., Peluso, E., & Trannoy, A. (2009). *American baby-losers? Robust indirect comparison of affluence across generations.* ECINEQ Working Paper 2009-133, September.

Mishel, L., Bernstein, J., & Allegretto, S. (2005). *The state of working America, 2004/2005.* Ithaca, NY: Cornell University Press.

Monea, E., & Sawhill, I. (2009). *Simulating the effect of the "Great Recession" on poverty* (September). Washington, DC: Brookings Institution, Center on Children and Families.

NBER. (2010). *Business cycle expansions and contractions.* Available at http://www.nber.org/cycles.html. Accessed on October 10, 2010.

Orszag, P. R. (2007). *Letter to the honorable Kent Conrad on federal tax revenues from 2003 to 2006* (May). Washington, DC: Congressional Budget Office.

Parker, J. A., & Vissing-Jorgensen, A. (2009). *Who bears aggregate fluctuations and how?* Papers and Proceedings of AEA, May.

Peichl, A., Schaefer, T., & Scheicher, C. (2010). Measuring richness and poverty: A micro data application to Europe and Germany. *Review of Income and Wealth, 56*(3), 597–619.

Petev, I., Pistaferri, & L., Saporta, V. (2010). Consumption and the great recession. Presented at Stanford Poverty Conference on the Great Recession, February, Stanford University.

Piketty, T., & Saez, E. (2003). Income inequality in the United States, 1913–1998. *Quarterly Journal of Economics, 118*(1), 1–39.

Piketty, T., & Saez, E. (2006). *The evolution of top incomes: A historical and international perspective.* NBER Working Paper no. 11955. National Bureau of Economic Research, Cambridge, MA.

Porter, E. (2006). After years of growth, what about workers' share? *New York Times,* October 15.

Poterba, J., Venti, S. F., & Wise, D. A. (2007). *Rise of 401(k) plans, lifetime earnings, and wealth at retirement.* NBER Working Paper no. 13091, May. National Bureau of Economic Research, Cambridge, MA.

Pryor, F. (2007). The anatomy of increasing inequality of US family incomes. *Journal of Socio-Economics, 36*(4), 595–618.

Reynolds, A. (2007). *Has U.S. income inequality really increased?* Policy Analysis no. 586, January. Cato Institute, Washington, DC.

Saez, E. (2010). *Striking it richer: The evolution of top incomes in the United States* (updated with 2008 estimates). Unpublished research note, July.

Schwabish, J. A. (2006). *Earnings inequality and high earners: Changes during and after the stock market boom of the 1990s.* Working Paper no. 2006-06, April. Congressional Budget Office, Washington, DC.

Sierminska, E., & Takhtamanova, Y. (2006). Wealth effects on consumption: Cross country and demographic group comparisons. Presented at 29th General Conference of the IARIW, Joensuu, Finland.

Slesnick, D. (1994). Aggregate consumption and saving in the postwar United States. *The Review of Economics and Statistics, 74*(4), 585–597.

Slesnick, D. (2001). Consumption, needs, and inequality. *International Economic Review, 35*(3), 677–703.

Smeeding, T., & Thompson, J. (2010). Inequality in the distribution of income from labor and income from capital over the recession. Presented at the Tobin Project Conference on Inequality, April–May 2010.

Smeeding, T. M. (2005). Public policy, economic inequality, and poverty: The United States in comparative perspective. *Social Science Quarterly, 86*(5), 955–983.

Tatom, J. A. (2007). *Is inequality growing as American workers fall behind?* Working Paper no. 2007-WP-07, February. Networks Financial Institute, Indiana State University, Indianapolis.

Taussig, M. K. (1973). *Alternative measures of the distribution of economic welfare.* Research Report Series no. 116. Industrial Relations Section, Princeton University, Princeton, NJ.

U.S. Census Bureau. (2010). *Income, poverty, and health insurance coverage in the United States, 2009.* Current Population Reports, P60-238. U.S. Census Bureau, Washington, DC.

Walker, R. (2005). *Superstars and renaissance men: Specialization, market size and the income distribution.* CEP Discussion Paper no. 707, November. Centre for Economic Performance, London School of Economics and Political Science, London.

Weisbrod, B. A., & Hansen, W. L. (1968). An income-net worth approach to measuring economic welfare. *American Economic Review, 58*(5), 1315–1329.

Wolff, E. N., & Zacharias, A. (2006a). *Household wealth and the measurement of economic well-being in the United States.* Levy Economics Institute Working Paper no. 447, May. Levy Economics Institute, Bard College, Annandale-on-Hudson, NY.

Wolff, E. N., & Zacharias, A. (2006b). *Wealth and economic inequality: Who's at the top of the economic ladder?* Annandale-on-Hudson, NY: Levy Economics Institute, Bard College.

TECHNICAL APPENDIX. CONSTRUCTING MCI AND ADDING TAXES

Income net wealth ("*income less capital*") is calculated by subtracting realized income from capital from the SCF income definition.[30] Hence, reported interest, rents, and dividends are excluded in the given income year. Capital gains income, realized from the sale of an asset, is retained in MCI.

In allocating the functional share of income between labor and capital, and further in accounting for capital income flows, we partition self-employment income as follows: in the cases where SEBI exceeds income from wages, 30 percent of SEBI is considered a return to capital and is also subtracted from SCF income to complete "less capital." In cases where SEBI is less than income from wages, we treat all SEBI as income from labor. This practice is the same as that employed by others who also split SEBI into labor and capital components (e.g., see Canberra Report, 2001).

After removing income from capital from SCF income, flows to assets are imputed for the full range of assets measured in the SCF data. Separate rates of return were applied for stocks, bonds, and housing assets. Specific rates applied to the assets are based on historic returns data described in greater detail below. The return to stocks is based on the Dow Jones Industrial Average. The return to bonds is based on 10-year U.S. Treasury notes. The return to residential real estate is based on Office of Federal Housing Enterprise Oversight (OFHEO) House Price Index. In addition, flows to assets are calculated gross of the inflation rate (CPI-U), while some flows are based on the average of two different types of return (the average of the return to stocks and bonds, for example). The details are contained in Table A1.

The following additive series of combined capital income flows are added to income, net of reported interest, rent, and dividends, in the order specified below:

- "*plus finance*" adds imputed flows to directly held stocks, stock mutual funds, combination mutual funds, bonds, other bond mutual funds, savings bonds, government bond mutual funds, and tax-free bond mutual funds, as well as "other managed assets," such as trusts and annuities to "*income less capital*";
- "*plus retire*" adds flows to "quasi-liquid retirement accounts," such as IRA/Keoghs and account-type pensions to "*plus finance*";
- "*plus home*" adds flows to owner-occupied home equity to "*plus retire*";

- "*plus oth invest*" adds flows to investment real estate equity, transaction accounts, certificates of deposit (CDs), and the cash value of whole life insurance to "*plus home*";
- "*plus business*" adds flows to other business assets and vehicles – only vehicles worth more than $50,000 – to "*plus oth invest*";
- *MCI* subtracts flows to non-real-estate debt, including credit card debt, installment loans, and other debt from "*plus business*" – after replacing observations, where "plus business" value incomes were below SCF income with the SCF income value.[31]

Separate estimates for each of these income concepts are created using both long-run (30-year) averages and short-run (3-year) time-specific rates. The long-run rates are based on the average annual return between 1977 and 2007, with the same long-run rate applied to each year of SCF data – 1989, 1992, 1995, 1998, 2001, 2004, 2007, and projections of the data into 2009.[32] Short-run returns are averages of the three years leading up to the survey year. The short-run return for income year 1989, for example, is based on the annual average return between 1987 and 1989. Income is from the completed calendar year prior to the survey. Assets are valued at the time of the survey, completed in the second half of the year. Imputed flows for 1989, for example, are based on wealth stocks reported between June and December of 1990.[33]

The long-run nominal rates of return for stocks, bonds, housing, and inflation are 7, 5, 6, and 3 percent, respectively, and are smaller than the 1977–2007 and 1989–2007 averages for this period. We believe that the long-run rates are modest and we know that they reflect estimates used by others. For instance, the 4 percent real return for stocks (7 percent minus 3 percent inflation adjustment) is the same as that used by the Social Security Advisory Board to score the net effects of investing Social Security funds in the private equities market. Also, the 6 percent rate of return for housing is identical to the real return that Case (2010) suggests homeowners should anticipate after maintenance. Finally, we assume a long-run nonhousing debt rate of 9 percent. Housing debt is factored in when determining net imputed rent on owned and other housing equity.

6.1. Incorporating taxes

In addition to the MCI concepts described above, three additional after-tax income concepts are calculated for each year up through 2007. Taxes for all

Table A1. Rates of Return Applied to Different Portions of Full-Income.

Type of Income	Definition	Return Categories	Long-Run Rates	1977–2007	1987–1989	1990–1992	1993–1995	1996–1998	1999–2001	2002–2004	2005–2007
SCF income	Fed gross income										
Less capital	SCF income less income from wealth (rent, interest, dividends, trusts, and annuities)										
Plus finance	+ imputed flows to stocks and bonds + imputed flows to annuities and trusts	SI	0.07	0.095	0.147	0.070	0.152	0.210	0.044	0.036	0.073
		SIBI[a]	0.06	0.085	0.116	0.074	0.108	0.135	0.050	0.039	0.059
		BI	0.05	0.076	0.086	0.078	0.065	0.060	0.055	0.043	0.045
		CPI	0.03	0.042	0.043	0.040	0.026	0.021	0.025	0.026	0.035
Plus retire	+ imputed flows to quasi-liquid retirement accounts	SI	0.07	0.095	0.147	0.070	0.152	0.210	0.044	0.036	0.073
Plus home	+ imputed flow to primary residence	HI	0.06	0.059	0.060	0.023	0.025	0.041	0.064	0.074	0.070
Plus oth invest	+ imputed flow to other residences and	SI	0.07	0.095	0.147	0.070	0.152	0.210	0.044	0.036	0.073
		CPI+1	0.04	0.052	0.053	0.050	0.036	0.031	0.035	0.036	0.045
		BI	0.05	0.076	0.086	0.078	0.065	0.060	0.055	0.043	0.045

investment real estate + imputed flow to transaction accounts + imputed flow to CDs and whole life insurance	BICPI[b]	0.04	0.059	0.064	0.059	0.046	0.041	0.040	0.034	0.040
Plus business + imputed flow to other assets and businesses + imputed flow to vehicle wealth	SI	0.07	0.095	0.147	0.070	0.152	0.210	0.044	0.036	0.073
MCI − imputed interest flow for remaining debts (after replacing plus business with SCF income when plus business < SCF income)	CPI + 6	0.09	0.102	0.103	0.100	0.086	0.081	0.085	0.086	0.095

[a] Average of **SI** and **BI** is for "combination" mutual funds, CPI is for tax-free bonds.
[b] Whole life insurance is given **BI** rate, CDs are given average of **BI** and CPI.

Table A2. Short-Run (3-Year Average) and Long-Run (1988–2007) Rates of Return.

	Housing Index (HI) (percent)	Stock Indices (SI) (percent)	Bond Indices (BI) (percent)	Inflation (CPI) (percent)
A. "Short Run"				
1989	6.0	14.7	8.6	4.3
1992	2.3	7.0	7.8	4.0
1995	2.5	15.2	6.5	2.6
1998	4.1	21.0	6.0	2.1
2001	6.4	4.4	5.5	2.5
2004	7.4	3.6	4.3	2.6
2007	7.0	7.3	4.5	3.5
B. "Long-run"[a]	6.0	7.0	5.0	3.0

[a]Rates used for 1988–1989 to 2006–2007.

three are federal income taxes calculated using the National Bureau of Economic Research (NBER) TAXSIM program. All of the required input for TAXSIM is generated based on programs developed by Fed economist Kevin Moore, and is available on the NBER web site.[34]

The first after-tax concept is simply reported SCF income less taxes, a version of disposable personal income (dpi). The second concept is income net wealth *and* net taxes. Income net wealth is defined as described above ("less capital") and the related taxes are calculated with TAXSIM by eliminating dividend and "other property" income, including interest, from the input file.[35] The final after-tax concept is based on MCI. In this case, the sum of the imputed flow to assets included in MCI is categorized as dividend income and the taxes calculated by TAXSIM.[36] The resulting federal taxes are subtracted from MCI to create "MCI less tax."

Table A3. Adjustments Made to SCF Income and Asset Categories for 2009 Projection.

Income	Matching Source. Table (Row Number)	Source Detail	Percent Change from 2007 Q3/4 to 2009 Q3/4
Interest	NIPA. 2.1 (14)		−5.8
Dividends	NIPA. 2.1 (15)		−28.6
Nontaxable investment income	NIPA. 2.1 (14)	"SCF detail refers to bonds"	−5.8
Other business/ investment/rent/ trust	NIPA. 1.12 (9, 39)	Combined rental and proprietor	5.7
Earnings	Analysis of CPS ORG, January to November		Varies by industry, education
Proprietors income	NIPA. 2.1 (9)		−4.4
Capital gains	CBO January 2009 budget outlook	Anticipated tax revenue decline of 40%	−40.0
Public transfers (excluding Social Security)	NIPA. 2.1 (17 less 18)		36.2
Retirement income (including Social Security)	NIPA. 2.1 (18)		15.3
Assets			
CDs	FOF. B.100 (12)	Time and savings deposits	4.9
Stocks	FOF. B.100 (24)	Corporate equities	−21.6
Stock mutual funds	FOF. B.100 (25)	Mutual fund shares	−12.6
Bonds	FOF. B.100 (18)	Treasury securities	404.2
Other bond mutual funds	FOF. B.100 (21)	Corporate and foreign bonds	21.9
Savings bonds	FOF. B.100 (17)	Savings bonds	−2.5
Government bond mutual funds	FOF. B.100 (19)	Agency and GSE- backed securities	−83.7
Tax-free bond mutual funds	FOF. B.100 (20)	Municipal securities	9.2
Combination and other mutual funds	FOF. B.100 (25)	Mutual fund shares	−12.6
Other (trusts, annuities, etc.)	FOF. B.100 (30)	Miscellaneous	10.8

Table A3. (*Continued*)

Income	Matching Source. Table (Row Number)	Source Detail	Percent Change from 2007 Q3/4 to 2009 Q3/4
Home equity	FOF. B.100(49)	Owner's equity in household real estate	−41.0
Quasi-liquid retirement	Urban Institute Analysis of FOF	www.urban.org/ retirement_policy/ url.cfm?ID = 41197	−14.0
Transaction accounts	FOF. B.100 (11)	(Checkable deposits)	140.1
Life insurance	FOF. B.100 (27)	Life insurance reserves asset	3.8
Nonresidential real estate	FOF. B.100 (49)	Owner's equity in household real estate	−41.0
Other residential real estate	FOF. B.100 (4)	Modify in same way as residential real estate	−21.4
Debt for other residential property	FOF. B.100 (33)	Home mortgages	−1.3
Other financial assets	FOF. B.100 (30)	Miscellaneous assets	10.8
Other nonfinancial assets	FOF. B.100 (7) and (30) combined	Consumer durables or miscellaneous assets	9.8
Business with active or nonactive household interest	FOF. B.100(29)	Equity in noncorporate business	−23.6
Vehicles	FOF. B.100 (7)	Consumer durables or miscellaneous assets	9.6
Total debt	FOF. B.100 (31)	Total liabilities	−1.4
Mortgages and home equity loans	FOF. B.100 (33)	Home mortgages	−1.3
Home equity lines of credit	FOF. B.100 (33)	Home mortgages	−1.3

Table A4. Change in Earnings between 2007 and 2009, by Education and Industry.

	Dropout (percent)	HS Only (percent)	Some College, No Degree (percent)	Bachelor's Degree or More (percent)
Agriculture, fish, forest, construction	−23.9	−13.1	−10.1	4.9
Manufacturing, information, publishing	−21.4	−12.7	−9.3	1.2
Trade, leisure, restaurants	−9.1	−3.4	−1.1	2.2
Utilities, professional, educational, health services	−10.0	2.0	7.1	6.9
Data, finance, other services	−6.1	−0.8	−2.5	2.7
Public administration	−22.0	3.4	3.8	9.4

Notes: Earnings change figures estimated from Current Population Survey, Outgoing Rotation Group data, for January through November of 2007 and 2009. The education and industry groupings are based on the categories in the public SCF data. Earnings change is the difference between the cumulative weekly earnings for each industry/education cell in 2007 and 2009. Differencing total earnings reflects changes in employment, weekly hours worked, and wages.

Table A5. Basic Trends from SCF – Comparisons Over Time – Long-Run Rates.

	1988–1989	1991–1992	1994–1995	1997–1998	2000–2001	2003–2004	2006–2007	2009 Projection
Panel A: MCI[a]								
99/10 ratio	50.5	40.9	45.3	54.2	71.7	63.0	71.6	63.2
99/50 ratio	11.5	10.2	10.4	13.5	17.4	15.6	18.8	17.5
10/50 ratio	0.23	0.25	0.23	0.25	0.24	0.25	0.26	0.28
Gini	0.560	0.526	0.540	0.561	0.595	0.579	0.608	0.600
Panel B: % change between SCF net some capital income and MCI[b]								
Mean	33.9	35.8	35.5	38.0	40.0	45.2	50.8	40.9
Median	20.0	21.9	17.2	19.6	22.4	21.9	25.6	20.8
99th percentile	65.2	58.1	68.9	77.0	90.4	104.2	99.8	78.3
99/10 ratio	32.7	29.9	37.1	41.2	63.6	69.7	57.8	59.1
99/50 ratio	37.6	29.7	44.1	48.0	55.6	67.5	59.1	47.6
10/50 ratio	3.6	−0.2	4.9	4.6	−5.1	−1.3	0.8	−7.2

Note: For details on the definitions and rates used in developing Full Income see Tables 3 and 4.
[a]MCI (more complete income) subtracts capital income (except realized capital gains) from gross income and adds back flows to assets and debt.
[b]SCF net some capital income takes gross income and subtracts interest, rent, dividends, and annuity and trust income, but retains realized capital gains.

Table A6.   Values of Net Worth by Alternative Rankings – 2007.

	By Net Worth	By SCF Income	By MCI	Addendum: MCI by Percentile (Short-Run Rates)
p10	11	68,039	23,112	25,664
p50	117,033	168,848	152,491	135,278
p90	870,988	876,835	864,138	761,991
p95	1,686,125	1,491,843	1,645,577	1,488,262
p99	6,252,244	5,607,287	6,509,146	6,443,411

CONSUMPTION AND INCOME POVERTY OVER THE BUSINESS CYCLE[☆]

Bruce D. Meyer and James X. Sullivan

ABSTRACT

We examine the relationship between the business cycle and poverty for the period from 1960 to 2008 using income data from the Current Population Survey and consumption data from the Consumer Expenditure Survey. This new evidence on the relationship between macroeconomic conditions and poverty is of particular interest, given recent changes in antipoverty policies that have placed greater emphasis on participation in the labor market and in-kind transfers. We look beyond official poverty, examining alternative income poverty and consumption poverty, which have conceptual and empirical advantages as measures of the well-being of the poor. We find that both income and consumption poverty are sensitive to macroeconomic conditions. A 1 percentage point increase in unemployment is associated with an increase in the after-tax income poverty rate of 0.9–1.1 percentage points in the long run, and an increase in the consumption poverty rate of 0.3–1.2 percentage points in

[☆] We have benefited from the comments of the editor, two referees, and participants at the IZA/OECD Workshop "Economic Crisis, Rising Unemployment and Policy Responses: What Does It Mean for the Income Distribution?".

Who Loses in the Downturn? Economic Crisis, Employment and Income Distribution
Research in Labor Economics, Volume 32, 51–82
ISSN: 0147-9121/doi:10.1108/S0147-9121(2011)0000032005

the long run. The evidence on whether income is more responsive to the business cycle than consumption is mixed. Income poverty does appear to be more responsive using national level variation, but consumption poverty is often more responsive to unemployment when using regional variation. Low percentiles of both income and consumption are sensitive to macroeconomic conditions, and in most cases, low percentiles of income appear to be more responsive than low percentiles of consumption.

Keywords: poverty; business cycles; unemployment; consumption; income

JEL Classification: D6; E31; I3

1. INTRODUCTION

There are two standard sets of tools that have been used to reduce poverty: programs that directly target poor populations and policies that alleviate poverty indirectly through economic growth that benefits the worst off. There is a consensus that the latter set of policies has greater potential impact.[1] In her essay on fighting poverty, Blank (2000) concludes that "a strong macroeconomy matters more than anything else." However, in some periods, the relationship between growth and poverty appears weak. There is also disagreement on the link between specific policies and the macroeconomy. We reexamine the relationship between the macroeconomy and poverty. We do this in part because past work has found a changing relationship between poverty and measures of the macroeconomy. Past work has emphasized that the relationship between official poverty and unemployment is very strong in some decades, but weak in others. There is even greater concern that the relationship may be different in recent years than in the past because our safety net has undergone a dramatic transformation. Policies such as welfare reform, Earned Income Tax Credit (EITC) expansions, expanded childcare, and restrictions on use of food stamps by the able bodied have pushed many low-income families to be more reliant on employment. We expect that the effects of macroeconomic conditions on poverty will be greater when the poor are more closely attached to the labor market. On the contrary, the argument that economic growth helps those at the bottom may also be less evident during times, such as recent decades, when growth is accompanied by a rise in income inequality. In addition, there are a number of groups that are less likely to be affected by macroeconomic fluctuations including those on disability or retirement benefits, both of which have grown recently.

Our analyses will consider several indicators of the well-being of those at the bottom of the distribution. Looking beyond official income poverty measures to improved, broader measures of well-being is important for several reasons. Official pretax income poverty has been widely criticized as poorly measuring the well-being of the worst off. The official measure fails to capture all the resources available to the family including in-kind transfers and tax credits that have been key tools in the antipoverty efforts of the last decades. Other flaws include an unattractive adjustment for family size and changes in the real value of the poverty thresholds over time due to biases in the Consumer Price Index (CPI) (Citro & Michael, 1995; Meyer & Sullivan, 2009).

More importantly, changes in consumption may provide a better measure of the effect of the economy on the well-being of the worst off than changes in income. Even when income changes, consumption may vary little if transfers from extended family members, in-kind government transfers, or access to savings or credit shield a families' living standards from transitory changes in income (Cutler & Katz, 1991; Slesnick, 1993, 2001; Meyer & Sullivan, 2008, 2009). If the importance of factors such as extended families and access to credit changes over time, the effect of the economy on well-being will likely change. Because consumption reflects home and car ownership, which provide a flow of consumption services to their owners even though not captured by income, consumption may provide a better picture of well-being if ownership rates differ across groups or over time.

The consumption and income data available in the United States are both subject to error, but there is evidence that consumption is reported better than income for those near the bottom of the distribution. For example, income is often far below consumption for those with few resources, even for those with little or no assets or debts (Meyer & Sullivan, 2003, 2011). Income measurement issues may be particularly important for this study because many of the types of income that may be more important in recessions seem to be poorly measured in household surveys. For example, in bad economic times, off-the-books income, interfamily transfers, and government transfers are likely to be more prevalent. Each of these sources is not well reported in household surveys (Edin & Lein, 1997; Meyer, Mok, & Sullivan, 2009). Our analyses will shed light on whether consumption poverty is less sensitive to macroeconomic conditions because of the wide variety of ways in which households can smooth their consumption and because mis-reporting of income is likely to be more cyclically sensitive than mis-reporting of consumption.

In addition to alternative poverty rates, we consider how the macro-economy affects low percentiles of the income and consumption distributions. These analyses provide a better picture of the sensitivity of the bottom of the distribution to economic conditions than focusing exclusively on a poverty rate, which is the cumulative distribution function of resources evaluated at a single point.

We find that both income and consumption poverty are sensitive to macroeconomic conditions. The evidence on whether income is more responsive to the business cycle than consumption is mixed. Income poverty does appear to be more responsive using national level variation, but consumption poverty is often more responsive to unemployment when using regional variation. Our results suggest that, for the period from 1981 to 2008, a 1 percentage point increase in unemployment is associated with an increase in the after-tax income poverty rate of 0.9–1.1 percentage points, and an increase in the consumption poverty rate of 0.3–1.2 percentage points. Results for the 2000s indicate that after-tax income poverty is responsive to changes in the national unemployment rate, although the point estimates are smaller than for the 1990s.

The evidence for low percentiles is consistent with that for poverty. Low percentiles of both income and consumption are sensitive to macroeconomic conditions, and in most cases, low percentiles of income appear to be more responsive than low percentiles of consumption. Across several low-income percentiles, we find that a 1 percentage point increase in unemployment is associated with a decline in these percentiles ranging from 4 to 10 percent. For low percentiles of consumption, this range is from 0 to 7 percent.

This chapter advances knowledge in a number of respects. First, we look beyond official poverty, examining alternative income poverty and consumption poverty. Second, we update the relationship between macroeconomic conditions and poverty through 2008. Given the sensitivity to time period found in past work, and recent policy changes, recent years are of special interest. Third, we examine low percentiles of income and consumption to provide a more complete picture of how macroeconomic conditions affect the worst off. Finally, we exploit both regional and national variations in economic conditions.

There are a number of limitations to any analysis of this kind. The relationship between economic conditions and poverty will depend on how government policy responds to a recession. We necessarily estimate the combined effect of macroeconomic conditions and any policy adjustments engendered by those conditions. Also, business cycles vary considerably in the extent to which they affect different industries, demographic groups, or regions. Thus, the relationship between macroeconomic conditions and poverty will differ across cycles. The unique nature of each business cycle makes it difficult to draw general conclusions about the impact of changes in macroeconomic conditions. Moreover, it is difficult to estimate precisely how the response of poverty to the business cycle changes over time, given the short time series for these subperiods. Our own robustness analyses, as well as comparisons of our results to others in the literature, demonstrate variation in estimates across equally plausible specifications for narrow time periods, such as a single decade.

In Section 2, we briefly summarize the key findings from previous studies of the effect of macroeconomic conditions on poverty. In Section 3, we describe the data used to construct alternative income and consumption measures of poverty and the methods used to examine how the macroeconomy is related to these outcomes. We present our results in Section 4. In Section 5, we briefly simulate poverty rates for the current recession, and we offer conclusions in Section 6.

2. PREVIOUS RESEARCH ON POVERTY AND MACROECONOMIC CONDITIONS

A long series of papers have examined the relationship between macroeconomic conditions and poverty.[2] The consensus from this literature is that the relationship between national unemployment and official poverty is strong, but the magnitude of the effect is sensitive to the years examined.[3] For example, using data from 1959 to 1983, Blank and Blinder (1986) find that a 1 percentage point rise in unemployment results in a 1.1 percentage point increase in poverty. Comparable estimates from Cutler and Katz (1991), whose sample period covers 1959–1989, indicate that a 1 point rise in the unemployment rate raises poverty by 0.43–0.69 points. These and other papers conclude that the effect of inflation on poverty is much more modest than that of unemployment.[4]

The literature has also emphasized that the relationship between macroeconomic conditions and poverty has changed over time. Early studies documented a strong relationship for the 1960s. However, there is evidence that this relationship weakened in the 1970s and particularly the 1980s (Blank, 1993). During the economic expansion from 1983 to 1989, real gross domestic product (GDP) grew by 27 percent, unemployment fell by 45 percent, but poverty fell a modest 16 percent. More recent studies have shown the relationship between unemployment and poverty to be stronger in the 1990s than in the 1980s, but still weaker than earlier years (Blank, 2000; Haveman & Schwabish, 2000).

A number of studies have documented how the relationship between macroeconomic conditions and poverty differs across demographic groups. Recent examples include Blank (2000, 2009) and Gundersen and Ziliak (2004). Blank (2000, 2009) finds that poverty is particularly responsive to unemployment for groups that have high exposure to public assistance: single mother families and black families. In the earlier paper, she finds for both of these groups that the relationship is stronger in the 1990s than in any earlier decade.

Our chapter contributes to the existing literature in several important ways. First, this literature has focused, almost exclusively, on officially measured poverty.[5] We consider alternative poverty measures that address known criticisms in the official measure. In addition to broader measures of income poverty, we examine consumption poverty, which is arguably a better measure of the well-being of the poor. As far as we know, we are the first to look at the relationship between macroeconomic conditions and consumption poverty. Second, we update past work by examining the relationship between macroeconomic conditions and poverty through 2008. This recent evidence is particularly interesting, given the flurry of antipoverty policies over the past two decades that have placed greater emphasis on participation in the labor market and in-kind transfers. Third, in addition to poverty measures, we will look at low percentiles of the distributions of income and consumption to provide a more complete picture of how the bottom of the distribution responds to the business cycle. Finally, we exploit both regional and national variations in economic conditions. This additional source of variation allows us to estimate more precisely how economic conditions are related to the well-being of the worst-off. In addition, we can estimate models with year fixed effects, which control for aggregate changes that have similar effects on poverty or low percentiles in all regions, such as changes in federal tax and transfer policies.

3. DATA AND METHODS

Our analyses of the relationship between macroeconomic conditions and the well-being of the worst off rely on official statistics on unemployment and poverty as well as alternative poverty measures and percentiles of the income and consumption distribution that we calculate using nationally representative survey data. The income data come from the ASEC/ADF Supplement to the Current Population Survey (CPS) and the consumption data come from the Interview component of the Consumer Expenditure (CE) Survey.

The CPS is the source for many official income statistics including poverty rates. Respondents to the CPS report information on a number of different sources of money income. In addition, the survey collects information on some noncash benefits such as food stamps, housing subsidies, and public health insurance. To calculate alternative income poverty measures and percentiles of the income distribution, we use the 1964–2009 CPS surveys, which provide data on income for the previous calendar year. In the analyses that follow, we consider three different measures of income: pretax money income, after-tax money income, and after-tax money income plus noncash benefits. Pretax money income is the measure used in official poverty statistics. To calculate after-tax money income, we add the value of tax credits such as the EITC and subtract state and federal income taxes and payroll taxes, as explained in the data appendix. Our measure of after-tax money income plus noncash benefits adds to after-tax money income the cash value of food stamps and imputed values for housing and school lunch subsidies and the imputed value of Medicaid and Medicare coverage. For more details, see the data appendix.

The CE survey is the most comprehensive source of spending data for the United States. To calculate the consumption poverty rate and percentiles of the consumption distribution, we use data from the CE survey for the years 1960–1961, 1972–1973, 1980–1981, and 1984–2008. The 1960–1961 surveys provide data on annual expenditures collected in a single interview, whereas the 1972–1973 surveys provide data on annualized expenditures collected from quarterly interviews. Since 1980, quarterly expenditures have been provided. To obtain annual measures, we multiply these quarterly measures by four. We do not use the data from the fourth quarter of 1981 through the fourth quarter of 1983 because the surveys for these quarters only include respondents from urban areas. We group the data for the 1960–1961 period because the data are only representative of the full population when the samples from these two years are combined.

Our measure of consumption includes both durable and nondurable goods. To convert reported expenditures into a measure of consumption, we make a number of adjustments. First, we convert vehicle spending to a service flow equivalent. Instead of including the full purchase price of a vehicle, we calculate a flow that reflects the value that a consumer receives from owning a car during the period that is a function of a depreciation rate and the current market value of the vehicle (see the data appendix). Second, to convert housing expenditures to housing consumption for homeowners, we exclude mortgage interest payments, property tax payments, and spending on insurance, maintenance, and repairs, and add the reported rental equivalent of the home. Third, for respondents living in government or subsidized housing, we impute a rental value using detailed housing characteristics available in the survey. Finally, we exclude spending that is better interpreted as an investment such as spending on education and health care, and outlays for retirement including pensions and social security.[6] For more details, see the data appendix.

Our measure reflects family consumption of goods and services but does not capture other important components of consumption such as home production of food, food preparation, and home repair and maintenance. It is important to note, however, that these components are also missed in an income measure.

Our poverty rates measure the fraction of all individuals who live in families with resources that are below a poverty threshold. Resources are measured at the family level. To adjust for differences in family size and composition, we scale all measures using an National Academy of Sciences (NAS)-recommended equivalence scale (Citro & Michael, 1995): $(A + 0.7K)^{0.7}$, where A is the number of adults in the family and K is the number of children. See Meyer and Sullivan (2009) for a discussion of the importance of equivalence scales for poverty measurement. For each scale-adjusted measure, the poverty threshold in 1980 is specified as the point in the distribution in 1980 such that the poverty rate for that measure is equal to that of the official poverty rate in 1980 (13.0 percent). To obtain thresholds for other years, these thresholds are adjusted for inflation using the CPI-U-RS.[7] Anchoring our alternative poverty measures to the official poverty rate in 1980 facilitates comparisons across measures, allowing us to examine the same point of the distribution initially so that different measures do not diverge simply because of differential changes at different points in the distribution. In addition to calculating a national level poverty rate for each year, we also calculate separate poverty rates for four geographic regions: the Northeast, Midwest, South, and West. These are the narrowest geographic regions identifiable in CE survey data for all years.

In addition to poverty rates, we also examine the relationship between macroeconomic conditions and low percentiles of the distribution of consumption or after-tax income. The percentiles of the distribution are determined in each year after adjusting for differences in family size using the NAS-recommended equivalence scale.

We focus on two annual measures of macroeconomic conditions. The first is the national unemployment rate for the U.S. civilian population age 16 and older. We also examine regional unemployment data, for each of the four regions that are identifiable in both the CPS and the CE survey.[8] Data

Table 1. Unemployment, Poverty, and the 10th Percentile, 1960–2008.

	National Unemployment Rate	Official Income Poverty	After-Tax Income Poverty	Consumption Poverty	10th Percentile of After-Tax Income	10th Percentile of Consumption
	(1)	(2)	(3)	(4)	(5)	(6)
Year						
1960	5.5	22.2				
1961	6.7	21.9		20.6		10,799
1963	5.7	19.5	25.0		8,016	
1972	5.6	11.9	14.2	14.2	11,832	12,860
1975	8.5	12.3	13.9		12,201	
1980	7.1	13.0	13.0	13.0	12,466	13,247
1985	7.2	14.0	14.5	14.0	11,548	12,668
1990	5.6	13.5	12.6	13.1	12,402	13,204
1995	5.6	13.8	11.3	12.5	13,349	13,522
2000	4.0	11.3	8.8	10.3	15,462	14,391
2005	5.1	12.6	9.7	9.1	14,731	15,034
2008	5.8	13.2	10.2	7.7	14,306	15,592
Percent change or difference						
1961–1972	−1.1	−10.0		−6.4		19.1%
1963–1972	−0.1	−7.6	−10.7		47.6%	
1972–1980	1.5	1.1	−1.2	−1.2	5.4%	3.0%
1980–1990	−1.5	0.5	−0.4	0.1	−0.5%	−0.3%
1990–2000	−1.6	−2.2	−3.9	−2.8	24.7%	9.0%
2000–2008	1.8	1.9	1.4	−2.5	−7.5%	8.3%

Notes: The statistics in columns (3)–(6) are based on the authors' calculations using CPS data for income or CE Survey data for consumption. The poverty rates in columns (3) and (4) are anchored at the official rate in 1980, as explained in the text. The 10th percentiles in columns (5) and (6) are expressed in constant 2005 dollars using the CPI-U-RS, adjusted for family size, and normalized to a three person family with one adult and two children.

on the national unemployment rate are available for our entire sample period, but data on the regional unemployment rate are only available for the years from 1976 through 2008.[9]

The national unemployment rate and our main outcome variables are shown for various years in Table 1. Over most periods, the unemployment rate and the poverty rate move in the same direction regardless of how poverty is measured. However, in some cases, the reverse is true. For example, the unemployment rate rises by 1.5 percentage points between 1972 and 1980, whereas the after-tax income and consumption poverty rates both fall by 1.2 percentage points. Changes in the 10th percentiles of income and consumption are similar, although the 10th percentile of income is a bit more volatile, and the two measures diverge between 2000 and 2008.

To determine how the poverty rate and percentiles are related to either national or regional variation in macroeconomic conditions, we estimate several different models. At the national level, we estimate

$$y_t = \alpha_1 + \beta_1 U_t + \lambda_1 y_{t-1} + \pi_1 \text{Inflation}_t + \tau_1 t$$
$$+ \sum_{d=1}^{D-1} [\delta_{1,d} \text{decade}_{d,t} + \kappa_{1,d} \text{decade}_{d,t} \times t] + \varepsilon_{1,t} \quad (1)$$

where y_t represents a national poverty rate or a percentile of income or consumption in year t and U_t is the national unemployment rate for year t. We include a lagged value of the dependent variable because poverty rates and percentiles are slow to change. Inflation$_t$, which is the change in the CPI-U-RS between years t and $t-1$, is included because past work has hypothesized that it might reduce the real incomes of the poor, such as those with unindexed pensions. Finally, we include a linear time trend, indicator variables for the D decades in the sample period, and the interaction of the time trend and the decade indicators. Because much of the previous literature has focused on how the relationship between macroeconomic conditions and poverty has changed over time, we also estimate models that allow the relationship to differ by decade:

$$y_t = \alpha_2 + \sum_{d=1}^{D} [\beta_{2,d} \text{decade}_{d,t} \times U_t] + \lambda_2 y_{t-1} + \pi_2 \text{Inflation}_t + \tau_2 t$$
$$+ \sum_{d=1}^{D-1} [\delta_{2,d} \text{decade}_{d,t} + \kappa_{2,d} \text{decade}_{d,t} \times t] + \varepsilon_{2,t} \quad (2)$$

For any given year, both the unemployment rate and the poverty rate will differ considerably across regions in the United States. This additional source of variation allows us to estimate more precisely how economic conditions are related to the well-being of the worst off. Another important advantage of examining this relationship regionally is that it allows us to include year fixed effects, which control for any aggregate changes that have similar effects on poverty or low percentiles in all regions, such as changes in federal tax and transfer policies. Specifically, we estimate a model that includes region (R_j) and year (γ_t) fixed effects:

$$y_{jt} = \alpha_3 + \beta_3 U_{jt} + \lambda_3 y_{jt-1} + R_j + \gamma_t + \varepsilon_{3,jt} \quad (3)$$

Alternatively, to consider whether the relationship between regional economic conditions and poverty has changed over time, we estimate models that allow the relationship to differ by decade:

$$y_{jt} = \alpha_4 + \sum_{d=1}^{D}[\beta_{4,d}\text{decade}_{d,t} \times U_{jt}] + \lambda_4 y_{jt-1}$$

$$+ R_j + \gamma_t + \sum_{d=1}^{D-1}[\delta_{4,d}\text{decade}_{d,t}] + \varepsilon_{4,jt} \quad\quad (4)$$

4. RESULTS

To examine the bivariate relationship between the macroeconomy and the well-being of the worst off, we construct scatter plots of annual unemployment and the official poverty rate for the years 1960 through 2008. These plots are shown for four separate time periods in Fig. 1. The results for the 1960s show the strong relationship between unemployment and official poverty for this decade that has been emphasized in many previous studies. Both unemployment and poverty fell sharply during this decade. This positive relationship is much less evident in the 1970s and 1980s, but is more noticeable again in the 1990s and 2000s.

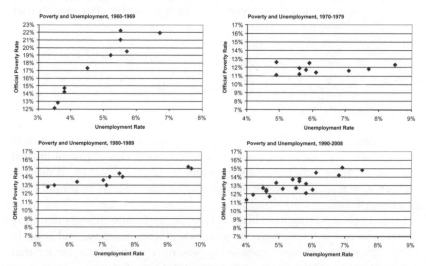

Fig. 1. Unemployment and Official Income Poverty, 1960–2008. *Notes*: Each data point represents a poverty rate and unemployment rate pair for a given year. The poverty rate is the official measure reported by the Census Bureau. The unemployment rate is measured at the national level and is reported by the Bureau of Labor Statistics.

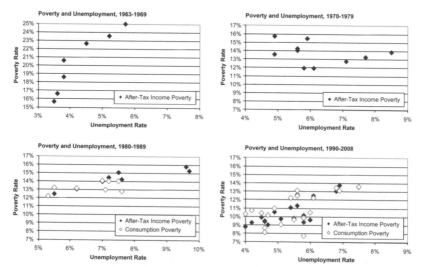

Fig. 2. Unemployment and After-Tax Income or Consumption Poverty, 1963–2008. *Notes*: Each data point represents a poverty rate and unemployment rate pair for a given year. After-tax income poverty is calculated using data from the CPS, while consumption poverty is calculated using data from the CE Survey. Data for consumption poverty is reported for 1980, 1981, and 1984–2008.

Fig. 2 provides similar plots for after-tax income and consumption poverty. The patterns for after-tax income poverty are fairly similar to those for official income poverty. For the 1960s, we again see a strong positive relationship between poverty and unemployment. The pattern is somewhat different for the 1970s, however, when unemployment and after-tax income poverty are inversely related for part of the decade. For the period from 1980 to 2008, we also show the relationship between consumption poverty and unemployment.[10] These scatter plots indicate a positive relationship between consumption poverty and unemployment that is fairly similar to that for after-tax income poverty.

Table 2 presents estimates of Eqs. (1) and (2) for three different measures of income poverty: official poverty, after-tax income poverty, and after-tax income plus noncash benefits poverty. We provide estimates for different sample periods so that we can compare estimates across outcomes for the same periods. Because all specifications include a lag of the dependent variable on the right-hand side, we also report in brackets the long-run derivatives, which are calculated as $\beta/(1-\lambda)$, where β is the point estimate for unemployment and

Table 2. The Relationship between National Unemployment and Income Poverty, 1964–2008.

Dependent Variable	Official Income Poverty		After-Tax Income Poverty						After-Tax Income Plus Noncash Benefit Poverty	
Period	1964–2008		1964–2008		1976–2008		1980–2008		1980–2008	
	(1)	(2)	(3)	(4)	(5)	(6)	(7)	(8)	(9)	(10)
Unemployment rate	0.377*		0.333*		0.507*		0.488*		0.482*	
	(0.074)		(0.076)		(0.068)		(0.078)		(0.097)	
	[0.624]*		[0.729]*		[1.018]*		[0.937]*		[1.004]*	
Unemployment rate × 1960s		2.202*		0.415						
		(0.465)		(0.517)						
		[3.518]*		[0.800]						
Unemployment rate × 1970s		0.210		0.092		1.095				
		(0.087)		(0.096)		(1.100)				
		[0.335]*		[0.177]		[1.991]				
Unemployment rate × 1980s		0.423*		0.599*		0.531*		0.526*		0.578*
		(0.111)		(0.120)		(0.105)		(0.109)		(0.134)
		[0.676]*		[1.154]*		[0.965]*		[0.948]*		[1.120]*
Unemployment rate × 1990s		0.609*		0.590*		0.563*		0.562*		0.501*
		(0.159)		(0.170)		(0.130)		(0.133)		(0.159)
		[0.973]*		[1.137]*		[1.024]*		[1.013]*		[0.971]*
Unemployment rate × 2000s		0.435*		0.420*		0.385*		0.382*		0.352*
		(0.148)		(0.159)		(0.126)		(0.129)		(0.159)
		[0.695]*		[0.809]*		[0.700]*		[0.688]*		[0.682]
Lagged poverty	0.396*	0.374*	0.543*	0.481*	0.502*	0.450*	0.479*	0.445*	0.520*	0.484*
	(0.110)	(0.100)	(0.101)	(0.102)	(0.072)	(0.090)	(0.084)	(0.093)	(0.107)	(0.116)
N	45	45	45	45	33	33	29	29	29	29

Notes: Standard errors are in parentheses. The numbers in brackets are long run derivatives calculated as $\beta/(1-\lambda)$, where β is the point estimate for unemployment and λ is the point estimate for lagged poverty. Poverty and unemployment are measured at the national level. In addition to the covariates listed, all regressions include controls for inflation and a linear time trend, decade dummies, and interactions of the time trend with the decade dummies.
*Significance at the 5% level.

λ is the point estimate for lagged poverty. We emphasize these long-run derivatives when summarizing the results. The results in columns (1) and (2) indicate a strong relationship between official income poverty and national unemployment. For the period from 1964 to 2008, a 1 percentage point increase in the unemployment rate is associated with a 0.6 percentage point rise in official poverty in the long run (column (1)). These results are comparable to estimates from the literature for earlier time periods, such at those from Cutler and Katz (1991) or Blank and Blinder (1986) discussed in Section 2. Consistent with previous research, we find a very strong relationship between poverty and unemployment in the 1960s, and a weaker relationship during the 1970s and 1980s (column (2)). The point estimate for the 1990s is slightly larger than that for the 1970s and 1980s.[11] For the 2000s, we find a statistically significant relationship between unemployment and poverty, but one that is slightly smaller than that for the 1990s.

Although our estimates are sensitive to which years are included in the sample period, the results are quite similar for different measures of income poverty.[12] For example, the results for after-tax income poverty (columns (3) and (4)) are similar to those for official income poverty (columns (1) and (2)), and the results for after-tax income poverty (columns (7) and (8)) are similar to those for after-tax income plus noncash benefits poverty (columns (9) and (10)). We should emphasize that the decade-specific estimates of the effect of unemployment on poverty in the even columns of Table 2 are sensitive to which covariates are included in the specification and to which years are included in the sample period.[13] Each of the specifications in Table 2 includes inflation as a control. As has been emphasized in past research (e.g., Blank & Blinder, 1986), we find the relationship between inflation and poverty to be weak. The point estimates for inflation (not reported) are considerably smaller than those for unemployment, and in all but one of the specifications reported in Table 2, this coefficient is not significantly different from zero.

Estimates for Eqs. 3 and 4, which consider the effect of regional unemployment on regional poverty, are presented in Table 3.[14] Focusing on the long-run derivatives, we again see that income poverty is sensitive to changing macroeconomic conditions, and the magnitudes of these estimates are similar to those using national variation in Table 2. For example, a 1 percentage point increase in regional unemployment is associated with a 1.1 percentage point increase in after-tax income poverty (column (3)), which is comparable to the analogous estimate using national variation (column (5) of Table 2). The results in Table 3 also indicate that the sensitivity of poverty to unemployment is similar for different measures of

Table 3. The Relationship between Regional Unemployment and Income Poverty, 1976–2008.

Dependent Variable	Official Income Poverty		After-Tax Income Poverty				After-Tax Income Plus Noncash Benefit Poverty	
Period	1976–2008		1976–2008		1980–2008		1980–2008	
	(1)	(2)	(3)	(4)	(5)	(6)	(7)	(8)
Unemployment rate	0.231* (0.070) [1.095]*		0.178* (0.062) [1.113]*		0.264* (0.077) [1.222]*		0.272* (0.090) [1.277]*	
Unemployment rate × 1976–79		−0.028 (0.135) [−0.104]		−0.048 (0.127) [−0.241]				
Unemployment rate × 1980s		0.272* (0.113) [1.015]*		0.243* (0.104) [1.221]*		0.227* (0.107) [1.032]*		0.248* (0.126) [1.148]
Unemployment rate × 1990s		0.465* (0.145) [1.735]*		0.318* (0.131) [1.598]*		0.329* (0.138) [1.495]*		0.321* (0.163) [1.486]*
Unemployment rate × 2000s		0.434 (0.250) [1.619]		0.259 (0.230) [1.302]		0.205 (0.237) [0.932]		0.183 (0.279) [0.847]
Lagged poverty	0.789* (0.052)	0.732* (0.055)	0.840* (0.042)	0.801* (0.046)	0.784* (0.052)	0.780* (0.054)	0.787* (0.056)	0.784* (0.058)
N	132	132	132	132	116	116	116	116

Notes: Standard errors are in parentheses. The numbers in brackets are long run derivatives calculated as $\beta/(1-\lambda)$, where β is the point estimate for unemployment and λ is the point estimate for lagged poverty. Poverty and unemployment are measured at the regional level. In addition to the covariates listed, all regressions include region and year fixed effects, and the specifications in even columns include decade dummies.

*Significance at the 5% level.

income poverty. As in Table 2, the estimates vary somewhat across decades (even columns). The point estimates for the 1990s are larger than those for the late 1970s and 1980s. The estimates for the 2000s are slightly lower than those for the 1990s, and these estimates are not significantly different from zero. The estimates for the region dummies (not reported) indicate the sharp differences in poverty across regions, with the south experiencing sharply higher rates than other regions regardless of how poverty is measured.

We also estimate Eqs. 1–4 for consumption poverty to determine how the response of consumption poverty to macroeconomic conditions compares to that of income poverty. We report estimates for both after-tax income poverty and consumption poverty for comparable years in Table 4. Estimates using national variation in unemployment and poverty are presented in columns (1)–(6), while those using regional variation are presented in columns (7)–(10). For each specification in Table 4, we allow the error term in the income poverty equation to be correlated with the error term in the corresponding consumption poverty equation, estimating these equations simultaneously using the Seemingly Unrelated Regressions approach proposed by Zellner (1962).[15]

The results in Table 4 indicate that both income and consumption poverty are sensitive to macroeconomic conditions. For the full time period (columns (1) and (4)), there is evidence that after-tax income poverty is more sensitive to the national unemployment rate than consumption poverty.[16] The former rises by 0.8 percentage points and the latter by 0.5 percentage points in response to a 1 point rise in unemployment. These responses are significantly different from each other. For the period from 1981 to 2008 (columns (2) and (5)), a 1 percentage point increase in unemployment is associated with an increase in the after-tax income poverty rate of 0.9 percentage points, and an increase in the consumption poverty rate of 0.3 points in the long run, but these responses are not significantly different from each other. For after-tax income poverty, the effect of the national unemployment rate (column (3)) is significant in each decade, and the effect is smaller in the 2000s than in previous decades. For consumption poverty, the effect of the national unemployment rate (column (6)) is not significant in any of the decades. The response to national unemployment for income poverty is greater than that for consumption in each decade, but these responses are only significantly different from each other for the 1990s.

Using regional variation, we also find that both income and consumption poverty are sensitive to macroeconomic conditions. For these specifications, however, there is little evidence that income poverty is more responsive than consumption poverty. None of the long-run estimates for consumption

Table 4. The Relationship between Unemployment and Income and Consumption Poverty.

	National Level Poverty						Regional Level Poverty			
	After-Tax Income Poverty			Consumption Poverty			After-Tax Income Poverty		Consumption Poverty	
Dependent Variable	(1)	(2)	(3)	(4)	(5)	(6)	(7)	(8)	(9)	(10)
Period	1963–2008	1981–2008	1981–2008	1961–2008	1981–2008	1981–2008	1981–2008	1981–2008	1981–2008	1981–2008
Unemployment rate	0.821* (0.256)	0.512* (0.078) [0.874]*		0.476*[1] (0.142)	0.242 (0.144) [0.281]		0.288* (0.078) [1.103]*		0.540* (0.185) [1.208]*	
Unemployment rate × 1980s			1.062* (0.358) [1.569]*			1.002 (0.672) [1.133]		0.290* (0.115) [1.090]*		−0.033 (0.273) [−0.069]
Unemployment rate × 1990s			0.734* (0.109) [1.084]*			0.334 (0.234) [0.378][1]		0.310* (0.111) [1.165]*		1.079*[1] (0.278) [2.257]*
Unemployment rate × 2000s			0.413* (0.090) [0.610]*			0.284 (0.167) [0.321]		0.195 (0.189) [0.733]		0.974 (0.492) [2.038]*
Lagged poverty		0.414* (0.073)	0.323* (0.074)		0.138 (0.154)	0.116 (0.176)	0.739* (0.052)	0.734* (0.052)	0.553* (0.082)	0.522* (0.080)
N	30	25	25	30	25	25	100	100	100	100

Notes: Corresponding income and consumption equations were estimated simultaneously using SUR. Standard errors are in parentheses. The numbers in brackets are long run derivatives calculated as $\beta/(1-\lambda)$, where β is the point estimate for unemployment and λ is the point estimate for lagged poverty. In columns (1)–(6), poverty and unemployment are determined at the national level, and specifications include inflation, a linear time trend, decade dummies, and interactions of the time trend with the decade dummies. In columns (7)–(10), poverty and unemployment are determined at the regional level, and specifications include region and year fixed effects. Columns (8) and (10) also include decade dummies. For comparability across measures, we use data from years when both income and consumption data are available. For the full time period, these years are 1961 or 1963, 1972, 1973, 1980, 1981, and 1984–2008.
*Significance at the 5% level.
[1] The effect for consumption is significantly different from that for income.

poverty are significantly different from those for income, and in most cases, the point estimates are larger when looking at consumption poverty. The point estimates indicate that a 1 percentage point increase in regional unemployment is associated with an increase in the after-tax income poverty rate of 1.1 percentage points and an increase in the consumption poverty rate of 1.2 points in the long run. The decade-specific estimates indicate that the regional unemployment rate (column (8)) has a significant effect on after-tax income poverty in both the 1980s and the 1990s, and the effect is smaller in the 2000s than in previous decades. For consumption poverty, the effect of the regional unemployment rate (column (10)) is greater than that of the national unemployment rate. Regional unemployment has a large and significant effect on consumption poverty in the 1990s and the 2000s.

To examine in more detail how the bottom of the distribution responds to the macroeconomy, we consider how low percentiles of income and consumption respond to the business cycle. In Table 5(a), we report these results for the 10th percentile using both national variation (columns (1)–(6)) and regional variation (columns (7)–(10)). We again find that both income and consumption are sensitive to macroeconomic conditions. In general, the effect of unemployment on the 10th percentile of income is larger than that on the 10th percentile of consumption. For example, a 1 percentage point rise in the national unemployment rate is associated with a 4.5 percent decline in the 10th percentile of income, and a 1 percent decline in the 10th percentile of consumption, and these responses are significantly different from each other. The decade specific estimates (columns (2) and (4)) indicate that in each decade the 10th percentile of income is more sensitive to the national unemployment rate than the 10th percentile of consumption, but these responses are only significantly different from each other in the 1990s and the 2000s. For the 10th percentile of after-tax income, the effect of the national unemployment rate is significant in each decade, and the effect is larger in the 1980s and 1990s than in the 2000s. The decade-specific effects of the national unemployment rate are smaller and insignificant for the 10th percentile of consumption. There is also evidence that the effect of unemployment on the 10th percentile of income is greater than that on the 10th percentile of consumption using regional variation (columns (7)–(10)). However, these responses are only significantly different from each other for the 1980s. The effect of the regional unemployment rate on the 10th percentile of consumption is large and significant for both the 1990s and the 2000s.

Tables 5(b) and (c) report analogous results for the 5th and 15th percentiles respectively. These results are quite similar to those reported in Table 5(a). Again, we see that low percentiles of both income and consumption are

Table 5(a). The Relationship between Unemployment and the 10th Percentile of Log Income and Consumption.

	National Level						Regional Level			
Dependent Variable	10th Percentile of Log After-Tax Income			10th Percentile of Log Consumption			10th Percentile of Log After-Tax Income		10th Percentile of Log Consumption	
Period	1963–2008	1981–2008	1981–2008	1961–2008	1981–2008	1981–2008	1981–2008	1981–2008	1981–2008	1981–2008
	(1)	(2)	(3)	(4)	(5)	(6)	(7)	(8)	(9)	(10)
Unemployment rate	-0.040* (0.009)	-0.026* (0.005) [-0.045]*		-0.015*[1] (0.004)	-0.008[1] (0.005) [-0.009]*[1]		-0.029* (0.005) [-0.063]*	-0.032* (0.007) [-0.068]*	-0.020* (0.006) [-0.043]*	-0.002[1] (0.008) [-0.004]*[1]
Unemployment rate × 1980s			-0.051* (0.024) [-0.079]*			-0.036 (0.022) [-0.037]		-0.032* (0.007) [-0.068]*		-0.002[1] (0.008) [-0.004]*[1]
Unemployment rate × 1990s			-0.036* (0.008) [-0.056]*			-0.011[1] (0.007) [-0.011]*[1]		-0.028* (0.007) [-0.059]*		-0.038* (0.008) [-0.075]*[1]
Unemployment rate × 2000s			-0.023* (0.006) [-0.036]*			-0.011* (0.005) [-0.011]*[1]		-0.023* (0.011) [-0.049]*		-0.038* (0.015) [-0.075]*[1]
Lagged 10th percentile		0.418* (0.079)	0.353* (0.087)		0.070 (0.167)	0.037 (0.184)	0.543* (0.057)	0.527* (0.057)	0.539* (0.078)	0.492* (0.075)
N	30	25	25	30	25	25	100	100	100	100

Notes: Corresponding income and consumption equations were estimated simultaneously using SUR. Standard errors are in parentheses. The numbers in brackets are long run derivatives calculated as $\beta/(1-\lambda)$, where β is the point estimate for unemployment and λ is the point estimate for the lagged 10th percentile. In columns (1)–(6), the 10th percentile and unemployment are determined at the national level, and specifications include inflation, a linear time trend, decade dummies, and interactions of the time trend with the decade dummies. In columns (7)–(10), the 10th percentile and unemployment are determined at the regional level, and specifications include region and year fixed effects. Columns (8) and (10) also include decade dummies. For comparability across measures, we use data from years when both income and consumption data are available. For the full time period, these years are 1961 or 1963, 1972, 1973, 1980, 1981, and 1984–2008.

*Significant at the 5% level.

[1] The effect for consumption is significantly different from that for income.

Table 5(b). The Relationship between Unemployment and the 5th Percentile of Log Income and Consumption.

Dependent Variable	National Level						Regional Level			
	5th Percentile of Log After-Tax Income			5th Percentile of Log Consumption			5th Percentile of Log After-Tax Income		5th Percentile of Log Consumption	
Period	1963–2008	1981–2008	1981–2008	1961–2008	1981–2008	1981–2008	1981–2008	1981–2008	1981–2008	1981–2008
	(1)	(2)	(3)	(4)	(5)	(6)	(7)	(8)	(9)	(10)
Unemployment rate	−0.058*	−0.061*		−0.013*[1]	0.000[1]		−0.042*		−0.023*	
	(0.015)	(0.010)		(0.005)	(0.005)		(0.009)		(0.007)	
		[−0.086]*			[0.000][1]		[−0.102]*		[−0.065]*	
Unemployment rate × 1980s			−0.021			−0.066		−0.041*		0.004[1]
			(0.048)			(0.022)		(0.014)		(0.010)
			[−0.027]			[−0.044]*		[−0.097]*		[0.009][1]
Unemployment rate × 1990s			−0.059*			−0.007[1]		−0.044*		−0.048*
			(0.014)			(0.006)		(0.013)		(0.010)
			[−0.077]*			[−0.005][1]		[−0.105]*		[−0.110]*
Unemployment rate × 2000s			−0.059*			−0.003[1]		−0.043		−0.062*
			(0.012)			(0.006)		(0.023)		(0.018)
			[−0.077]*			[−0.002][1]		[−0.102]		[−0.143]*
Lagged 5th percentile		0.292*	0.234*		−0.431*	−0.514*	0.590*	0.579*	0.644*	0.565*
		(0.088)	(0.088)		(0.207)	(0.173)	(0.065)	(0.066)	(0.078)	(0.075)
N	30	25	25	30	25	25	100	100	100	100

Notes: See notes to Table 5(a).

Table 5(c). The Relationship between Unemployment and the 15th Percentile of Log Income and Consumption.

Dependent Variable	National Level						Regional Level			
	15th Percentile of Log After-Tax Income				15th Percentile of Log Consumption		15th Percentile of Log After-Tax Income		15th Percentile of Log Consumption	
Period	1963–2008	1981–2008	1981–2008	1961–2008	1981–2008	1981–2008	1981–2008	1981–2008	1981–2008	1981–2008
	(1)	(2)	(3)	(4)	(5)	(6)	(7)	(8)	(9)	(10)
Unemployment rate	-0.036* (0.008)	-0.023* (0.004) [-0.043]*		-0.014*[1] (0.004)	-0.006[1] (0.004) [-0.007][1]		-0.019* (0.003) [-0.058]*		-0.015* (0.005) [-0.033]*	
Unemployment rate × 1980s			-0.052* (0.018) [-0.081]*			-0.016 (0.020) [-0.019]		-0.021* (0.005) [-0.062]*		0.002[1] (0.008) [0.004][1]
Unemployment rate × 1990s			-0.034* (0.006) [-0.053]*			-0.006[1] (0.007) [-0.007][1]		-0.017* (0.005) [-0.050]*		-0.030* (0.008) [-0.061][1]
Unemployment rate × 2000s			-0.018* (0.004) [-0.028]*			-0.008 (0.005) [-0.010]		-0.016* (0.008) [-0.047]*		-0.027 (0.014) [-0.055]*
Lagged 15th percentile		0.460* (0.079)	0.356* (0.081)		0.154 (0.147)	0.177 (0.171)	0.671* (0.050)	0.659* (0.050)	0.550* (0.079)	0.505* (0.078)
N	30	25	25	30	25	25	100	100	100	100

Notes: See notes to Table 5(a).

responsive to macroeconomic conditions. And, using national variation, there is evidence that low percentiles of income are more responsive than low percentiles of consumption. The response of the 5th percentile of the income distribution to unemployment is somewhat greater than that for the 10th percentile. For example, 1 percentage point rise in the national unemployment rate is associated with an 8.6 percent decline in the 5th percentile of income, as compared to a 4.5 percent decline in the 10th percentile. The point estimates for the effect of unemployment on the 15th percentile of both income and consumption (Table 5(c)) are very similar to those on the 10th percentile.

We also examine higher percentiles of the distributions of income and consumption. As with the 10th percentile, estimates for the 50th percentile indicate that both median after-tax income and median consumption are responsive to unemployment (results available from the authors). The point estimates for the effect of unemployment on median income are slightly smaller than those on the 10th percentile, and in all cases, the long-run effect of unemployment is greater on median after-tax income than on median consumption. However, we cannot reject the hypotheses that these responses are the same.

All of the poverty results presented thus far are for absolute measures of poverty using a poverty line that does not change over time in real terms. We focus on absolute measures because the official poverty measure in the United States is designed to capture absolute poverty, and the previous work looking at changes in income poverty over the business cycle in the United States has focused on absolute poverty. The European Union and other areas rely on relative poverty measures that are based on a poverty line that can rise (or fall) over time. The expected effects of macroeconomic conditions on relative poverty are unclear. On the one hand, if improved economic conditions benefit the middle of the distribution more than the bottom, then low unemployment could lead to a rise in relative poverty. On the other hand, if the bottom of the distribution benefits the most from low unemployment, then we would expect relative poverty to fall as macroeconomic conditions improve.

In Table 6, we examine the relationship between the unemployment rate and both income and consumption relative poverty, where relative poverty is defined as the fraction of individuals with resources below 50 percent of median resources. In general, the results show that there is a weaker relationship between unemployment and relative poverty than between unemployment and absolute poverty. In most cases, the estimates in Table 6 are smaller than those in Table 4. At the national level, the relationship between unemployment and relative poverty is weak regardless of whether poverty is measured using income or consumption. The relationship between unemployment and relative

Table 6. The Relationship between Unemployment and Income and Consumption Relative Poverty.

Dependent Variable	National Level Poverty						Regional Level Poverty			
	After-Tax Income Relative Poverty			Consumption Relative Poverty			After-Tax Income Relative Poverty		Consumption Relative Poverty	
Period	1963–2008	1981–2008	1981–2008	1961–2008	1981–2008	1981–2008	1981–2008	1981–2008	1981–2008	1981–2008
	(1)	(2)	(3)	(4)	(5)	(6)	(7)	(8)	(9)	(10)
Unemployment rate	0.156	0.173		0.107	−0.214		0.240*		0.371*	
	(0.082)	(0.095)		(0.096)	(0.161)		(0.088)		(0.174)	
		[0.210]			[−0.186]^1		[0.654]*		[0.890]*	
Unemployment rate × 1980s			0.369			1.203		0.279*		−0.168
			(0.472)			(0.665)		(0.137)		(0.248)
			[0.418]			[0.872]		[0.723]*		[−0.381]
Unemployment rate × 1990s			0.293*			−0.237^1		0.258*		0.899*^{1}
			(0.136)			(0.209)		(0.124)		(0.251)
			[0.332]*			[−0.172]^1		[0.668]*		[2.039]*
Unemployment rate × 2000s			0.095			−0.060		0.048		0.682
			(0.121)			(0.173)		(0.216)		(0.445)
			[0.108]			[−0.043]		[0.124]		[1.546]
Lagged poverty		0.178	0.118		−0.151	−0.380	0.633*	0.614*	0.583*	0.559*
		(0.155)	(0.155)		(0.382)	(0.355)	(0.070)	(0.071)	(0.086)	(0.083)
N	30	25	25	30	25	25	100	100	100	100

Notes: The consumption (income) relative poverty rate is defined as the fraction of individuals with consumption (income) below 50 percent of median consumption (income). See Table 4 for additional notes.

poverty is significant at the regional level, and there is some evidence that consumption relative poverty is more responsive than income relative poverty, but the difference is only significant for the 1990s.

The unemployment rate is only one indicator of macroeconomic conditions. To assess whether our main findings are sensitive to how we specify the business cycle, we consider other measures of macroeconomic conditions. In Table A1 we present the results for GDP per capita. At the national level, a rise in GDP per capita is associated with a decline in both income and consumption poverty. Income poverty appears more responsive than consumption poverty and the differences are significant in some cases. As was the case for the results using unemployment, consumption poverty appears more responsive to GDP per capita when using regional variation. For the relationship between regional GDP per capita and regional income poverty (column (8)), the test for a unit root is marginally significant. Therefore, we have added an additional specification with the first difference of income poverty as the dependent variable (column (9)). In both of these specifications, the relationship between regional income poverty and regional GDP per capita is weak.

We also consider other measures of macroeconomic conditions including lagged unemployment, GDP, lagged GDP, and median income (these results are available from the authors). The results from the other alternative specifications are also qualitatively similar to those focusing on unemployment.

5. PREDICTED EFFECTS OF THE CURRENT RECESSION

If we were to extrapolate the estimated effects over the 1981–2008 period to the next few years, the predicted changes in poverty are very large. Unemployment rose 4.7 percentage points between 2007 and 2009 and averaged an additional 0.3 percentage points higher over the first 10 months of 2010. The predicted change over three years can be obtained by inserting coefficient estimates in the expression

$$\beta[\Delta U_{t-2}(1 + \lambda^2) + \Delta U_{t-1}(1 + \lambda) + \Delta U_t] \tag{5}$$

On the basis of the estimates in Table 4, the increase in unemployment would be predicted to raise after-tax income poverty by 2.4–3.4 percentage points and consumption poverty by 1.3–3.9 percentage points in 2010 over the 2007 level. This is a very large and troubling possible increase in poverty. These forecasts should be interpreted cautiously, though, given that such forecasts do not reflect changes in government policy in response to the recent recession and given the instability of the effect of economic conditions on poverty over the past 50 years. Monea and Sawhill (2009) provide another set of estimates. They suggest that the recession will have much smaller effects on income poverty than we estimate, raising poverty about 1.7 percentage points between 2007 and 2010. The smaller estimated effect is due to their reliance on a smaller coefficient on unemployment than ours, based on Blank (2009).

6. CONCLUSIONS

This chapter examines the relationship between poverty and macroeconomic conditions in the United States from 1960 through 2008. Overall, we find that consumption and income poverty rates respond strongly to economic conditions, whether they are measured by unemployment rates, per capita GDP, or median incomes. The response of poverty to macroeconomic conditions is similar across several different measures of income poverty, although the magnitude of the response is somewhat sensitive to the years included in the sample period. The results indicate that, for the period since 1981, a 1 percentage point increase in unemployment is associated with an increase in the after-tax income poverty rate of 0.9–1.1 percentage points in the long run.

Although we expect consumption poverty to be less sensitive to unemployment than income poverty given the ability of some households to smooth their consumption, the poor measurement of some cyclically large components of income may reverse this relationship. The empirical evidence on whether income poverty is more responsive to macroeconomic conditions than consumption poverty is mixed. Income poverty does appear to be more responsive using national level variation, but consumption poverty is often more responsive to unemployment when using regional variation. We find that a 1 percentage point increase in unemployment is associated with an increase in the consumption poverty rate of 0.3–1.2 percentage points in the long run.

The effects of unemployment on low percentiles of income and consumption have a similar pattern to that for the poverty rate. Low percentiles of both income and consumption are sensitive to macroeconomic conditions, and in most cases, low percentiles of income appear to be more responsive than low percentiles of consumption. Our results for the 5th, 10th, and 15th percentiles indicate that a 1 percentage point increase in unemployment is associated with a decline in these percentiles ranging from 4 to 10 percent. For low percentiles of consumption, this range is from 0 to 7 percent. Consistent with the permanent income hypothesis, median consumption is in all cases less sensitive to unemployment than median income.

NOTES

1. For example, see Blank and Blinder (1986), Blank (2000), and Haveman and Schwabish (2000).

2. See Haveman and Schwabish (2000) for a brief review of this literature.

3. Studies using regional or state variation in poverty and macroeconomic conditions have found similar evidence (Blank & Card, 1993; Tobin, 1994; Freeman, 2001; Gundersen & Ziliak, 2004; Hoynes, Page, & Stevens, 2006).

4. Several papers have considered the effect that government transfer spending has on poverty (Gottschalk & Danziger, 1984; Blank & Blinder, 1986; Haveman & Schwabish, 2000; Blank, 2009). These studies typically find that greater transfer spending is associated with reduced poverty, but the estimates are imprecise.

5. One exception is Gundersen and Ziliak (2004), who look at an after-tax income poverty measure.

6. We also exclude spending on individuals or entities outside the family, such as charitable contributions and spending on gifts to nonfamily members. This category is very small relative to total consumption.

7. The official poverty thresholds are adjusted for inflation using the CPI-U. The CPI-U-RS corrects for many, but not all, of the biases in the CPI-U. See Meyer and Sullivan (2009) for more details.

8. We also estimate specifications using GDP and median family income as a measure of macroeconomic conditions. We discuss these results briefly in Section 5.

9. The unemployment data are available at the Bureau of Labor Statistics (www.bls.gov/data/#unemployment).

10. We do not show consumption poverty for the 1960s and the 1970s because data for consumption are only available for a few years (1960–1961, 1972, and 1973). During the 1980s, data for consumption poverty is reported for 1980, 1981, and 1984–1989.

11. Looking at the period from 1959 to 1998, Haveman finds the largest effect for the 1959–1972 period and then for the 1993–1998 period.

12. As explained in Section 3, our measures of alternative poverty differ from official poverty not just in how resources are measured, but also in how differences in family size are accounted for and in how thresholds are adjusted for inflation.

13. For example, the results in column (4) suggest a weak relationship between unemployment and after-tax income poverty for the 1964–1969 period. However, when the interaction terms between the linear time trend and the decade dummies are excluded, this point estimate is much closer to the one for official poverty in column (2).

14. These results do not include data from the 1960s and early 1970s because the regional unemployment rate series provided by the Bureau of Labor Statistics (BLS) only goes back to 1976.

15. For example, the specifications in columns (1) and (4) are estimated simultaneously, as are those in columns (2), (5), and so on.

16. For the full time period, we do not include a lagged dependent variable because we only observe one observation for consumption poverty in the 1960s and only two observations in the 1970s.

17. This adjustment is made because $\exp(x_i\hat{\beta})$ will tend to underestimate y_i.

18. The ASEC/ADF also includes an imputed value for taxes and credits, but this information is only available starting with the 1980 survey.

REFERENCES

Bakija, J. (2008). *Documentation for a comprehensive historical U.S. federal and state income tax calculator program*. Williams College Working Paper, January.

Blank, R. (1993). Why were poverty rates so high in the 1980s? In: D. B. Papadimitriou & E. N. Wolff (Eds.), *Poverty and prosperity in the late twentieth century* (pp. 21–55). London: Macmillan Press.

Blank, R. (2000). Fighting poverty: Lessons from recent U.S. history. *Journal of Economic Perspectives, 14*(2), 3–19.

Blank, R. (2009). Economic change and the structure of opportunity for low skill workers. In: M. Cancian & S. Danziger (Eds.), *Changing poverty, changing policy* (pp. 71–87). New York: Russell Sage Foundation.

Blank, R. M., & Blinder, A. S. (1986). Macroeconomics, income distribution, and poverty. In: S. Danziger (Ed.), *Fighting poverty: What works and what does not* (pp. 180–208). Cambridge: Harvard University Press.

Blank, R. M., & Card, D. (1993). Poverty, income distribution, and growth: Are they still connected? *Brookings Papers on Economic Activity, 2*, 285–339.

Citro, C. F., & Michael, R. T. (1995). *Measuring poverty: A new approach*. Washington, D.C.: National Academy Press.

Cutler, D. M., & Katz, L. F. (1991). Macroeconomic performance and the disadvantaged. *Brookings Papers on Economic Activity, 2*, 1–74.

Edin, K., & Lein, L. (1997). *Making ends meet: How single mothers survive welfare and low-wage work*. New York: Russell Sage Foundation.

Feenberg, D., & Coutts, E. (1993). An introduction to the TAXSIM model. *Journal of Policy Analysis and Management, 12*(1), 189–194. http://www.nber.org/~taxsim/.

Freeman, R. (2001). The rising tide lifts...? In: S. Danziger & R. Haveman (Eds.), *Understanding poverty* (pp. 97–126). Cambridge, MA: Harvard University Press.

Gottschalk, P., & Danziger, S. (1984). Macroeconomic conditions, income transfers, and the trend in poverty. In: D. L. Bawden (Ed.), *The social contract revisited* (pp. 185–215). Washington, D.C.: The Urban Institute.

Gundersen, C., & Ziliak, J. (2004). Poverty and macroeconomic performance across space, race, and family structure. *Demography, 41*(1), 61–86.

Haveman, R., & Schwabish, J. (2000). Has macroeconomic performance regained its antipoverty bite? *Contemporary Economic Policy, 18*(4), 415–427.

Hoynes, H. W., Page, M. E., & Stevens, A. H. (2006). Poverty in America: Trends and explanations. *Journal of Economic Perspectives, 20*, 47–68.

Meyer, B. D., Mok, W. K. C., & Sullivan, J. X. (2009). *The under-reporting of transfers in household surveys: Its nature and consequences*. NBER Working Papers 15181, July.

Meyer, B. D., & Sullivan, J. X. (2003). Measuring the well-being of the poor using income and consumption. *Journal of Human Resources*, *38*(S), 1180–1220.

Meyer, B. D., & Sullivan, J. X. (2011). Viewpoint: Further results on measuring the well-being of the poor using income and consumption. *Canadian Journal of Economics*, *44*(1), 52–87.

Meyer, B. D., & Sullivan, J. X. (2008). Changes in the consumption, income, and well-being of single mother headed families. *American Economic Review*, *98*(5), 2221–2241.

Meyer, B. D., & Sullivan, J. X. (2009). *Five decades of consumption and income poverty*. NBER Working Paper no. 14827.

Monea, E., & Sawhill, I. (2009). *Simulating the effect of the "Great Recession" on poverty* (September 10. Available at http://www.brookings.edu/papers/2009/0910_poverty_monea_sawhill.aspx). Washington, DC: Brookings Institution, Center on Children and Families.

Slesnick, D. T. (1993). Gaining ground: poverty in the postwar United States. *Journal of Political Economy*, *101*(1), 1–38.

Slesnick, D. T. (2001). *Consumption and social welfare*. Cambridge: Cambridge University Press.

Tobin, J. (1994). Poverty in relation to macroeconomic trends, cycles, and policies. In: S.H. Danziger, G.D. Sandefur, & D.H. Weinberg (Eds.), *Confronting poverty, prescription for change* (pp. 148–167). Cambridge, MA: Harvard University Press.

Zellner, A. (1962). An efficient method of estimating seemingly unrelated regressions and test for aggregation bias. *Journal of the American Statistical Association*, *57*, 348–368.

DATA APPENDIX: MEASURING CONSUMPTION IN THE CE SURVEY

Consumption includes all spending in the CE survey measure of total expenditures less spending on out-of-pocket health care expenses, education, and payments to retirement accounts, pension plans, and social security. In addition, housing and vehicle expenditures are converted to service flows. For homeowners, we subtract spending on mortgage interest, property taxes, maintenance, repairs, insurance, and other expenses and add the reported rental equivalent of the home.

Because a rental equivalent is not reported in the 1960–1961 and 1980–1981 surveys, we impute a rental equivalent for these years. Using data from the 1984 survey, we regress log reported rental equivalent on the log market value of the home, log total nonhousing expenditures, family size, and the sex and marital status of the family head. Estimates from these regressions are used to impute a value of the rental equivalent for respondents in the 1980–1981 surveys. A similar approach is used to impute a rental equivalent value for the 1960–1961 surveys using data from the 1972–1973 surveys.

For those in public or subsidized housing, we impute a rental value using reported information on their living unit including the number of rooms, bedrooms, and bathrooms and the presence of appliances such as a microwave, disposal, refrigerator, washer, and dryer. Specifically, for renters who are not in public or subsidized housing, we estimate quantile regressions for log rent using the CE survey housing characteristics mentioned above as well as a number of geographic identifiers including state, region, urbanicity, and Standard Metropolitan Statistical Area (SMSA) status, as well as interactions of a nonlinear time trend with appliances (to account for changes over time in their price and quality). We then use the estimated coefficients to predict the 40th percentile of rent for the sample of families that do not report full rent because they reside in public or subsidized housing. We use the 40th percentile because public housing tends to be of lower quality than private housing in dimensions we do not directly observe. Evidence from the Panel Study of Income Dynamics (PSID) indicates that the average reported rental equivalent of public or subsidized housing is just under the predicted 40th percentile for these units using parameters estimated from those outside public or subsidized housing.

For vehicle owners, we subtract spending on recent purchases of new and used vehicles as well vehicle finance charges. We then add the service flow value of all vehicles owned by the family. The service flow for each vehicle is a function of the market price of the vehicle and a depreciation rate. We determine a current market price for each vehicle in the CE survey in one of three ways. First, for vehicles that were purchased within 12 months of the interview and that have a reported purchase price (the estimation sample), we take the current market price to be the reported purchase price. Second, for vehicles that were purchased more than 12 months before the interview and that have a reported purchase price, we specify the current market price as a function of the reported purchase price and an estimated depreciation rate as explained below.

Finally, for the remaining vehicles, we impute a current market price because the purchase price is not reported. Using the estimation sample, we regress the log real purchase price on a cubic in vehicle age, vehicle characteristics, family characteristics, and make-model-year fixed effects. The vehicle characteristics include indicators for whether the vehicle has automatic transmission, power brakes, power steering, air conditioning, a diesel engine, a sunroof, four-wheel drive, or is turbo charged. Family characteristics include log real expenditures (excluding vehicles and health), family size, region, and the age and education of the family head. Coefficient estimates from this regression are then used to calculate a predicted log real purchase price for the ith vehicle ($x_i\hat{\beta}$). The predicted current market value for each vehicle without a reported purchase price is then equal to

$\hat{\alpha} \times \exp(x_i\hat{\beta})$, where $\hat{\alpha}$ is the coefficient on $\exp(x_i\hat{\beta})$ in a regression of y_i on $\exp(x_i\hat{\beta})$ without a constant term.[17]

To estimate a depreciation rate for vehicles, we compare prices across vehicles of different age, but with the same make, model, and year. In particular, from the estimation sample, we construct a subsample of vehicles that are in a make-model-year cell with at least two vehicles that are not the same age. Using this sample, we regress the log real purchase price of the vehicle on vehicle age and make-model-year fixed effects. From the coefficient on vehicle age (β), we calculate the depreciation rate (δ): $\delta = 1 - \exp(\beta)$. The service flow is then the product of this depreciation rate and the current market price. If the vehicle has a reported purchase price but was not purchased within 12 months of the interview, we calculate the service flow as (real reported purchase price) $\times \delta(1-\delta)^t$, where t is the number of years since the car was purchased.

Measures of Income in the CPS ASEC/ADF

Money Income
This measure follows the Census definition of money income that is used to measure poverty and inequality. Money income sources, as reported in the ASEC codebook, include earnings; net income from self employment; social security, pension, and retirement income; public transfer income including Supplemental Security Income, welfare payments, veterans' payment or unemployment and workmen's compensation; interest and investment income; rental income; and alimony or child support, regular contributions from persons outside the household, and other periodic income.

After-Tax Money Income
Adds to money income the value of tax credits such as the EITC and subtracts state and federal income taxes and payroll taxes and includes capital gains and losses. Federal income tax liabilities and credits and FICA taxes are calculated for all years using TAXSIM (Feenberg & Coutts 1993).[18] State taxes and credits are also calculated using TAXSIM for the years 1977–2008. Before 1977, we calculate state taxes using IncTaxCalc (Bakija, 2008). We confirm that in 1977, net state tax liabilities generated using IncTaxCalc match very closely those generated using TAXSIM.

Table A1. The Relationship between GDP per Capita and Income and Consumption Poverty.

Dependent Variable	National Level Poverty						Regional Level Poverty (1981–2008)						
	After-Tax Income Poverty			Consumption Poverty			After-Tax Income Poverty				Consumption Poverty		
	Level	Level	Level	Level	Level	Level	Level	Level	First Difference	Level	Level	Level	Level
Period	1963–2008	1981–2008	1981–2008	1961–2008	1981–2008	1981–2008	1981–2008				1981–2008		
	(1)	(2)	(3)	(4)	(5)	(6)	(7)	(8)	(9)	(10)	(11)	(12)	(13)
Log GDP per capita	−54.436* (5.453)	−14.996* (4.378) [−25.417]*		−27.903*[1] (3.361)	−5.002 (6.049) [−5.927][1]		−10.117* (3.209) [5.549]	0.899 (1.716)	3.022 (1.640)		−30.582* (4.301)	−18.127* (4.929) [−30.466]*	
Log GDP per capita × 1980s			7.124 (45.755) [12.368]			39.199 (59.557) [43.554]				−1.640 (1.883) [−6.721]			−21.712* (5.039) [−33.925]*[1]
Log GDP per capita × 1990s			−15.051* (6.948) [−26.130]*			−10.587 (11.769) [−11.763]				3.439 (1.771) [14.094]			−16.345* (5.321) [−25.539]*[1]
Log GDP per capita × 2000s			−15.245* (6.264) [−26.467]*			−2.158 (8.158) [−2.398]				1.399 (1.732) [5.734]			−15.014* (5.088) [−23.459]*[1]
Lagged poverty		0.410* (0.101)	0.424* (0.122)		0.156 (0.159)	0.100 (0.231)		0.838* (0.049)		0.756* (0.060)		0.405* (0.095)	0.360* (0.095)
N	30	25	25	30	25	25	100	100	100	100	100	100	100

Notes: The dependent variable is either the poverty rate (level) or the change in the poverty rate from the previous year (first difference). See Table 4 for additional notes. See online Appendix Tables 1–3 at www.nd.edu/~jsulliv4/PovertyandBusinessCycles_Appendix_Tables.pdf

After-Tax Money Income Plus Noncash Benefits
This adds to after-tax money income the cash value of food stamps and imputed values for housing subsidies, school lunch programs, Medicaid, and Medicare.

PATTERNS OF EMPLOYMENT DISADVANTAGE IN A RECESSION

Richard Berthoud and Lina Cardona Sosa

ABSTRACT

There has been much commentary on the consequences of a recession on the incomes of households. This short chapter aims to contribute to the debate about the current recession by analysing the impact of the recessions of the early 1980s and 1990s on non-employment patterns among people in the main range of working ages in Great Britain. The hypothesis is that the effects observed in earlier business cycles are likely to be repeated now. The chapter uses a series of General Household Surveys over a 32-year period, to show, first, the impact of cyclical factors on overall patterns of non-employment (including mothers and disabled people, as well as the unemployed), and second, which social groups are most affected. A key question is whether types of people who are already disadvantaged are especially sensitive to a downturn. Recent data can be used to test how far the experience of previous business cycles is being repeated in the current recession.

Keywords: Employment; unemployment; recession; disadvantage

JEL Classification: J21; J64; J82

Who Loses in the Downturn? Economic Crisis, Employment and Income Distribution
Research in Labor Economics, Volume 32, 83–113
Copyright © 2011 by Emerald Group Publishing Limited
All rights of reproduction in any form reserved
ISSN: 0147-9121/doi:10.1108/S0147-9121(2011)0000032006

1. AIMS

The economic downturn following the crisis in the financial services industry has stimulated a spate of commentary on the likely consequences for households and families. Obvious potential economic impacts on unemployment (Stafford & Duffy, 2009), poverty (Muriel & Sibieta, 2009) and mortgage repossessions (*Daily Telegraph*, 2009) may lead to less obvious adverse personal outcomes, including rises in burglaries (*Guardian*, 2009), divorce (Blekesaune, 2008), mental illness (*Time*, 2009) and child abuse (Independent, 2008).

This chapter focuses on the labour market, but has obvious implications for the distribution of income. The US National Bureau of Economic Research defines a recession as:

> a significant decline in economic activity spread across the economy, lasting more than a few months, normally visible in real GDP, real income, employment, industrial production and wholesale-retail sales (NBER, 2009).

This broad definition is often operationalised statistically to identify a recession as a period of two consecutive quarters of negative economic growth measured by GDP. But the NBER definition stresses a range of potential indicators, and some economists argue for an increase in the rate of unemployment – by more than (say) 1.5 or 2 percentage points in 12 months – as the best single indicator (Eslake, 2008). Unemployment statistics are both understood by, and potentially threatening to, the general public, and therefore play an important political role. The UK claimant count rose from 2.4 per cent in the first quarter of 2008 to 5.0 per cent in the last quarter of 2009.

What types of people are likely to find themselves out of work in consequence? Does the lack of demand in the labour market primarily affect people who were disadvantaged already? Or is it 'ordinary people' with average characteristics who find themselves at heightened risk of unemployment? Or does a recession tend to eat away at the privilege of those who had previously been almost certain of carrying on in work?

The existing literature on the relationship between unemployment trends and social disadvantage has been usefully reviewed by Stafford and Duffy (2009). The evidence base is patchy. Much of it looks at trends over a single recession, often analysing data about the downturn before information about the upturn is available. It focuses mainly on unemployment itself (i.e. people actively looking for a job) as the undesirable outcome, without much attention being paid to the impact of recessions on the number of people out of work for other (reported) reasons. Many studies have focused on one particular disadvantaged group (lone parents, disabled people, ethnic minorities and so on) without direct comparisons between groups, or allowing for the interactions between characteristics.

The underlying assumption is that people whose employment is adversely affected by slump in the demand for labour are likely to face a significant reduction in their household incomes. This will affect the overall distribution of the income, and the risk of poverty (Muriel & Sibieta, 2009).

This chapter aims to contribute to the debate about the current recession by analysing the impact of the recessions of the early 1980s and 1990s on non-employment patterns among people in the main range of working ages (20–59) in Great Britain. Two complete business cycles are observed, while long-term trends in patterns of non-employment are also taken into account. Although unemployment rates are used as the measure of the level of demand in the labour market (a predictor variable), overall non-employment probabilities are used as the outcome measure (the dependent variable), including a cyclical rise in the number of people not even looking for work as part of the potential problem. The analysis systematically compares the experiences of different social groups, defined by gender and family structure, age, education, health, ethnicity and region, allowing for and investigating the effects of combinations of these characteristics.

Although most of the chapter uses the past to predict the present, the historical analysis is complemented with very recent data about the actual consequences of the fall in labour demand that occurred in Great Britain between 2008 and 2009. This helps to show whether the effects of a downturn are generalisable from one cycle to the next, or whether each recession should be viewed as an independent event.

The next section describes the main data source – an almost-annual sequence of General Household Surveys (GHSs) over three decades. Section 3 describes the analytical approach, followed, in Section 4, by aggregate findings about the overall effect of a recession on the number of adults not in work. Section 5 shows how much more or less sensitive the non-employment rates of particular groups are to cyclical variations. Section 6 compares the predictions based on previous cycles with early data about the actual outturn. Section 7 discusses the findings, looking for a link between long-term disadvantage and short-term problems.

2. DATA: THE GENERAL HOUSEHOLD SURVEY

The main aim of this chapter is to distinguish between long-term and cyclical trends in the non-employment rates of different social groups. It is based mainly on a long-running population survey, rather than on published statistics on unemployment and other benefit claims.

The GHS is a continuous multipurpose survey of large random samples of households across Great Britain. The survey has been conducted, using a new sample each time, every year since 1973, with the exception of 1997 and 1999. The latest evidence in the data set analysed here relates to 2005.[1] In practice the 1973 survey did not have full data on economic activities, and the 1977 and 1978 surveys did not carry the standard question on limiting long-standing illness. These three annual surveys were therefore dropped from the analysis. The database therefore provides 28 annual observations, over a 32-year period.[2]

2.1. Structure of the Sample Being Analysed

The analysis in this chapter is based on adults aged 20–59. Young adults, aged 16–19, have not been included because such a high proportion of them are still in full-time education. Men aged 60–64 have been omitted because, although still below pensionable age in Britain, a high proportion of them have in fact retired – and in this age group, 'early retirement' is sometimes a marker of privilege and sometimes a marker of disadvantage. Where an adult within the age range has a partner under 20 or over 59, the former is included and the latter excluded – but we know whether the excluded partner had a job.

Each of the 28 annual GHSs included in the analysis covers between 10,000 and 16,000 men and women within this age range, with an overall total of 360,672 respondents. Weighting factors have been applied so that each annual survey represents the composition of the relevant year's population by age and sex. These weights are calculated as population size/ sample size, so that they can be used as grossing up factors to estimate the number of people in the population who have been affected.

All the annual surveys asked questions about respondents' economic activity, and about the set of personal characteristics that are known to be associated with people's job prospects. Some of these questions (notably age and sex) were asked and coded identically in every survey, and could easily be compared across the sequence. Others, notably educational qualifications and ethnic group, were asked and/or coded in different ways across the sequence, and an important preparatory task was to ensure that these data were re-coded to be as comparable as possible from year to year.

As with all research of this kind, the findings should be treated just as 'estimates', with a margin of error either way associated with sampling considerations, measurement uncertainties and analytical simplifications. It is the broad differences and trends that matter. The appendix provides details of sampling errors in the main analytical model.

Section 6 of this chapter uses a different data set, the Labour Force Survey (LFS). It will be described then.

2.2. Definitions of Non-Employment and Unemployment

People have been defined as 'not in work' if they did not have a job, and were not studying at the time they took part in the survey. The definition is as close as the survey data can get to the concept of 'NEET' – not in employment, education or training.[3]

A job of less than 16 hours per week was counted as 'not in work', on the grounds that very short hours cannot be considered either a primary activity or a means of earning a living. The 16-hour cut-off is enshrined in current UK social security and tax-credit legislation, although the formal boundary was at 30 hours at the beginning of the period under review. It is acknowledged that some of the people defined here as 'not in work' may have had small part-time earnings, mainly mothers.

Full-time education has been classified as 'in work', because it is long-term economic investment, strongly supported by government policy.[4]

All references in this chapter to 'non-employment' and synonyms such as 'out of work' refer to this NEET-based definition. In 2005 (the most recent GHS year in the data set), the non-employment rate ('out of work' as a proportion of all adults in the age range) was 25 per cent, the converse of an overall employment rate of 75 per cent.

But the words '*un*employed' and '*un*employment' refer more narrowly to people seeking work. In between the unemployed and people in work is a group of those who have no job, but are not looking for one, known as 'economically inactive'. The unemployment rate reported by the GHS in 2005 (the 'ILO definition') was 3.3 per cent.

The best-known measure of unemployment, and the one that can be kept up to date from month to month, is based on a count of the number of people claiming the relevant benefits (in the UK mainly the Jobseekers' Allowance and its predecessors Unemployment Benefit and Income Support). Fig. 1 plots changes over the period in three measures of unemployment:

- the figure based on the LFSs, using the ILO definition for those of working age in Great Britain – this is the source used for official estimates of long-term trends;

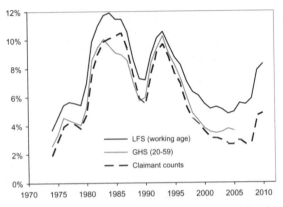

Fig. 1. Annual Unemployment Rates, 1974–2008, Measured by the Labour Force Survey, by the General Household Survey and by Official Claimant Counts. *Note:* Figures for 2010 based on the first quarter only.

- the GHS based figure, again using the ILO definition, confined to 20–59-year-olds in Great Britain;
- the claimant count figure, for those of working age across the UK – this is the headline figure used to monitor short-term rises and falls in unemployment.

The ebbs and flows that are crucial to the analysis in this chapter are clearly visible in Fig. 1, and the three rather different measures of unemployment track each other with almost uncanny consistency. The main differences are as follows:

- the GHS indicated a peak in unemployment in 1983, and the LFS in 1984, while the claimant count reported a continuing increase through to 1986;
- the LFS figures have been rather higher than the other two versions, especially in the early 1980s and over the most recent period.

The current recession is indicated by the upturn in unemployment rates between 2008 and 2010. In detail,

- the claimant count rose from 2.4 per cent in the first quarter of 2008 to 5.0 per cent in the last quarter of 2009;
- the LFS measure of ILO unemployment rose from 5.4 per cent to 8.1 percent over the same period;

- but UK unemployment rates have not (yet) reached the levels observed in the recessions of the 1970s and 1980s. Monthly figures (not shown in Fig. 1) suggest that the increase levelled off in 2009, though at the time of writing the possibility of a 'double-dip' recession, with a second stage rise in unemployment, cannot be ruled out.

3. ANALYTICAL APPROACH

The chapter uses logistic regression techniques to estimate the probability that any member of the GHS sample was not in work in any year. That probability will be influenced both by the supply side (the individual's preference for work and the set of skills s/he has to offer) and by the demand side (employers' need for workers). The question to be addressed is how sensitive individuals' non-employment probabilities are to variations in aggregate demand, holding supply-side characteristics constant.

1. The analysis focuses mainly on whether an individual is not in work, rather than whether s/he is unemployed. Clearly the unemployed (looking for a job) are the group of primary concern, given that their current situation is one that they are positively trying to escape. It is often assumed that economically inactive people have chosen not to work and are not of concern. The extent to which these choices are freely made in the long term is open for discussion (Berthoud & Blekesaune, 2007). But the important point in the current context is that any *increase* in the non-employment rates of (e.g.) mothers or disabled people *directly attributable to a cyclical scarcity of job*s is unlikely to have been the outcome of autonomous changes in their preferences, and so should be considered one of the outcomes of a recession.
2. It is important to take account of *all* the influences on people's job prospects before reaching conclusions about the importance of any *one* of them. A multivariate analysis is proposed, in which gender and family structure, age, education, health, ethnicity and region are all considered as potentially independent predictors of non-employment probabilities. Rather than simply report how many (e.g.) disabled people do not have a job, the approach offers the opportunity to show how much higher the non-employment rate of disabled people is than that of non-disabled people with otherwise similar characteristics. This net difference – a 'disability employment penalty' (Berthoud, 2008) – can be compared with

similarly-calculated penalties for mothers, ethnic minority groups and so on (Berthoud & Blekesaune, 2007).

3. The analysis compares year-by-year changes in the labour market advantages or disadvantages experienced by different social groups, with year-by-year changes in the unemployment rate, used as an indicator of ups and downs in the business cycle. If the non-employment rate of any group remained constant, regardless of booms and busts, then it could be concluded that the group was unaffected by recessions. If their non-employment rate fluctuated widely in a pattern closely synchronised with the national indicator of labour demand, then it could be concluded that the group was highly sensitive to market conditions – and the analysis provides an estimate of the numbers affected. The analysis projects the conclusions about the early 1980s and 1990s forward to the late 2000s, effectively 'predicting' the detail of what is happening now.

4. A constant non-employment rate is not necessarily the appropriate counterfactual baseline against which to compare the outcome of a recession. While the overall proportion of GHS sample members in and out of work remained fairly steady over the long term (once cyclical effects have been ironed out), some of the social groups of interest (e.g. mothers) have seen a fairly steady improvement in their job expectations, while others (e.g. disabled people) have seen a fairly steady deterioration (Berthoud & Blekesaune, 2007). For these groups, what matters is the extent to which their non-employment rate departed from their under-lying trend during a recession and recovery.

   Fig. 2 plots year-by-year changes, for one sample group whose non-employment rate fell over the period and another whose rate rose. The analytical challenge is to identify the M-shaped pattern of response to cyclical variations (see Fig. 1) superimposed on a steady trend. If the underlying trend was not taken into account, the cyclical effect would be substantially under-estimated when the trend is upwards, and over-estimated when the trend is downwards.

5. The fifth point is obvious, but needs to be made explicit. The past is the only, but not an ideal, guide to the future. Analysis of the impact of the recessions in the early 1980s and 1990s is intended to illustrate the likely consequences of the recession now in progress. There are all sorts of differences between the three events – in the starting situation, in the causes of the crisis and in the policy responses – which mean that study of the first two cannot be used to predict the pattern of the third with any precision. The analysis should nevertheless offer a good guide to the likely impact of the current downturn on the welfare of individuals.

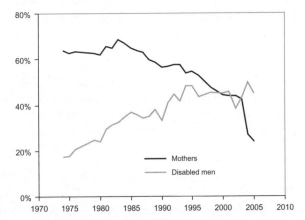

Fig. 2. Illustration of Rising and Falling Trends in Annual Non-Employment
Rates among Specific Groups.

6. It is nevertheless possible to provide a preliminary check on the
conclusions derived initially from the 1980s and 1990s. Since the
historical analysis was originally undertaken, early data from the LFS
have become available, from which it is possible to observe the actual
changes in employment rates that occurred between 2008 and 2009.
Preliminary analysis, reported in section 6, help to show how far the
experience of a recession is generalisable from cycle to cycle.

4. OVERALL TRENDS IN NON-EMPLOYMENT PROBABILITIES

A first step is to establish that cyclical variations in the proportion of
potential workers who report that they are unemployed are associated with
parallel trends in the proportion of adults who are not in work for other
stated reasons. Table 1 does this using a multinomial regression equation, in
which each of the alternatives to being in work (16 hours plus) is analysed
distinctly. The equation controls for underlying trends by including the
sequence of years as a predictor (1974–2005, numbered 0 through 31), and
also the square of the numerical sequence. This incorporates an assumption
that any long-term rises or falls were continuous, but not necessarily linear.

Table 1. Multinomial Regression Equation Using Annual Unemployment Rate and Annual Trend to Predict Specific Labour Market Activities.

	Proportion of All, 2005 (per cent)	Multinomial Coefficients		
		Annual unemployment rate	Trend (year)	Trend (year^2)
a. In work, 16 hours or more	73	Reference category		
b. Work, less than 16 hours	5	*0.021*	*0.022*	*−0.001*
c. Student	2	0.018	*0.049*	0.000
d. Unemployed	3	*0.152*	*0.032*	*−0.001*
e. Incapable of work	5	0.011	*0.096*	*−0.001*
f. Retired	2	0.024	*0.166*	*−0.003*
g. Home or family	8	*0.038*	*−0.043*	0.000
h. Other/not known	2	−0.023	−0.001	*0.001*

Notes: GHS 1974–2005, adults aged 20–59. Coefficients in italics are significant ($p < 0.05$). Pseudo-R^2 for the multinomial equation as a whole was 1.4 per cent.

Since the annual unemployment rate is calculated from the number of people reporting that they were unemployed, it is hardly surprising that the one strongly predicts the other. The important point of the analysis in Table 1 is that all the other alternative outcomes also tended to rise during periods of rising unemployment, and fall during periods of falling unemployment (with the exception of the unimportant 'other/not known' category).

The temptation is to use this multinomial approach to predict how sensitive disabled people, older workers and women are to changing market conditions, using the categories 'incapable of work', 'retired' and 'home or family' as indicators of the three groups' experiences. The difficulty with such a solution is that the choice of label is often subjective, depending partly on what the individual was doing before, and partly on current normative considerations about appropriate social and economic roles. These norms have changed over time, leading to trends in the number of people explaining their non-work in different ways, which do not necessarily match rises or falls in their non-employment probabilities.

Instead, the analysis later in this chapter shows how many members of each specific group did not have a job (as defined). Not having a job seems a more objective fact than the reason given. Moreover, the chosen approach allows finer-grain analysis, controlling for more factors than the categorisation used in Table 1.

Note that the definition of non-work used in the analysis is based on categories b, d, e, f, g and h as labelled in the table, so the overall non-work rate was 25 per cent in 2005. $(5+3+5+2+8+2)$. The ILO definition of unemployment rates expresses category d as a percentage of $a+b+d$. This gives a figure of 3.3 per cent in 2005. Because the bases for the percentages are not the same, a percentage point change in non-employment would refer to more actual people than a percentage point change in unemployment. This will become clear as examples are given in the following paragraphs.

A first step is to analyse annual non-work rates, using the annual characteristics – current unemployment rate and trend – as the predictor variables. There are three ways of doing this.

• The first column of Table 2 shows the results of an ordinary least squares (OLS) regression in which each year in the sequence is treated as an observation, using the annual unemployment rate and the year-on-year trend as the predictors. It shows that for every rise or fall of 1 percentage point in the unemployment rate, the non-work rate rose or fell by 1.1 percentage point. This means that if unemployment in 2005 had doubled,

Table 2. Three Ways of Explaining the Relationship between Annual Unemployment Rates and Annual Non-Work Rates.

| | Analysis of Yearly Averages (OLS) | Analysis of Individual Probabilities (Logistic Regression) | |
		Without controls	With controls
Annual unemployment rate	*0.011*	*0.051*	*0.066*
Trend (per year)	*−0.003*	*−0.009*	0.006
(year squared)	*0.000*	0.000	0.000
(Pseudo) R^2	97%	0.4%	25.5%
Number of observations	28	360,672 individuals in 28 clusters	
Effect of increasing unemployment by 3.3%	3.49%	3.59%	3.25%

Notes: See the appendix for full details of the logistic regression equation with controls. Coefficients in italics are significant at the 95% confidence level.

from 3.3 to 6.6 per cent, the non-work rate would have increased by 3.5 percentage points.

• The second column of Table 2 shows the results of a logistic regression equation, predicting the probability of non-employment of each individual in the sample, again using the annual unemployment rate and the year-on-year trend as the sole predictors.[5] The logistic regression coefficient of 0.051 is not easy to interpret, but it can be calculated that doubling the 2005 unemployment rate from 3.3 to 6.6 per cent would lead to an increase in the non-work rate of 3.6 percentage points.

• The last column of Table 2 shows the results of a similar logistic regression equation, which also controls for the effects of a wide range of other personal characteristics on non-work probabilities. These other effects are recorded in the appendix and may be interesting in their own right, but the important point for the current objective is that controlling for these characteristics suggests a slightly weaker underlying relationship between unemployment and non-work than appeared in the logistic specification without controls – a doubling (3.3 percentage point rise) in the 2005 unemployment rate would lead to a rise of just under 3.25 percentage points in the overall non-employment rate.[6]

The estimate of the effect of doubling the 2005 unemployment rate will be used again and again in the following text, to illustrate the predicted effects of the recession on particular groups of people. It is calculated by

1. using the logistic regression equation to predict the non-employment probability of each 2005 sample member under 2005 conditions; and
2. adding 3.3 × the relevant coefficient to the prediction formula,[7] and re-predicting the non-employment probabilities in 2005 under the hypothetically revised conditions.

The approach is similar in concept to the calculation of marginal effects, except that the estimate refers to a plausible change in actual conditions rather than to an infinitesimal change. Year 2005 is used because it is the most recent year available in the data set. Doubling the unemployment rate is assumed because that is what happened (according to the claimant counts) between 2008 and 2009.

So the best estimate is that a rise of 3.3 in the percentage unemployment rate is matched by a rise of 3.25 in the overall percentage non-work rate. Applying these figures to 2005 conditions implies that:

• Doubling the unemployment rate represents an increase of 812,000 in the number of unemployed people aged 20–59 (defined as looking for work).

- An increase of 3.25 percentage points in the proportion of all adults (in that age range) not working represents a total rise of joblessness attributable to weakened demand of 1,034,000.
- It can be concluded that the number of jobs directly affected by cyclical factors is about 127 for every 100 individuals recorded as unemployed.

The rise in unemployment therefore undercounts the total number of people whose jobs are affected by a recession. The difference between the two counts is not massive, and it can be concluded that the number of people not working on grounds of disability, early retirement and motherhood is somewhat, but not exceptionally, sensitive to fluctuations in the number of jobs available.

5. EFFECTS ON SOCIAL GROUPS

The overall effect of fluctuations in labour demand on the number of people out of work is not difficult to estimate and the fact that some 'unemployment' is hidden among people who report other reasons for not having a job is not a new idea (Beatty & Fothergill, 2005). But the detailed year-by-year data provided by the GHS offers an opportunity to analyse the rises and falls in joblessness among different social groups, to show, for example, whether it is men or women, well-qualified or poorly qualified, whose prospects are most sensitive to market conditions. Do disabled people, or members of minority ethnic groups, face additional disadvantage during downturns in the economy, or is their position already so weak that macro-economic changes make no difference?

The main logistic regression equation covering all groups and the whole period is set out in the appendix. Including (say) education and the annual unemployment rate in the same model tells us that people with no qualifications are generally less likely to have a job than graduates in all years, and that the overall non-employment rate fluctuates with the business cycle for people of all educational backgrounds. But this does not differentiate between the effects of the business cycle on those with low and high qualifications. The analysis needs to estimate the pattern of changes over time for each social group.

This has been done by adding a set of interaction terms to the equation, which provide estimates of the effects of both underlying trends and cyclical variations in demand, on each of the original predictor variables. The detailed results are in the appendix, together with a summary of the Stata commands used to generate the estimates. The model takes account of the direct effects on non-work probabilities of 30 characteristics, and also allows for 30 distinct trends and 30 distinct cyclical patterns.

Models with large numbers of interaction terms are too complex to be interpreted directly. The trick is to repeat the approach already used to summarise the overall cyclical effect.

- The current non-work probability of each member of the 2005 sample is predicted, taking account of all characteristics and their interactions.
- A hypothetical non-employment probability is then calculated for each 2005 sample member, assuming a 3.3 percentage point increase in the unemployment rate, and applying that to all the interactions between characteristics and unemployment rates.
- This provides, for every sample member, an estimate of their increased risk of non-employment. Variations in this increased risk can be analysed across the key characteristics of interest.
- Reported effects are averaged across adults in the 2005 sample.

That is done in the following paragraphs, for the following characteristics in order: gender/family structure, age, disability, educational qualifications, ethnic group and region.

5.1. Gender and Family Structure

Preliminary analysis suggested that the most efficient way of describing variations in non-employment patterns was to compare all men (excluding the small number of lone fathers), women without dependent children living with them and mothers (plus lone fathers). This three-way distinction provides the basis for Table 3, illustrated by Fig. 3.

By 2005, the estimated non-employment rate among men (as defined) had risen to nearly 15 per cent as the result of long-term trends. Among parents (mostly mothers, as defined), it had fallen to about 38 per cent, while childless women were in between at 27 per cent. But a rise of 3.3 per cent in the unemployment rate is expected to have substantially more impact on men (4.0 percentage points) than on parents (3.1 points), with childless women least affected (1.6 points).

The second half of Table 3 presents the percentages in terms of the number of people affected. Two million 'men' would have been out of work for one reason or another in 2005 anyway. They would have been joined by more than a further half million if unemployment had doubled. Larger numbers of 'women' and 'parents' who would not have been working in any case are relatively unaffected by a potential recession. The number of men

Table 3. Logistic Regression Predictions of the Relationship between Annual Unemployment Rates and Overall Non-Work Probabilities, by Gender and Family Structure.

	Men (Except Lone Fathers)	Women (Except Mothers)	Parents (Mothers + Lone Fathers)
Percent predicted not to be working in 2005	14.7%	27.0%	37.8%
Predicted if unemployment doubled	18.7%	28.6%	41.0%
Predicted increase, percentage points	4.0%	1.6%	3.1%
Number not working in 2005 (thousands)	2,196	2,335	3,111
Predicted increase (thousands)	603	135	258
Proportionate increase	27%	6%	8%

Note: Estimates derived from the model reported in the appendix.

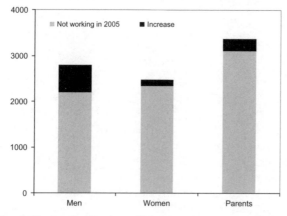

Fig. 3. Predicted Changes in Number of Non-Employed People in 2005 Conditions, by Gender and Family Structure. *Note*: Estimates derived from the model reported in the appendix. See text for the definition of categories.

out of work would increase by more than a quarter, and the number of childless women by little more than 1 in 20.

5.2. Age

Table 4 reports estimates for a series of other population groups, calculated in the same way as, though presented in less detail than, the results by

Table 4. Logistic Regression Predictions of the Relationship between Annual Unemployment Rates and Non-Work Probabilities, by Other Social Characteristics.

	Per cent Predicted not to be Working in 2005	Predicted Increase		
		Percentage points	Thousands	Proportionate (per cent)
Age				
20–24	22.4	5.7	215	26
25–29	22.9	4.8	189	21
30–34	24.2	4.1	167	17
35–39	23.1	3.3	140	14
40–44	19.4	2.6	113	13
45–49	19.9	2.1	81	10
50–54	26.5	1.7	62	7
55–59	36.3	1.3	53	4
Disability				
Not disabled	19.2	3.3	890	17
Limiting long-standing illness	53.5	2.1	99	4
Education				
No qualifications	46.1	4.0	176	9
Lower	30.8	4.6	137	15
O level/GCSE	25.7	2.7	198	11
A level	18.7	2.2	106	12
Higher/degree	16.5	2.5	243	15
Ethnic group				
White	23.2	2.9	815	12
Caribbean	27.7	5.2	24	19
Indian	28.3	4.2	36	15
Pakistani/Bangladeshi	47.0	6.9	44	15
Other	35.0	5.2	70	15
Region				
Scotland	22.2	2.0	55	9
North East	27.0	1.5	20	6
North West	24.5	3.4	101	14
Yorks and Humber	25.5	3.0	109	12
East Midlands	24.7	3.8	96	15
West Midlands	25.8	5.1	144	20
Wales	26.1	2.3	36	9
Eastern	22.3	3.2	102	14
London	26.8	3.8	144	14
South East	23.2	2.7	122	12
South West	21.9	2.1	58	10

Note: Estimates derived from the model reported in the appendix.

gender and family structure. Analysis by age shows that the overall proportion not working in baseline 2005 conditions tended to be higher in the 50s, and especially the late 50s, compared with younger age groups. But it is clearly people at the beginning of the age-sequence analysed who are most susceptible to the potential impact of a recession. The non-employment rate among 20–24-year-olds would soar by a quarter, while the rate for 55–59-year-olds would rise by only 1 in 25.

5.3. Disability

There has been much discussion of the possibility that the rapid rise in the number of disabled people claiming out-of-work benefits over the 1980s and early 1990s was caused by the industrial restructuring and fiscal retrenchment associated with the Thatcher administration (Beatty & Fothergill, 2005). A more detailed analysis of trends in the non-employment rates of disabled people (using the same GHS data set) suggests that disabled people are highly sensitive to *geographical* variations in the health of the labour market, but not very sensitive to variations *over time* (Berthoud, 2011).

The GHS does not carry detailed questions on the nature and severity of people's impairments, such as would be required to define 'disability' with any precision. Instead, it identifies sample members who report a limiting long-standing illness – a question which has been shown to exaggerate estimates of the number of disabled people in the working age population, and under-estimate the extent of their labour market disadvantage (Berthoud, 2007).

If disabled people (i.e. those reporting a limiting long-standing illness) followed a similar trajectory in the current downturn as they did in the 1983 and 1993 recessions, they would experience a 2.1 percentage point rise in their non-employment rate – rather lower than that faced by non-disabled people. The rise would be only a small proportionate increase, compared with the very high rate of non-employment already faced by disabled people.

5.4. Education

Educational qualifications have a strong influence on people's chances of having a job, as well as on the type of work and level of earnings they can expect.[8] Nearly half of the shrinking group of people with no qualifications are estimated to have been out of work in 2005 conditions, even before the hypothesised recession. But only one sixth of the growing group of graduates, and others with higher educational qualifications, would have been out of work in baseline 2005 conditions.

The third panel of Table 4 shows that under-qualified potential workers have been exceptionally sensitive to previous recessions, and are predicted to suffer a substantial increase in non-employment during the current period, while well-qualified individuals are much better protected against the vagaries of the labour market.

Unlike the analyses by gender/family, age and disability, the analysis by education suggests that those already disadvantaged will be most at risk of further disadvantage. One consequence is that the proportionate increase, recorded in the final column of Table 4, is fairly constant across qualification categories.

5.5. Ethnic Group

It has long been observed that the unemployment rates of ethnic minorities are 'hypercyclical' (Smith, 1977; Jones, 1993), rising faster than white unemployment rates during recessions, but falling faster during periods of economic growth. This means that an assessment of minority non-employment rates is sensitive to the period in the cycle that is under consideration.

The current analysis estimates overall non-employment rates (not just unemployment), and differentiates between the main minority groups. A complication is that the composition of the minority population has changed over the decades being analysed, following migration, so the projection of 1980s and 1990s experience to the 2000s is less reliable.

Nevertheless, the conclusions are largely consistent with previous studies. Pakistanis and Bangladeshis, already among the most disadvantaged groups in the country, are also shown to be highly sensitive to a potential recession, with an estimated increase in non-employment of nearly 7 percentage points. All the other minorities, though less disadvantaged in normal times, also exhibit the hypercyclical pattern.

5.6. Region

The non-employment rate in the base conditions of 2005 ranged between just under 22 per cent in the South West, and 27 per cent in the North East. It is well known that unemployment rates vary between regions, but Fig. 4 shows that long-term prosperous and disadvantaged regions have fluctuated over

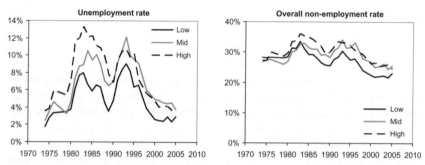

Fig. 4. Variations in Raw Unemployment and Overall Non-Employment Rates across the Business Cycle, in Regions of Low, Middle and High Underlying Unemployment. *Note*: Underlying unemployment is calculated as the mean unemployment rate in each region, over the whole 32-year period. Low rates are in Eastern, South East, South West and East Midlands (<6 per cent); mid rates are in London, Wales and North West (6–6.9 per cent); high rates in West Midlands, Yorkshire/Humberside, Scotland and North East (≥7 per cent).

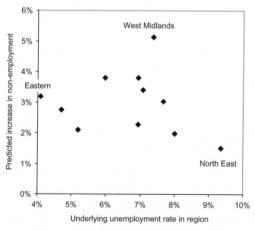

Fig. 5. Predicted Increase in Non-Employment Associated With a Recession: Regions Plotted against Their Underlying Unemployment Rate. *Note*: Derived from the logistic regression equation reported in the appendix.

the business cycle in parallel with each other. Table 4 shows that doubling the 2005 unemployment rate is estimated to increase the proportion of people out of work by between 1.5 percentage points in the North East, and just over 5 percentage points in the West Midlands.

Table 4 listed the regions in an order roughly from north to south. There is no obvious north/south divide in the sensitivity of labour markets to cyclical effects. An alternative perspective is offered in Fig. 5, which plots the estimated increase in non-employment in each region, against the region's underlying unemployment rate (calculated as its mean unemployment rate across the 32-year period). Again, there is no obvious relationship between the underlying health of a regional economy and its response to a downturn.

6. COMPARING THE PREDICTIONS WITH THE OUTCOME (SO FAR)

The preceding sections of this chapter have used data about the recessions in the early 1980s and 1990s to predict the probable impact of the recession of the late 2000s. The analysis was initially undertaken with the short-term objective of identifying the social groups who might be in most need of policy intervention to protect their employment options and living standards. But a longer-term objective of this formally published version of the chapter is to assess the extent to which the experience of earlier recessions can be generalised to cover later recessions – or whether, on the contrary, each turn of the cycle should be thought of as an independent event.

At the time of writing (October 2010) early data from the UK Labour Force Survey (LFS) can be used to describe the actual changes in the rates of employment reported by the social groups of interest between the spring of 2008 and the summer of 2009.[9] Fig. 6 briefly illustrates the differences between the effects of the recession actually observed in the 2008 and 2009 LFSs, and the effects predicted from the GHS analysis of the previous two recessions. To the extent that the actual outcome matches the prediction, the comparison confirms that all three recessions showed similar patterns of job loss. To the extent that the outcome varies from the prediction, the implication is that the current downturn differs from the previous two.

The overall increase in non-employment observed so far in the LFS was rather less than that assumed in the GHS analysis, but it is the distribution of the job losses that matters for this comparison.

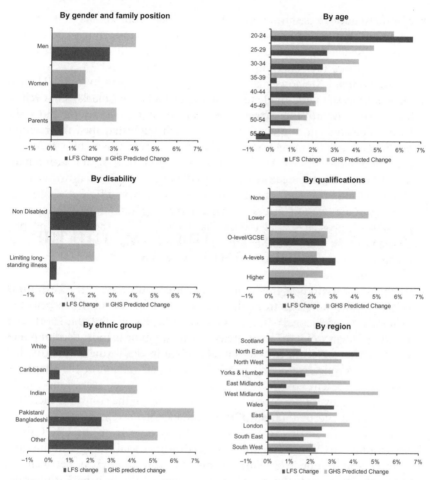

Fig. 6. Increases in Non-Employment Rates: Comparison between Change Predicted from the GHS Analysis of Previous Recessions and Actual Change Reported in LFS.

- The analysis of previous recessions predicted that men would experience a higher rate of job loss than childless women – and this is borne out by the actual changes observed between 2008 and 2009. But the expectation that parents (mostly mothers) would be more affected than childless women has not been confirmed.

- The prediction based on analysis of the sequence of GHS data sets suggested that young people were much more sensitive to recessions than older ones. This systematic age pattern is even more strongly visible in the LFS reports of the actual outturns (though the result for 35–39-year-olds is anomalous).
- Disabled people were predicted to be relatively unaffected by the 2008–2009 recession, and this expectation is clearly confirmed by the outturn.
- Both the prediction and the outcome suggest that people without qualifications are more likely to suffer the adverse effects of a recession than graduates, though this trend is much less clear in the event than might have been expected from the prediction.
- But the outcome for ethnic minorities is rather different from the prediction. People of Caribbean origin have seen a minimal deterioration in their job prospects, and Indians have suffered less than white people. Pakistanis and Bangladeshis are still worse off than average, but these exceptionally disadvantaged groups seem to have suffered less this time than in previous recessions.
- The regional pattern of employment reductions recorded in the 2008–2009 LFSs is quite different from the prediction based on previous decades. Whereas the prediction pointed to the West Midlands, East Midlands and London as the worst affected areas, it was the North East, Scotland and Wales which faced the largest actual decline in employment rates.

7. CONCLUSIONS

Rises and falls in job opportunities are so directly linked to cyclical patterns of growth and decline in national output that some experts propose trends in unemployment statistics as the key measure of the health of a national economy. The claimant count rose from 2.4 per cent in the first quarter of 2008 to 5.0 per cent in the last quarter of 2009; the LFS measure of ILO unemployment rose from 5.4 to 8.1 per cent over the same period.

This chapter mainly uses survey data covering a 30-year period, analysing the experience of the past two recessions, to predict the probable impact of the current downturn on individuals. Of course no two circuits of the economic cycle are identical, but the past is the only, if imperfect, guide to the future. The analysis is designed to show, first, whether the reduction in the number of people in work will be confined to, or larger than, the number reporting themselves to be unemployed (i.e. available for and actively looking for work); and, second, what kinds of people (men or women, young or old, and so on) are likely to be affected. The analysis is based on a multivariate logistic regression equation which takes account both of changes in the characteristics of the population, and (crucially) of longer-term trends in the non-employment risks of particular groups. An analysis of the whole 32-year period covered by the GHS is used to 'predict' the outcome of a hypothetical recession occurring in 2005 (the latest year in the data sequence). The inference is that this is what is happening now, in 2010. The hypothesised macro-economic event is a doubling of the national unemployment rate, from 3.3 to 6.6 per cent.

At an aggregate level, the analysis confirmed that the reduction of the number of people in work would be larger than the increase in the number of unemployed. Bear in mind that macro-economic trends impact on a continuous process by which men and women leave work and find new jobs. An increase of 100,000 in the unemployment count does not mean that exactly that number of people were made redundant. It is the net outcome of a rise in the rate at which people leave work, and/or a fall in the rate at which they start new jobs. Other non-workers, besides the unemployed, participate in these outflows and inflows, so that scarcity of jobs might (for example) encourage a disabled person to give up work a little earlier than he might otherwise have done, or discourage a mother from finding a job until a little later than she might otherwise have done. The scale of this rise in the number of 'discouraged workers' during a recession is not as great as might perhaps have been feared – an increase of 127 in the total number of people not in employment, for every 100 who say they are unemployed.

The GHS data provide a unique opportunity to identify the social characteristics of those most and least affected by recessions. For adults aged 20–59 taken as a whole, the increase in the non-employment rate, predicted if the strictly measured unemployment rate doubled, was 3.25 percentage points. For the sub-groups identified in Tables 3 and 4, this effect fell as low as 1.3 percentage points (55–59-year-olds) and as high as 6.9 percentage points (Pakistanis and Bangladeshis). The groups most affected are men, younger adults, not disabled, with poor educational records, members of ethnic minorities, living in the West Midlands. Those least affected, conversely, are women without children, in older age groups, disabled, with good qualifications, whites, living in the North East of England.

A test of the reliability of these estimates is offered by the LFSs conducted between the spring of 2008 and the summer of 2009. Preliminary analysis of these data sets provides an indication of the early actual effects of the current recession, for comparison with the predictions based on analysis of earlier cycles. In some respects, the actual outturn is similar to that of previous recessions: men, younger people, non-disabled people and those with poor qualifications are all shown to have been more sensitive to cyclical trends in the demand for labour than women, older people, disabled people and graduates – though even here there are differences in detail between the prediction and the actual experience. But the patterns of change affecting ethnic minorities, and variations between regions, have been quite different in the late 2000s than would have been expected from the 1980s and 1990s.

It is far from easy to generalise from these observed patterns. It has been suggested that those already facing labour market disadvantage would be most likely to face additional problems if jobs are scarce. That is not the consistent conclusion of the analysis.

- The GHS findings for education and ethnic group tend to support the vicious-circle-of-disadvantage hypothesis.
- The findings for gender, age, and disability tend to the opposite, implying that existing disadvantage is stable across business cycles. This is particularly surprising for disabled people, whose deteriorating job prospects over the decades have often been blamed on the experience of earlier recessions.
- There is no consistent pattern suggesting that already disadvantaged regions are either more or less sensitive to cyclical factors than more prosperous regions.

The output from the logistic regression equations can be used to address the relationship between baseline prospects and cyclical sensitivity more directly. The analysis predicts the non-employment probability of every member of the (2005) GHS sample, based on his or her characteristics; and the change in that predicted probability associated with a hypothesised recession. Those with low baseline probabilities of being out of work (positioned on the left of the graphs in Fig. 7) tend to be men, young, not disabled, with degrees, white, living in the South West. Those with poor prospects, a high baseline probability of non-employment, are depicted on the right of the graphs – they tend to be mothers, older, disabled, with no qualifications, members of minority groups, living in the North East. The graph in the left-hand panel illustrates the baseline distribution of non-work probabilities, and also the predicted outcome of a recession. It can be seen that the increase in non-work risk is broadly spread across the

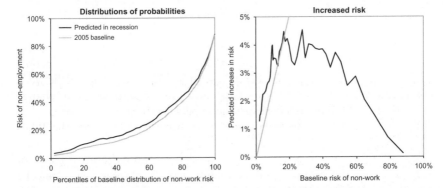

Fig. 7. Relationships between Baseline Non-Employment Probabilities and the Increased Risk Associated With a Recession. *Note*: Both graphs are based on dividing the distribution of baseline risks into 50 equal groups (using the logistic regression equation reported in the appendix), each covering 2 per cent of the total. The left-hand graph plots these according to their number in the sequence; the right-hand graph plots them at their mean baseline risk.

distribution of initial probabilities, rather than bunched mainly at one end or the other.

The right-hand panel re-presents the data from the left-hand panel, this time plotting the average increase in non-work probabilities directly against the baseline probability. The pattern can be summarised in three stages:

- Among adults with a fairly low risk of being out of work – up to about 20 per cent – a recession can be expected to increase that (low) risk by about one fifth. That is, 1 percentage point for people with a 5 per cent starting risk, rising to 4 percentage points for those with a starting risk of 20 per cent. (The pattern is illustrated by the sloping straight line.) About 6 out of 10 adults are in this range with a steady *proportionate* increase in their risk.
- Across the middle of the range of initial disadvantage, between about 20 and 50 per cent, the further increase in risk is steady at about 4 percentage points. About 3 out of 10 adults are in this already disadvantaged range, facing a steady *absolute* increase in their risk.
- The most disadvantaged people are relatively unaffected by a recession. More than half of them are out of work in any case. About 1 in 10 adults are in this position of extreme disadvantage, who could hardly be further affected by temporary labour market fluctuations.

NOTES

1. Between 2000 and 2004, the annual sample was based on financial years, e.g. April 2003 to March 2004, but they are labelled here according to the first-named year, e.g. 2003, for convenience. In 2005, the first three months of the calendar year were allocated to the 2004/2005 survey (and labelled here 2004), while a new (and larger) sample was drawn for the remaining months (and labelled here 2005).

2. That is, 1974–2005, excluding 1977, 1978, 1997 and 1999.

3. 'NEET' was a definition introduced by the UK government in 2000 as a way of focussing on young people (aged 16–24) who were not engaged in any productive activity. It has since been adopted by other countries, e.g. Japan. The analysis here is not confined to young people, and addresses lack of employment (or training) by all adults aged 20–59.

4. The proportion of those defined as 'in work' and who were students rose from 1.1 per cent in 1974 to 3.6 per cent in 2003. They were concentrated among those in their 20s. It is possible that scarcity of jobs is one of the factors that encourages young people to stay on in the education system, but that issue is not addressed in this analysis.

5. All the members of each year's GHS sample have identical values for the annual unemployment rate and the year. Estimates of sampling errors have taken account of the non-independence of these variables at the individual level by treating each year as a cluster.

6. It is interesting to note that while the raw trend in the non-employment rate is slightly negative in the first two columns of Table 2 (without controls), it is slightly positive in the third column when characteristics are controlled for. This suggests that the reduction in overall non-work rates is more than accounted for by the reduction in the number of people with a high risk of non-employment in any case – e.g. people with no qualifications, women with children.

7. The formula for predicting probabilities from a logistic regression equation is $1/(1 + \exp(-x\beta))$, where $x\beta$ is the sum, for each member of the sample, of the values of the predictor variables times their coefficients.

8. O levels (before 1988) and GCSE (since 1988) are qualifications obtained at the end of compulsory schooling, typically at age 16. A levels are obtained on completion of secondary education, typically at age 18. Higher qualifications are typically obtained at university, though some advanced vocational training is counted.

9. The preliminary analysis of the LFS is based on 2008 Q1 (all waves) plus 2008 Q2 (wave 1 only) for the 'before' sample, and 2009 Q2 (wave 5 only) plus 2009 Q3 (all waves) for the 'after' sample. Analysis is confined to Great Britain to be consistent with the GHS. The classifications by family status, age, disability and so on in the LFS analysis are designed to be equivalent to the classifications used in the GHS analysis, but are not necessarily identical.

10. These are not the commands actually used, but rewritten to make the method as clear as possible to the reader.

ACKNOWLEDGMENTS

This chapter derives from a programme of research on disability and employment funded by the Nuffield Foundation. Additional work was undertaken under the auspices of ISER's Research Centre on Micro-Social Change, supported by the UK Economic and Social Research Council. The chapter is based on an analytical approach and data-set used in earlier projects sponsored by the Joseph Rowntree Foundation, the Department for Work and Pensions and the Equalities Review.

It is based mainly on GHS and LFS data collected by the Office for National Statistics and made available to analysts via the UK Data Archive.

We are grateful to all of the organisations or individuals mentioned above. As always, none of them is responsible for the content of the chapter.

REFERENCES

Beatty, C., & Fothergill, S. (2005). The diversion from 'unemployment' to 'sickness' across British regions and districts. *Regional Studies, 39*, 837–854.

Berthoud, R. (2008). Disability employment penalties in Britain. *Work, Employment and Society, 22*(1), 129–148.

Berthoud, R. (2011). *Trends in the employment rates of disabled people in Britain.* ISER working paper 2011-03. University of Essex.

Berthoud, R., & Blekesaune, M. (2007). *Persistent employment disadvantage.* DWP Research Report 416. Department for Work and Pensions.

Blekesaune, M. (2008). *Unemployment and partnership dissolution.* ISER Working Paper 2008–21. University of Essex.

Daily Telegraph. (2009). *Repossessions double in a year as a family loses their home every seven minutes,* January 22.

Eslake, S. (2008). What is the difference between a recession and a depression? Available at <http://clubtroppo.com.au/2008/11/23/>

Guardian. (2009). *Increase in burglaries shows effect of recession,* January 22.

NBER. (2009). See <http://www.nber.org/cycles.html#announcements>

Independent. (2008). *Recession could put children at risk of abuse, warns Bar Council chief,* 8 December.

Jones, T. (1993). *Britain's ethnic minorities.* London: Policy Studies Institute.

Muriel, A., & Sibieta, L. (2009). *Living standards during previous recessions.* IFS Briefing Note 85. Institute for Fiscal Studies.

Smith, D. (1977). *Unemployment and ethnic minorities.* London: PEP.

Stafford, B., & Duffy, D. (2009). *Review of evidence on the impact of economic downturn on disadvantaged groups.* DWP Working Paper 68. Department for Work and Pensions.

Time. (2009). *Suicides: Watching for a recession spike,* February 9.

APPENDIX. DETAILS OF MAIN LOGISTIC REGRESSION EQUATION

Table A1 presents the details of a logistic regression equation predicting adults' probability of not working (at least 16 hours per week, using the definition explained in Section 2.2). The main coefficients show that, as expected, some types of people are systematically more or less likely to have a job than other types of people.

Table A1. Logistic Regression Equation Predicting Non-Employment Probabilities – GHS 1974–2005.

	Mean (in 2005)	Main coefficient		Interactions With					
				Year		Year^2		Unemployment rate	
		B	z	B	z	B	z	B	z
Family structure									
Lone man	12%	0.704	11.2	−0.005	−0.3	0.000	−0.3	−0.006	−0.4
Man with partner (base)	38%								
Lone woman	15%	1.721	28.8	−0.033	−2.0	0.000	−0.3	−0.064	−4.1
Woman with partner	35%	2.970	37.2	−0.049	−3.5	0.000	0.1	−0.084	−5.7
Age of children[a]	−3	−0.185	−29.8	0.000	0.0	0.000	2.6	0.001	1.3
Has a working partner	53%	−0.695	−8.5	−0.063	−3.6	0.002	2.8	0.019	1.1
Age (spline)									
Per year, 20–45	37.6	0.010	2.5	0.002	3.2	0.000	−3.9	-0.003	−3.4
Per year, 45–59	2.7	0.102	27.8	0.001	1.9	0.000	−1.8	-0.004	−4.5
Disability									
None (base)	85%								
Limiting long-standing illness	15%	1.118	15.3	0.024	1.8	0.000	−0.4	-0.036	−2.4
Education									
No qualifications	14%	0.145	2.5	0.037	3.3	−0.001	−1.8	0.019	1.7
Less than O level/GCSE	9%	−0.082	−1.6	0.010	1.0	0.000	−0.6	0.027	2.7
GCSE (base)	23%								
A level	15%	−0.145	−2.4	0.004	0.3	0.000	−0.5	−0.013	−1.1
Higher	30%	−0.442	−7.7	−0.017	−1.8	0.000	1.5	0.010	1.0
Not known	8%	0.571	4.7	−0.030	−1.5	0.000	0.4	−0.007	−0.4

Table A1. (*Continued*)

	Mean (in 2005)	Main coefficient		Interactions With					
				Year		Year^2		Unemployment rate	
		B	z	B	z	B	z	B	z
Ethnic group									
White (base)	90%								
Caribbean man	1%	0.138	0.9	0.037	1.3	-0.001	-0.6	0.012	0.4
Caribbean woman	1%	−1.136	−10.4						
Indian	3%	0.290	1.4	−0.028	−0.8	0.001	1.1	−0.009	−0.2
Pakistani/Bangladeshi man	1%	0.424	1.7	0.029	0.8	−0.001	−0.6	0.010	0.2
Pakistani/Bangladeshi woman	1%	*1.218*	5.3						
Other minority group	4%	−0.102	−0.5	0.023	0.8	0.000	0.1	−0.002	−0.1
Region									
Scotland	9%	−0.061	−1.1	*0.052*	6.0	−0.002	−5.4	−0.017	−1.6
North East	4%	*0.166*	3.8	*0.053*	3.6	−0.002	−3.5	−0.028	−1.9
North West	9%	0.010	0.2	0.015	1.3	−0.001	−1.4	0.004	0.3
Yorks and Humber	11%	−0.116	−2.2	0.026	2.9	−0.001	−2.4	0.000	0.0
East Midlands	8%	−0.177	−3.0	0.008	0.6	0.000	−0.4	0.016	1.0
West Midlands	9%	−0.193	−2.6	−0.010	−0.6	0.000	0.8	*0.036*	2.4
Wales	5%	*0.212*	3.8	0.020	1.7	−0.001	−2.2	−0.011	−0.9
Eastern	10%	−0.006	−0.1	0.000	0.0	0.000	−0.2	0.005	0.4
London	12%	−0.230	−4.0	0.014	1.3	0.000	−0.2	0.002	0.2
South East (base)	14%								
South West	9%	0.095	1.3	0.021	1.4	−0.001	−1.7	−0.011	−0.8
Trend									
Year	31	−0.045	−1.5						
Year^2	961	*0.003*	3.4						
Unemployment rate									
This year	0.033	*0.215*	7.0						
Constant		−4.262	−29.2						

[a]Someone whose youngest child was aged 0, was scored −18, and whose youngest child was 18, was scored 0. Women with no children scored 0. Men were scored 0 unless they were lone parents.

- Men and women without a partner have lower job expectations than men with a partner.
- Over the period as a whole, women with a partner were even less likely to have a job than single men and women (though this disadvantage has decreased over the years).
- The younger a mother's, or lone father's, youngest child, the less likely s/he was to be employed.
- The individual's own age had no effect on job chances up to 45, but expectations declined steadily from 45 onwards.
- Disabled people (LLI) were less likely to have a job.
- The better someone's educational qualification, the more likely they were to be in employment.
- Members or minority ethnic groups were often at a disadvantage. Pakistani and Bangladeshi women were exceptionally unlikely to have a job. In contrast, Caribbean women were more likely to have a job than white women with otherwise similar characteristics.
- People living in some regions have less chance of being in work than in other regions, all other characteristics held constant.

While these findings are of interest in their own right, showing which social groups are most and least disadvantaged, the task on this occasion is to show how the non-employment rates of each group changed from year to year, controlling for long-term trends in order to focus on short-term variations in the national unemployment rate. The logistic regression equation therefore included terms interacting all the 'social group' variables with both year-on-year trends and the annual unemployment rate. The coefficients of these interaction terms are shown on the right of Table A1.

The Stata commands producing the model were in the following form,[10] where A to Z represent the predictor variables ranging from 'Lone man' to 'South West'; 'year' is the numerical year in the sequence (1974 = 0), 'year2' is its square and 'ueyear' is the national average unemployment rate in each year.

```
foreach a in A-Z{
    gen I'a'year = 'a'*year
}
foreach a in A-Z{
    gen I'a'year2 = 'a'*year2
}
foreach a in A-Z{
    gen I'a'ue = 'a'*ueyear
}
logit nonwork A-Z year IAyear-IZyear year2 IAyear2-IZyear2 ueyear IAue-IZue
```

Post-estimation commands were used to estimate, first, each sample member's current probability of being out of work

predict prednw

and then each sample member's counterfactual probability of being out of work if the annual unemployment rate was increased by 3.3 per cent

predict XB, xb
gen counterpred $= 1/(1 + \exp(-(XB + .033*(\_b[ueyear] + A*\_b[IAue] + . \quad . \quad . \quad . + Z*\_b[IZue]))))$

The effect of a hypothesised recession is then the difference between the counterfactual prediction and the actual prediction. All the analysis in the chapter reports the effect in 2005, although in principle the same output could be applied to other years in the sequence.

The results of the analysis are shown in Table A1. The equation was based on 360,672 observations, clustered in 28 annual surveys, weighted as described in Section 2.1. The ratios of coefficients to their standard errors are indicated by the z-statistic, and coefficients significant at the 95 per cent confidence limit are italicised. The pseudo-R^2 (a measure of the accuracy with which the equation was able to predict individual non-work probabilities) was 25.4 per cent.

JOB FLOWS, DEMOGRAPHICS, AND THE GREAT RECESSION [☆]

Eva Sierminska and Yelena Takhtamanova

ABSTRACT

The recession the US economy entered in December of 2007 is considered to be the most severe downturn the country has experienced since the Great Depression. The unemployment rate reached as high as 10.1% in October 2009 – the highest we have seen since the 1982 recession. In this chapter, we examine the severity of this recession compared to those in the past by examining worker flows into and out of unemployment taking into account changes in the demographic structure of the population. We identify the most vulnerable groups of this recession by dissaggregating the workforce by age, gender, and race. We find that adjusting for the aging of the US labor force increases the severity of this recession. Our results indicate that the increase in the unemployment rate is driven to a larger extent by the lack of hiring (low outflows), but flows into unemployment are still important for understanding unemployment rate dynamics

[☆] We dedicate this chapter to Emil – who waited till the end. The views expressed in this chapter are solely the responsibility of the authors and should not be interpreted as reflecting the views of the Federal Reserve Bank of San Francisco or the Board of Governors of the Federal Reserve System. This chapter was prepared for the IZA/OECD Workshop "Economic Crisis, Rising Unemployment and Policy Responses: What Does It Mean for the Income Distribution?" taking place on Feb 8–9, 2010 in Paris.

Who Loses in the Downturn? Economic Crisis, Employment and Income Distribution
Research in Labor Economics, Volume 32, 115–154
Copyright © 2011 by Emerald Group Publishing Limited
All rights of reproduction in any form reserved
ISSN: 0147-9121/doi:10.1108/S0147-9121(2011)0000032007

(they are not as acyclical as some literature suggests) and differences in unemployment rates across demographic groups. We find that this is indeed a "mancession," as men face higher job separation probabilities, lower job finding probabilities, and, as a result, higher unemployment rates than women. Lastly, there is some evidence that blacks suffered more than whites (again, this difference is particularly pronounced for men).

Keywords: Unemployment; worker flows; job finding rate; separation rate; demographics; gender

JEL Classification: J1; J6

1. INTRODUCTION

In August 2007, the US and global economy were hit by a financial crisis. Many argued that it is the worst financial crisis in the postwar period, and some went as far as suggesting it might be the worst in modern history.[1] The colossal losses faced by financial institutions (and stunning failures of some of them) led to a credit crunch. At the same time, the extremely poor performance of housing and stock market led to an enormous wealth loss by households (over 25% of US households' net worth was destroyed in the crisis). With weakening demand, the labor market tumbled, as businesses laid off workers. The US economy entered the recession in December 2007. Early on, job losses were low in comparison to previous recessions and the downturn appeared to be mild (in fact, some questioned if a recession was imminent). As financial panic intensified in the fall of 2008, massive job losses followed, and it was clear that not only the country entered a recession, but that this was going to be a deep one.

The National Bureau of Economic Analysis (NBER) announced that the recession ended in June 2009. Yet, it took until March 2010 for the US economy to start registering job gains, and in the summer of 2010 the economy hit a soft patch. Overall, the US economy lost over 8.6 million jobs during December 2007 to February 2010. The unemployment rate reached as high as 10.1%. While the pace of the job losses subsided and the unemployment rate came down from the peak, the multitude of public and private forecasts suggest that it would take years for the US labor market to recover. And, thus, while the recovery has begun, "it is likely to be painfully slow."[2]

The extreme weakness of the labor market became the focus of attention of many US policymakers. Policy response was comprehensive and involved measures aimed at the stabilization of the financial system, improvements in credit and liquidity and the American Recovery and Reinvestment Act (ARRA) – an aggressive fiscal expansion. One of the goals of ARRA was to create and save jobs.

How does this recession compare to the other ones? What is the main driving force of rising unemployment? Is it fueled by higher worker inflows into unemployment or decreasing worker outflows? Are some demographic groups affected more than others? Is ARRA helping the most vulnerable? We take a stab at answering these important questions by examining labor market experiences of several demographic groups. We compare the experiences of men and women and control for age and race – an important variable in the United States. As is highlighted in Smith (2009), "gendered understanding of the current crisis is important to both understand the likely outcomes and also avoid ineffective policy responses or unintended increases in inequality." It is also important to note that the recession of 2007 is different from previous downturns given the increased vulnerability of women to the business cycle (Joint Economic Committee Majority Staff, 2010; Smith, 2009; Antonopoulos, 2009). Other authors, such as Elsby, Hobijn, and Sahin (2010) also examine differences across demographic groups, but subsequently focus on reasons of unemployment loss and on the outlook for recovery, whereas our focus is the distributional effects of employment loss particularly with respect to gender and race. We note that part of our analysis is similar to the work of Elsby et al. (2010), and although the results reconfirm each other, the analysis was conducted independently.

We find that both outflows and inflows to unemployment need to be considered when explaining differences in unemployment experiences during this recession. Men's decline in the job finding probability and women's decline in the job separation probability during this recession seem particularly important. We also find that it is important to be mindful of the changes in labor force composition when comparing aggregate measures of labor market performance over time. For instance, when the aging of the labor force in the US economy is taken into account, this recession looks even more severe.

The chapter is organized as follows. Section 2 discusses reasons to expect heterogeneity in employment experiences during economic downturns and briefly summarizes the relevant literature. The data is discussed in Section 3. We present our empirical methodology in Section 4. Section 5 documents the current state of the US labor market for different demographic groups and compares it to previous recessions. Section 6 discusses policy response and Section 7 concludes.

2. HETEROGENEITY IN EMPLOYMENT EXPERIENCES AND BACKGROUND LITERATURE

There are reasons to expect labor market experiences to differ across demographic groups during expansions and even more so during recessions. Job segregation, differences in labor market attachment and job tenure, and employment discrimination all could serve as mechanisms by which work experiences could differ during times of economic downturn. With regard to race and age, one motivation is theoretical work by Blanchard (1995), which argues that economic downturns have "ladder effects" adversely affecting lower-income individuals. In this section, we outline the potential reasons for expecting differential employment responses during changing economic conditions in the labor market. We focus mainly on gender differences as in many cases these remain stronger than racial differences.

2.1. Employment Segregation

Empirical evidence in OECD countries indicates that women tend to work in a different and narrower range of occupations than men, leaving the possibility of unevenly distributed employment effects during times of economic change.[3] Traditionally, men are more likely to be employed in manufacturing and agricultural professions, while women tend to concentrate in administrative, public, and service sector occupations in a more restricted range of professions. In the 1990s, OECD countries saw the beginning of a greater demand for women in the labor market due to technological change that allowed substitution of men and women workers, the rise of the service sector and the decline of the production sector, increased education levels of women, and effective anti-discrimination policy measures. As discussed in the next section, while women's labor market attachment increased, occupation and industry segregation, although declining, has remained an issue (Dolado, Felgueroso, & Jimeno, 2002). Given the existence of occupational and industry segregation, a differential employment effect by gender due to the onset of a recession can be expected, if these sectors have, for example, differing degrees of interest rates sensitivity. Cyclical properties of certain industries and occupations could also result in a gendered employment effect. For example, in the European Union (EU) countries, women's relative lower unemployment rates in the past have been attributed to female labor shifts from manufacturing to the service sector, the latter being less affected by the business cycle. Hence, women, by concentrating in industries less sensitive to business cycle swings, shelter themselves from both negative and positive business cycle effects (Buddelmeyer, Mourre, & Ward, 2004b). More recently, the influences of changes in occupational distribution, rather than distributions by industry, have been highlighted as having a greater effect on employment. Using UK data, Rives and Sosin (2002) show that although at times of recession, unemployment rises for both genders, the occupational distribution favors women's employment. More specifically, within occupations, women's unemployment rates are consistently higher than men's, but the distribution of occupations favors women because low unemployment occupations have relatively higher proportions of women. This evidence suggests the possibility of gender-specific employment effects, although the direction of that effect is ambiguous.

Occupational segregation according to race is also present, although it has been steadily declining since the early 1980s (Queneau, 2005). Blacks are now more present in favorable managerial position, but remain overrepresented in some laborer professions. Nevertheless, according to Hegewisch, Liepmann, Haves, and Hartmann (2001), gender remains the predominant factor in the occupational segregation in all major race and ethnic groups.

2.2. Labor Market Attachment

Men's and women's employment effects due to changing economic conditions may also take place due to gender differences in the division of part-time and full-time work and labor market attachment (resulting from men's and women's different roles in the care economy) and its correlation with occupational segregation. In both Europe and the United States, women have a considerably lower presence in full-time work compared to men (see, e.g, Blank, 1998; Buddelmeyer, Mourre, & Ward, 2004a; Bardasi & Gornick, 2008) and concentrate in temporary and part-time jobs, which are more sensitive to economic downturns and upswings. In addition, higher labor market attachment for women compared to previous recession will increase their vulnerability and potentially could make the impact of the crisis more equal in terms of losses. Occupational segregation is also positively correlated with the share of part-time jobs, as these jobs tend to be in occupations traditionally held by women. During recessionary times, women are also encouraged to take up and remain in part-time jobs and leave the full-time positions for men (Smith, 2009).

2.3. Job Tenure

A third reason we could expect differential employment responses is differences in job tenure across groups (Munasinghe & Reif, 2008). It has been shown that females and nonwhite employees have shorter tenure (see, e.g., Mumford & Smith, 2003) and consequently may be laid off faster (see Booth, Francesconi, & Garcia-Serrano, 1999 for the case of women in the United Kingdom). However, workers with substantial tenure may also be disproportionately hurt in terms of employment during economic down-turns. Ruhm (1987) finds that although the inverse relationship between job duration and turnover rates holds in the United States, workers with substantial tenure in recently held jobs are more vulnerable during cyclical fluctuations. This effect is strengthened in sectors that are hit particularly hard by recessions. It should be noted that overall, differences in job tenure exist between men and women, between whites and nonwhites, and as a result tenure affects employment responses to economic conditions.

2.4. Discrimination

Employer discrimination either due to gender or race can also result in employment segregation and cause a employment effect during recession. Employers may perceive the productivity of certain demographic groups differently and prefer to hire one over the other, either in hiring/firing the more productive or hiring/firing the seemingly less productive and offering a lower wage. This type of behavior may not be evident when the economy is operating close to full employment but can certainly be in effect in times of economic downturns. Although the argument of employer discrimina-tion is difficult to maintain with the existence of widespread occupational segregation, there is empirical evidence for the United States showing that in male-dominated occupations and industries, the unemployment rate for women has in the past increased more at the cycle troughs (see the literature review in Rives and Sosin, 2002 and Azmat, Guell, & Manning, 2006). More recently, Singh and Zammit (2002) found that women in developing countries were fired at substantially higher rates than men after the Asian financial crisis. Another study also found that employers in developing countries may prefer to hire men as a means of reducing costs in recessionary times given that women are more likely to go on leave due to maternity or illness despite the fact that they are perceived as reliable employees (Seguino, 2003). During this recession, age discrimination rather than race discrimination has been more prominently discussed in the popular press,[4] although it would be hard to provide quantitative evidence to support this claim.

3. DATA

We use current, publicly available data from the Current Population Survey (CPS). The CPS is a monthly survey of households conducted by the US Bureau of Census for the Bureau of Labor Statistics. It provides data on the labor force, employment, unemployment, persons not in the labor force, hours of work, earnings, and other demographic and labor force characteristics. We use monthly aggregated unemployment data disaggregated by age, gender, and race. Unless otherwise stated. The three main unemployment series are the number of unemployed, the unemployment rate, and the number of short-term unemployed (those unemployed for less than 5 weeks).[5] The unemployment rate and the number of unemployed is available for the whole sample (1948:1 to 2009:12), and the data for short-term unemployed is often available from mid-1970s (1976:1 to 2009:12). Thus, the beginning of our period of analysis is driven by the availability of the data, yet our results and discussion are focused on the current recession.

4. EMPIRICAL METHODOLOGY

We first examine unemployment rates, which give us an idea of the share of people in the labor force that are not working in a given period of time or the probability that a randomly chosen person in the labor force will be unemployed. Next, we take a dynamic approach and estimate the underlying movements of workers into and out of unemployment. These are typically referred to as the inflow rate (s_t), which is the pace at which workers move *into* unemployment and the outflow rate (f_t), the pace at which workers move *out of* unemployment.

During recessions, we see more people losing jobs and becoming unemployed, hence we expect the inflow rate to increase. At the same time, it is harder for people to find jobs, hence we expect the outflow rates to decrease. Yet, there is quite a disagreement in the literature as to which is the main driver of the unemployment rate. Earlier literature found flows into unemployment to be the main driver of unemployment hence "The Ins Win" title of the seminal chapter by Darby, Haltiwanger, and Plant (1986). Later work claimed the opposite with Robert Hall (e.g., 2005a, 2005b) and Robert Shimer (e.g., 2005, 2007) being, perhaps, the strongest voices arguing that "outs" of unemployment explain much of unemployment dynamics. Finally, a recent strand of literature finds that "everyone's a winner" – that is, both ins and outs are important in a complete understanding of cyclical unemployment (Elsby et al., 2009). In this chapter, we revisit this issue during the most recent downturn with a particular focus on differences across demographic groups. We find that to explain these differences both ins and outs into unemployment need to be considered as their contribution varies over time and across population groups.

We use Shimer's methodology for computing flows into and out of unemployment. We assume that during period t, the job finding (outflow) rate and job separation (inflow) rate are governed by a Poisson process with arrival rate f_t and s_t, respectively. That is unemployed workers find a job according to $f_t \equiv -\log(1-F_t) \geqslant 0$ and employed workers lose a job according to $s_t \equiv -\log(1-S_t) \geqslant 0$. F_t and S_t are finding and separation probabilities.[6]

We follow the model outlined in Shimer (2007) in which unemployment and short-term unemployment increase and fall according to

$$\dot{u}_{t+\tau} = e_{t+\tau}s_t - u_{t+\tau}f_t \tag{1}$$

$$\dot{u}_t^s(\tau) = e_{t+\tau}s_t - u_t^s(\tau)f_t \tag{2}$$

where $e_{t+\tau}$ is the number of employed workers at time $t + \tau$, $u_{t+\tau}$ is the number of unemployed workers, and $u_t^s(\tau)$ is short-term unemployment, that is, workers who are unemployed at time $t + \tau$, but were employed at some time before $t' \in [t, t + \tau]$. Once the equation is solved and a number of simplifying assumption imposed, the number of unemployed workers at time $t + 1$ is equal to the number of workers at time t who do not find a job $(1-F_t = \exp^{-f_t})$ plus the number of short-term unemployed workers u_{t+1}^s those who are unemployed at $t + 1$, but held a job at some point during time t.

$$u_{t+1} = (1-F_t)u_t + u_{t+1}^s \tag{3}$$

Thus, the monthly job finding probability is equal to

$$F_t = 1 - \left[\frac{u_{t+1} - u_{t+1}^s}{u_t} \right] \tag{4}$$

and the outflow hazard then

$$f_t \equiv -\log(1-F_t) = -\log\left[\frac{u_{t+1} - u_{t+1}^s}{u_t} \right] \tag{5}$$

Finding the inflow hazard is more complicated as some workers that flow into the unemployment pool exit unemployment before the next period, hence they are not counted and as a result the measured stock of short-term unemployed is in fact underestimated. One can solve Eq. (1) to obtain an implicit expression for the separation probability

$$u_{t+1} = \frac{(1-\exp^{-f_t-s_t})s_t}{f_t + s_t} l_t + \exp^{-f_t-s_t} u_t \tag{6}$$

where $l_t \equiv u_t + e_t$ is the size of the labor force during period t.

This continuous time formulation allows to avoid the time aggregation bias that occurs in a discrete time model in which the information on workers that lose and find a new job within the same period is omitted. For more details, see Shimer (2007).[7]

It is important to note that this approach assumes that all inflows into unemployment come from employment, whereas flows into unemployment can also originate from previous nonparticipation in the labor force. However, one of the requisite series for such analysis, the number of unemployed for less than 5 weeks by reason of unemployment, is not readily available for the demographic groups this project focuses on. This is indeed an important consideration as the labor market entrants made up about 30–40% of unemployed during 1990–2008 period, and this share tends to rise in recessions (Frazis & Ilg, 2009). Sahin, Song, and Hobijn (2010) show that during this recession the increase in flows from labor force non-participation to unemployment increased more for men than for women. They also point out that, on average, men are more likely to leave unemployment for employment while women are more likely to drop out of the labor force. Research indicates that during the recession of 2007 declines in wealth and liquidity drove some nonparticipants into the labor market (retirees, students, and married women 25–54) to look for work

(Daly, Kwok, & Hobijn, 2009b). Elsby et al. (2010) examine unemployment flows by reason for unemployment at the aggregate level and find that in the beginning of the recession the inflow rate was driven by entrants into the labor force, and subsequently the inflow rate of layoffs was the driving force of the aggregate inflow rate.

4.1. Demographic Adjustment

The sample of analysis spans over six decades, which represents over two generations. During this time, there have been many cultural and demographic changes in the United States, which may have affected the unemployment rates and subsequently the job finding and job separation probabilities. We take this into account by comparing actual measures with adjusted-hypothetical ones that keep labor force shares of certain sub-groups constant, thereby "purging out" the effects of changes in the labor force composition.

Let the aggregate unemployment rate be expressed in the following way:

$$U_t = \sum_{i \in I} \omega_t(i) u_t(i) \tag{7}$$

where $\omega_t(i)$ is the fraction of workers at age i at time t, so $\sum_{i \in I} \omega_t(i) = 1$ for all t; $u_t(i)$ is the unemployment rate at age i time t. Here the aggregate unemployment may rise if the unemployment rate of different workers ($u_t(i)$) rises or the population shifts toward groups with higher unemployment rates, so either $w_t(i)$ rises for those with high $u_t(i)$ or falls for those with low $u_t(i)$.

Next, in order to understand what would be the unemployment rate if there were no changes in the age structure of the population, we create a hypothetical unemployment rate by assuming for the entire sample period constant shares of employment at each age[8]i and summing them across each age group j. In other words, we assume $\omega_t(i) = \omega(i) = \text{const}$[9] for all t and we group the population into the following age groups: $J = \{16-19, 20-24, 25-34, 35-44, 55+\}$. Our hypothetical unemployment rate is then of the following form:

$$U_t^h = \sum_{j \in J} \omega(j) u_t(j) \tag{8}$$

where $\sum_{j \in J} \omega(j) = 1$. The gap between the two series (U_t and U_t^h) will indicate the extent to which changes in the aggregate unemployment rate are due to changes in demographics.

Similarly, we construct hypothetical job finding and separation probabilities. That is, we fix each subgroup's weight and allow group-specific job finding or separation rates to fluctuate across time.

4.2. Impact of Flows into and Out of Unemployment on the Unemployment Rate

In addition to computing flows into and out of unemployment, we also look at the contribution of these flows to increases in unemployment rate during recessions. As Elsby et al. (2009) point out, all that is necessary is to compare the log variation in the two rates. In order to see this, first note that several studies have shown that actual unemployment rate ($\tilde{u}_t$) dynamics is closely approximated by the steady-state unemployment rate (u^*):

$$\tilde{u}_t \equiv \frac{u_t}{l_t} \approx \frac{u_t^*}{l_t} = \frac{s_t}{s_t + f_t} \qquad (9)$$

Log differentiate the above to obtain

$$d \log \tilde{u}_t \approx ((1 - \tilde{u}_t)[d \log f_t - d \log s_t] \qquad (10)$$

One can also multiply both sides by $\tilde{u}_t$ to obtain an expression for the change in unemployment rate:

$$d\tilde{u}_t = \tilde{u}_t(1 - \tilde{u}_t)[d \log f_t - d \log s_t] \qquad (11)$$

Either way, this yields a separable decomposition of unemployment rate changes into contributions from inflow and outflow rates. We use this decomposition to study increases in the unemployment rate during every recession in our sample. As a first step, we identify start and end dates for the unemployment increase associated with each recession. We identify the start date as the minimum quarterly unemployment rate preceding each NBER recession start date.[10] The end date is the date of the unemployment rate peak during or following the recession.[11]

5. THE CURRENT STATE OF THE US LABOR MARKET

During the recent downturn about 8.6 million jobs have been lost in the US The national unemployment rate reached a high of 10.1% (October 2009), bringing back memories of unemployment rates as high as 10.8% reached during the recession of the early 1980 (see Fig. 1).[12] To gain additional insight into which forces lead to high unemployment rates during recessions, we examine job finding and separation probabilities. The average job finding probability (F_t) during the whole sample period (January 1948 – March 2010) is rather high at 43 percentage points and volatile, while the average separation probability (S_t) is rather low at 3.3 percentage points and exhibits less variation (see Fig. 2).

The extent to which flows into and out of unemployment contributed to the increase in unemployment during this recession and how that compares to previous recessions can be seen in Fig. 3. We find that until the 1990s, both separation and finding probability played a role in unemployment rate increases. As is highlighted in Daly, Hobijin, and Kwok (2009a), in those cases when both flows played a significant role, large recessionary increases in unemployment were accompanied by strong declines. In contrast, the recessions of the 1990s were characterized by large declines in job finding probability, and job separation played a relatively minor role in the aggregate unemployment rate dynamics. Thus, unemployment rate increases during those two recessions were driven more by the lack of hiring than firing of workers. The return of unemployment to lower levels after those two recessions was much more gradual (hence, these recoveries are often described as jobless). Our results indicate that the current downturn is similar to the two preceding it in a sense that the decline in the job finding

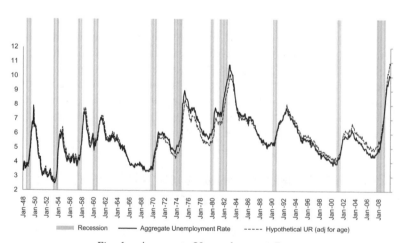

Fig. 1.   Aggregate Unemployment Rates.

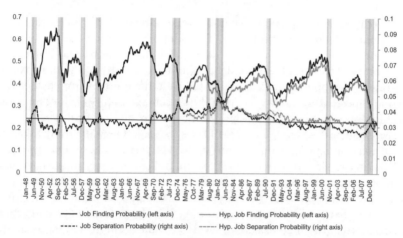

Fig. 2. Aggregate Job Finding and Separation Probabilities.

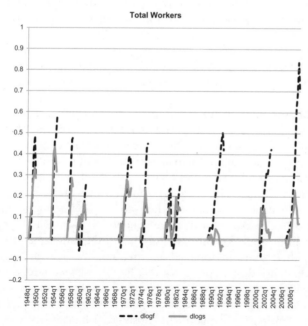

Fig. 3. Changes in Aggregate Log Inflow (Solid line) and Outflow (Dashed line) Rates by Recession.

rate is playing a much larger role in driving up the unemployment rate than the increase in the separation rate. This supports the view that it will take the unemployment rate a while to recover following the current downturn.

To give the reader a bit more detail about the severity of the most recent downturn, the job finding probability fell from the prerecession peak of just above 40 percentage points to a low 17 percentage points. This level is the lowest observed since 1948. The decline in job finding probability from prerecession peak to trough is 57%. This is the largest peak-to-trough decline observed since data collection began (the next largest decline observed is equal to 45% (in the 1950s)). This decline in job finding probability to a historic low is also emphasized by Elsby et al. (2010). The separation probability increased from a prerecession low of slightly below 2% to a peak of just above 3% over the course of the most recent recession. At 3%, the separation probability is not extraordinarily high as similar levels were observed during the previous recession and higher levels were observed in prior recessions.

Shimer (2007) points out the secular decline in separation probability since the early 1980s. Recent data does not contradict this conclusion. However, the increase in the job separation probability over the course of the most recent recession allows for a possibility of a reversal of this trend.

5.1. Age

One possible explanation for the changes in the aggregate unemployment rate and probabilities of losing and finding a job is the change in the composition of the labor force. One dimension of the changing labor force discussed here is the aging of the baby boomers and resulting increase in the share of prime age adults.[13] This change in the labor force composition is emphasized by Shimer (1998, 2001). On average, older age groups have lower unemployment rates and also have lower job finding, and separation probabilities (see Table 1 for average gender-specific unemployment rates, job finding, and separation probabilities during the sample period). Thus, an increase in their share in total labor force might drive the aggregate job finding probability down. To verify this hypothesis, we next examine how the unemployment rate and probabilities would have evolved if the population shares had remained constant and whether the aging of the population can partly explain the observed changes in the aggregate unemployment rate. As is pointed out in Valletta and Hodges (2005), this technique is widely used in the literature at least since Perry (1970).

Table 1. Average Unemployment Rate (*UR*), Job Finding (*F*), and Separation (*S*) Probabilities (May 1976–February 2010)(Standard Errors in Parenthesis).

	Men			Women			Differences		
	UR	F	S	UR	F	S	UR	F	S
16–19	0.19	0.52	0.15	0.16	0.56	0.15	0.02 ***	−0.04 ***	0.01
	(0.00)	(0.00)	(0.00)	(0.00)	(0.00)	(0.00)	(0.00)	(0.01)	(0.01)
20–24	0.11	0.43	0.06	0.09	0.49	0.07	0.01***	−0.06***	−0.01***
	(0.00)	(0.00)	(0.00)	(0.00)	(0.00)	(0.00)	(0.00)	(0.01)	(0.00)
25–34	0.06	0.37	0.03	0.06	0.43	0.04	0.00***	−0.06***	−0.01***
	(0.00)	(0.00)	(0.00)	(0.00)	(0.00)	(0.00)	(0.00)	(0.01)	(0.00)
35–44	0.04	0.33	0.02	0.05	0.39	0.02	0.00***	−0.06 ***	−0.01 ***
	(0.00)	(0.00)	(0.00)	(0.00)	(0.00)	(0.00)	(0.00)	(0.01)	(0.00)
45–54	0.04	0.30	0.01	0.04	0.36	0.02	0.00	−0.06***	0.00***
	(0.00)	(0.00)	(0.00)	(0.00)	(0.00)	(0.00)	(0.00)	(0.01)	(0.00)
55+	0.04	0.31	0.01	0.04	0.34	0.02	0.00***	−0.03***	0.00***
	(0.00)	(0.00)	(0.00)	(0.00)	(0.00)	(0.00)	(0.00)	(0.01)	(0.00)

Source: Authors' calculations.
Note: ***, **, * designate that the difference between the coefficients for men and women is statistically significantly different from zero at the 1%, 5%, and 10% level, respectively.

In Fig. 1, we plot the actual and hypothetical unemployment rate. In the 1970s, we begin to see the effect of demographic changes on the aggregate unemployment rate as the baby boomers are entering the labor market and are driving the aggregate unemployment rate up compared with the hypothetical situation where the population age shares would be constant. This is taking place as young workers' unemployment rate is much higher than the rate for adult workers (see Fig. 4 for age group shares in the labor force and age-specific unemployment rates). In the late 1990s, the actual unemployment rate is lower than the hypothetical one because of the aging of the baby boomers and a larger share of the population is with a lower unemployment rate. During this last recession the gap is even larger. Again, thanks to the aged baby boomers the unemployment rate is about one percentage point lower than it would have been if the demographic structure had not been changing in favor of those traditionally with lower unemployment rates (adult and older workers).[14]

Fig. 1 illustrates the importance of taking into account changes in the composition of the labor force when making comparisons of aggregate statistics across time. Aggregate unemployment rate series suggest that this

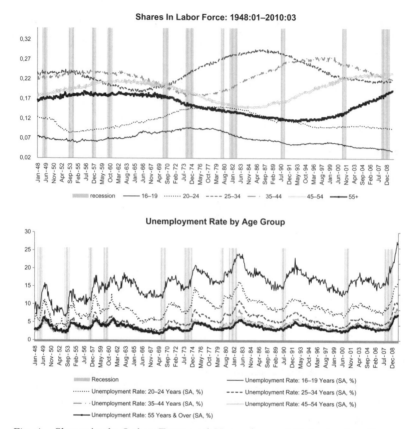

Fig. 4.   Shares in the Labor Force and Unemployment Rates by Age Groups.

recession is not as severe as those of the 1980s, as the peak of the unemployment rate reached during this recession (10.1%) is below that of the 1980s (10.7%). However, a look at the hypothetical unemployment rate reveals that if population shares were held constant this recession would be the most severe one in the sample period (this is consistent with the findings of Elsby et al. (2010)).

These demographic adjustments also prove important for comparing probabilities of losing and finding a job across time and particularly for the job separation probability (to our knowledge, this point has not been emphasized in other research focused on unemployment flows). The hypothetical/adjusted probabilities in Fig. 2 suggest a lower job finding probability throughout the sample period. The separation probability would have been lower in the late 1970s and since then higher. This is again due to the aging of the baby boomers. As shown in Table 1, those in younger age groups tend to have higher separation and finding probabilities (particularly the job separation probabilities of those in the 16–19 and 20–24 age groups compared to those in the other age groups). The decline in the share of those 24 and younger in the labor force since the early 1970s causes the actual job separation probability to be lower than the adjusted one for the period of decline in the share of the young ones. As for the job finding probability, the calculation of the adjusted series assumes a higher share for those 45 and older. Since the job finding probability for these age groups is lower, the adjusted job finding probability falls below the actual one. The main conclusion we reach from looking at hypothetical probabilities is that the decline in the job separation probability since the early 1980s is not nearly as pronounced when we control for the change in the age structure of the labor force (i.e., this change is driven, in part, by demographics).

Our findings indicate that this recession in many ways is different from those in the past (in terms of the degree of severity and the driving forces behind the increase in the unemployment rate), and as a result will have different implications for the well-being of households and individuals. In order to get a better understanding of those most affected, we proceed by examining differences in employment experiences in the most recent recession among men and women and by race. We note that while the understanding of the experiences of certain demographic groups may not be necessary for those trying to understand aggregate unemployment rate dynamics, others, for instance, those interested in policies aimed at sheltering the most vulnerable might benefit from such discussion.

5.2. Who Are the Most Vulnerable?

Examining the composition of employment and job losses suggests that some demographic groups have been hit harder than others. Table 2 shows the share in the labor force (LF) as of December 2007; the share in the cumulative increase in the number of unemployed (Un.) and the share in the cumulative change in employment (Emp.) from the beginning of the recession until November 2009 for several demographic groups.[15] According to this table, the young and blacks are disproportionately affected by this recession as both the share of increase in unemployment and the share of decline in employment exceed the group's share in the labor force.

Table 2. Demographic Composition of the Labor Force (LF), Increases in Unemployment (Un.) and Declines in Employment (Emp.), Percent.

	Men			Women			Total		
	LF	Un.	Emp.	LF	Un.	Emp.	LF	Un.	Emp.
<25	13	20	32	14	19	47	13	18	37
25–54	69	64	78	68	61	78	69	65	78
55+	19	16	−10	18	20	−25	18	16	−15
	100	100	100	100	100	100	100	100	100
White	83	80	79	81	77	74	81	79	78
Black	10	15	13	12	16	18	11	15	15
Other	7	5	7	7	7	8	8	6	7
	100	100	100	100	100	100	100	100	100
Total	54	65	68	46	35	32	100	100	100

Source: Authors' calculations and Bureau of Labor Statistics.
Note: Employment composition in 12/07. Job losses and change in employment during 12/07–11/09.

Elsby et al. (2010) look at the ratios of the rise in group unemployment rate to the rise in the overall unemployment rate and also identify male workers, young workers, and ethnic minorities as the groups that have been hit the hardest. Overall, the oldest group appears to have suffered disproportionately less as for this group the share in the overall unemployment increase is below that in the labor force and actual employment gains are observed (employment loss is negative). One might wonder why despite added jobs this group experienced a rise in unemployment. One characteristic of this recession is that older workers are reentering the labor force from non participation, thus, even though jobs became available, it was not enough to counteract the increase in job seekers. In addition, it appears that older women suffered relatively more than men.

5.2.1. Gender
As previously mentioned, looking at the labor market performance with a gender perspective is important for those thinking about effective policy responses of the economic downturn of 2007. In the United States, the unemployment rate for men had been lower than for women until the early 1980s. Since then the situation reversed. Unemployment rates for males and females moved rather closely, although the gender unemployment gap widened during recessions (see Fig. 5 for gender-specific unemployment rates).

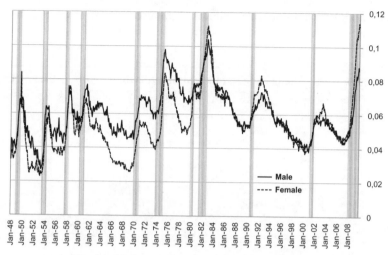

Fig. 5. Male and Female Unemployment Rate.

The convergence of gender-specific unemployment rates was driven by higher labor force participation of women and by changes in the labor force composition, as female-dominated sectors (education and health care) thrived, while male-dominated sectors (manufacturing) deteriorated (Mishel, Burnstein, & Allegretto, 2007). The recession of 2007 saw a dramatic increase in the unemployment rate gap. In August 2009, the male unemployment rate was 2.7 percentage points higher than that for females – the largest unemployment rate gap observed in the history of the series. When comparing unemployment rates between men and women for different age groups (results available upon request), we find similar results. This is particularly visible for prime age workers, where the male and female unemployment rate tends to converge since the 1980s (unemployment rate gap is close to zero), but during the recent recession, the gap increases dramatically.

This unusually large gap between male and female unemployment is driven by historically high unemployment rates for males. At 11.4% in October 2009, the unemployment rate for males stands at its highest level since 1948. The last time male unemployment rate reached the teens was during the recessions of the 1980s (the peak back then was 11.2% in December 1982). For females, unemployment rate stands at 8.8%. While this is the highest unemployment rate we have observed for females in more than two decades, it is not an unprecedented high as unemployment level for females reached 10.4% in December 1982.[16]

Fig. 6 shows the gender-specific job finding and separation probabilities since 1976. At the beginning of the sample period, the job finding probability for males is lower than for females. The two probabilities start converging in the early 1990s and move closely together during the most recent downturn. The decline in job finding probability from peak to trough during the recession of 2007 was 64.8% for men and 58.5% for women.

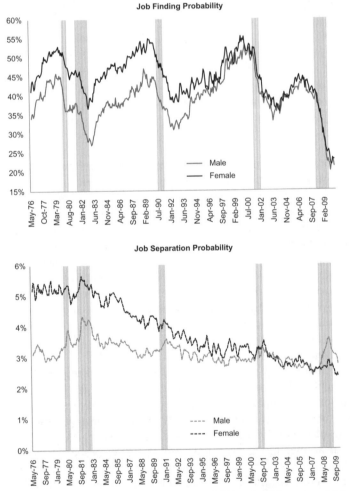

Fig. 6.   Job Finding and Separation Probabilities for Women and Men.

Both groups experienced the largest decline in the job finding probability during the sample period. The job finding probability during the current recession is at historically low levels for both women and men.

The job separation probability for men is also below that for women, but the decline in the job separation probability seen in the aggregate (shown in Fig. 2) is driven by women, as men's does not have as pronounced a decline. The current downturn is a noticeable exception as the job separation probability for men increased and became higher than that for women. These results suggest that the gender gap differential observed (higher unemployment rate for men) in the current downturn can be explained by differences in job separation probabilities (with job separation probability for men exceeding that for women) and not job finding probabilities (this is consistent with the findings of Elsby et al. (2010) and Sahin et al. (2010)). As we have shown this phenomena has not been observed during previous recessions and is driving the current results.

The hypothetical probabilities shown in Fig. 7 indicate that age matters when it comes to comparing the job separation probability (dashed line) across time. For example, for men the unadjusted aggregate job separation probability in the current downturn seems to be below that of the 1980s, but once we adjust for age, it seems that this recession is as bad as that of the 1980s in terms of the probability of losing jobs. The changing age composition does not have a very large effect on the job finding probability during the current recession (solid line), although it does matter overall.

Lastly, we look at contributions of the job finding and separation flows to the unemployment rate by gender (Fig. 8). We find that job separation tends to exert larger pressure on unemployment of men than of women for the four recessions in our sample, but this is particularly pronounced in the most recent downturn, which confirms our conclusions from Fig. 6 regarding the smaller role of the job finding probability during this recession.

5.2.2. Race and Gender

Next, we take a look at the labor market indicators by race. We focus on blacks and whites, which are the two demographic groups for whom the necessary data is readily available for our sample period. The unemployment rate of whites stands below that of blacks (see Fig. 9) during the entire sample period. The available data show that the race gap has been growing during the double dip recessions of the early 1980s, and then reversed course until the early 2000s, when it was relatively stable until 2007 and then increased considerably during the most recent recession. The trend has been for a decreasing race gap, although in four out of five recessions the gap

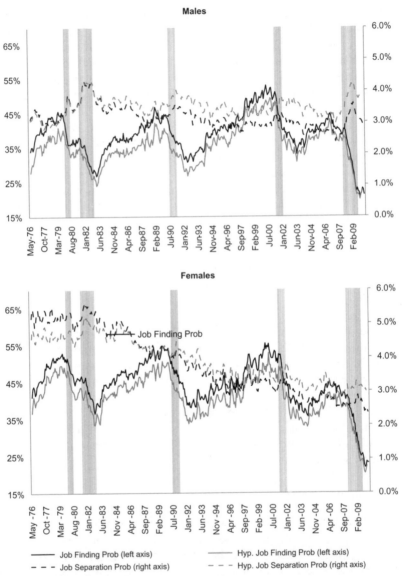

Fig. 7. Actual and Hypothetical Job Finding and Separation Probabilities by Gender.

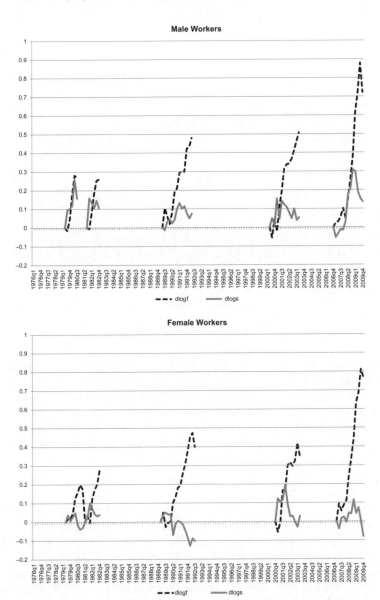

Fig. 8.   Changes in Log Inflow (Solid line) and Outflow (Dashed line) Rates by Recession: Males vs. Females.

EVA SIERMINSKA AND YELENA TAKHTAMANOVA

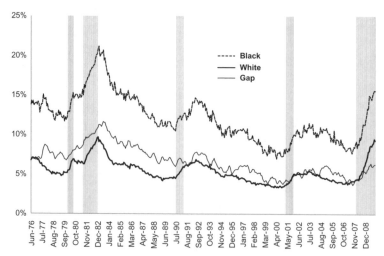

Fig. 9. Unemployment Rate and Unemployment Rate Gap by Race (3-Month Moving Average). *Note*: Gap shown is the difference between black and white unemployment rates.

increased (the recession of the early 1990s is an exception). As a result, the increase observed during the most recent downturn is not unusual, although it is rather large in magnitude. The peak of 6.4% reached in September 2009 is about half of what was observed during the recession of the 1980s (e.g., the gap reached 12.1% in January of 1983). Comparing the unemployment rate by race and gender (Fig. 10) reveals that the increase in the race unemployment gap during the current recession is driven by the increase in the unemployment rate gap for males as the unemployment rate gap for females actually declined.

Turning to job finding and separation probabilities (Figs. 11 and 12, respectively), we find that for whites job finding probabilities are for the most part higher than for blacks. During the current economic downturn, peak-to-trough decline in job finding probability was higher for blacks. Job separation probabilities have remained lower for whites, although for blacks, they have been steadily declining since 1976 for both women and men. Since the mid-1990s there is about a 1 percentage point difference in probabilities between the two race groups. Elsby et al. (2010) also look at job finding and separation by race. However, they do not look at race and gender and do not address racial occupation segregation.

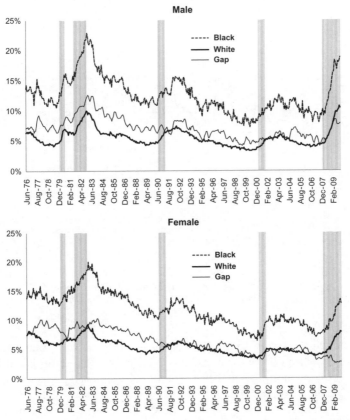

Fig. 10. Unemployment Rate and Unemployment Rate Gap by Race and Gender. *Note*: Gap shown is the difference between black and white unemployment rates.

The race unemployment gap for women has decreased, resulting from the convergence of the two probabilities for women. It seems that for men, the observed increase in the race unemployment gap is driven by differences in job separation probabilities, as job separation probability for blacks jumped noticeably above that for whites during the recent recession (see Fig. 12). Thus, once again, we see that the job separation rate is playing an important role in explaining the differences between unemployment rates across demographic groups.

The main driver of the recessionary increases in the unemployment rate, for both black and white workers (men and women), is the reduction in the

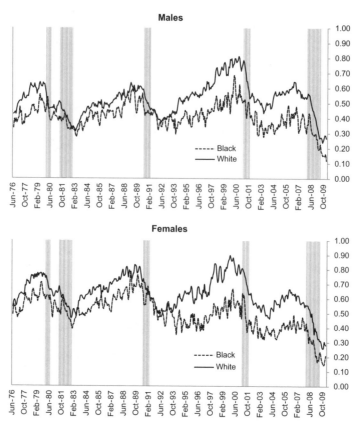

Fig. 11. Job Finding Probabilities by Race and Gender.

job finding probability (see Fig. 13). For either race, the job separation probability played a larger role in the increase in the male rather than the female unemployment rate.[17] (Fig. 13)

Part of the explanation of the disproportionate job losses among blacks could be occupation segregation. In Table 3, we find the representation ratios of blacks by major occupational groups. This ratio is defined as the percentage of black workers in an occupation divided by the percentage of minority workers in total employment. The group is overrepresented in an occupation if the ratio is greater than 1 and underrepresented if it is less than 1. The next column in the table is the change in US full-time employment by occupation during 2005 and 2009. We find that blacks are

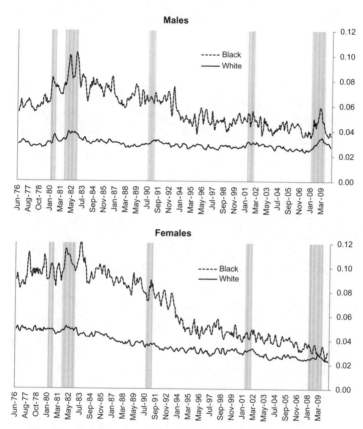

Fig. 12. Job Separation Probabilities by Race and Gender.

overrepresented in most occupations with a negative change in employment (particularly in transportation (−11%) and production (−24%)). On the other hand, a positive change in employment during this recession is observed in occupations where blacks are underrepresented.

To summarize our results, we find that in the recession of 2007, young men, older women, and racial minorities (of both genders) can be thought of as those who have been hit the hardest by the Great Recession of 2007. We caution the reader that our work focuses on unemployment rates to measure the impact of the recession, which is an imperfect metric (see Humphries, 1988). However, our findings that males and ethnic minorities

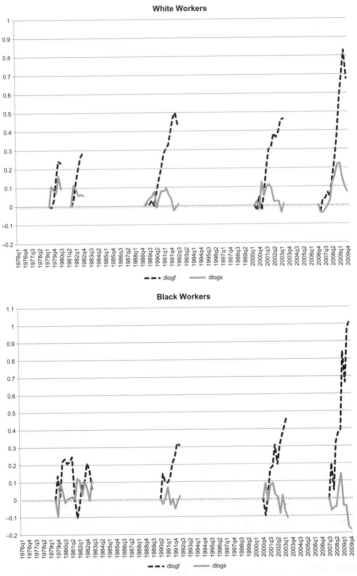

Fig. 13. Changes in Log Inflow (Solid lines) and Outflow (Dashed lines) Rates by Recession: White vs. Black Workers.

Table 3. Representation Ratios of Blacks (in 2002) and Changes in US Full-Time Employment (2005–2009) by Occupation.

Occupations	Ratios	Emp. change
Executive	0.70	6%
Professional	0.76	3%
Health care and technical	0.89	13%
Sales	0.78	−6%
Office/admin	1.20	−8%
Protective	1.83	0%
Handlers, laborers	1.31	
Production: precision and inspectors	0.68	−24%
Production: operators	1.37	
Service, private household	1.13	−1%
Service, except private and protective	1.61	
Transportation	1.47	−11%

Source: Queneau, 2005 and Smeeding and Thompson, 2010.
Note: Ratios – percentage of black workers in an occupation divided by the percentage of minority workers in total employment.

are disproportionately affected by this recession via a rise in unemployment is consistent with findings of those that focus on employment (Engemann & Wall, 2009). We note, however, that looking at unemployment rate increases is not the same as looking at job losses as not everyone who loses a job transitions into unemployment; some may drop out of the labor force. In addition, focusing on the conventional unemployment rate measure (i.e., defining unemployed as those who do not have a job, have actively looked for work during 4 weeks, and are currently available for work) also misses persons in the labor force that are available for work but have not searched for a job in the past 4 weeks (discouraged workers). To our knowledge, such data is not readily available for the demographic groups and sample period in question, but based on data available since the early 1990s we find that the two rates are highly correlated.

Examining gender-specific statistics is important, but may still miss important within-group variation. For instance, it has been shown that single mothers in the labor force experienced a dramatic increase in unemployment rates during this recession. The unemployment rate for single mothers increased from 8% to 13.6%, and for single mothers of young children (under the age of 6), the unemployment rate peaked at

17.5% (Joint Economic Committee Majority Staff, 2010). Married women on the other hand have been returning to the labor force (Daly et al., 2009b). Our ability to look into the experiences of women during this recession is limited by the lack of all the necessary series for the flow analysis undertaken here; looking further into experiences of single mothers and women in general during this recession and comparing it to past downturns would be a productive venue for future research. This could also be informative for policy decisions, as the fiscal challenges currently faced by the states are likely to affect women disproportionately more, as women are concentrated in the public sector.

6. POLICY RESPONSE

After documenting the current state of the US labor market and identifying more vulnerable groups, we turn to policy response. In particular, we look into the American Recovery and Reinvestment Act of 2009, whose purpose (among others) is to save and create jobs. The Council of Economic Advisers (CEA) (an agency within the executive office of the US president charged with offering the president objective economic advice on the formulation of both domestic and international economic policy) estimates that ARRA would increase employment by 3.5 million by the end of 2010 and 6.8 million by the end of 2012 (Council of Economic Advisers, 2009).

As our analysis thus far shows, the employment and unemployment experiences during economic downturns, however, vary by demographic group. The Obama administration recognizes this, and one of ARRA's aims is to protect the most vulnerable from the deep recession. The administration estimates that roughly 42% of jobs created will go to women, which as of December 2007 held about 46% of jobs and initially (until the end of November 2008) accounted for about 27% of the job losses during the current recession (Romer & Bernstein, 2009).[18] In order to assess whether this recovery package favors one demographic group over another (e.g., women over men), we would first need to understand the reasons behind lower employment shares of, for example, women in certain industries (due to discrimination or individual preferences). As a result assessing the equity of the stimulus package based on raw data alone is not fully satisfactory. Other evidence on the demographic split of jobs created by the ARRA forecasts that less jobs will go to whites compared to their initial employment share before the recession, while nonwhites will not gain significantly.

The highest job losses not addressed by ARRA will be for those with low education levels (high school or less) (Zacharias, Masterson, & Kim, 2009).

Compared to the above studies, which forecast the likely path of recovery, the most recent estimates of the impact of the ARRA published by the CEA (2009, 2010a) examine the effect of the stimulus plan relative to a baseline scenario. Using past data of GDP and employment and actual data from 2009, these estimates indicate that employment would be about 2 million jobs lower without the ARRA. In Table 4, Bureau of Labor Statistics data indicate the extent to which there has been a systematic decrease in the number of jobs lost since the onset of the recession.

Using the employment effects calculated by the CEA, we estimate the possible job effects by gender by industries, given the share of groups employed in each of the industries (see Table 5). We see that for some industries the net gain of total jobs considering the baseline scenario is larger than their share in total employment (in bold: construction, manufacturing, trade, and to the largest extent professional and business services) as compared to the other sectors (education and health services, leisure, and government). Taking into account the equity effects of the ARRA, one should note that in the former industries the majority of employees are men and minorities as compared to the latter group. In Table 5 besides the estimates of the CEA, for comparison purposes, we also include two types of estimates of jobs created performed by the Levy Institute based on different assumptions.[19] These matched well with CEA estimated considering the total number of jobs created in 2009–2011 (about 6.2 million), but there is some variation when comparing the results by industry (particularly for manufacturing, professional and business services, and government).

Finally, we compare the impact of the fiscal stimulus on employment by demographic groups with the employment composition and job losses until late 2009 (see Table 6). We find that men and the young have suffered in terms of job loss relatively more then their share in employment would suggest. Job creation estimates suggest that the nonwhite will benefit

Table 4. Change in Payroll Employment 2007–2009.

	Q1	Q2	Q3	Q4
2007	133	82	2	167
2008	−113	−153	−208	−553
2009	−691	−428	−199	−69

Source: Department of Labor (Bureau of Labor Statistics).

Table 5. Employment Effects of the Recovery Act by Sector, 2009:Q4.

Factor	Empl. Share (%)	Share of Total Jobs Created			Total Jobs (000s)	Fraction Female (%)	Jobs of Women (000s)
		Levy (%)		CEA (%)	CEA		CEA
		Gov.	Private				
Mining and logging	1	**2**	**2**	0	8	13	1
Construction	5	5	**10**	**13**	262	13	34
Manufacturing	9	8	9	**17**	354	29	103
Trade, transportation and utilities	19	15	16	**22**	459	43	197
Information	2	2	2	**5**	101	42	42
Financial activities (FIRE)	6	5	5	3	61	59	36
Professional and business services	13	12	13	**25**	510	44.7	228
Education and health services	15	10	13	2	46	77	35
Leisure and hospitality	10	8	7	8	165	53	87
Other services	4	4	4	2	43	52	22
Government	17	**29**	**19**	3	60	57	34
Total nonfarm employment	100	100	100	100	2068		955

Source: Authors' calculations; Bureau of Labor Statistics; Council of Economic Advisers, 2009; Zacharias et al., 2009.
Note: Items may not add to total due to rounding. In bold if estimate of share of jobs created is larger than the share in employment. Employment composition in 12/07. Levy estimates are ARRA employment estimated as in Zacharias et al., 2009 considering two scenarios (government and private) (see text).

Table 6. Demographic Composition of Employment, Job Losses and ARRA Employment.

	Emp. Comp.	Job Loss	ARRA Emp.	
			Gov.	Priv.
Gender				
Men	54	65	60	63
Women	46	35	40	37
Race				
White	81	79	61	61
Nonwhite	19	21	40	39
Age				
<25	13	18	10	12
25+	87	80	90	88

Source: Authors' calculations based on data from the Bureau of Labor Statistics; Zacharias et al., 2009.
Note: Employment composition in 12/07. Job losses as of 11/09. ARRA employment estimated as in Zacharias et al., 2009 considering two scenarios (government and private) (see text).

relatively more than the white from ARRA job creation and the young relatively less than prime-age adults.[20]

6.1. ARRA and the Income Distribution

Our results indicate that men, nonwhite, and particularly the young have been affected relatively more (in terms of percentages) by unemployment during the current recession than their employment share would suggest. To some extent, this seems to be addressed by ARRA thus affecting the distribution of earnings, although it still leaves out the most vulnerable. Zacharias et al. (2009) estimate that jobs created by ARRA will provide higher average earnings than the earnings of earners in non-ARRA jobs by 3%. Particularly affected will be those in the bottom quintile of the earnings distribution compared to the rest of the distribution. There will be some gain for those with high school diploma, nonwhites, and women compared to men, although these will not be sufficient to close the respective earnings gaps. These authors also find that the gain in average income resulting from the ARRA stimulus package will benefit those in the lower quintiles relatively more than those in the higher quintiles, but the pro-poor pattern

Table 7.   Distribution of ARRA Programs (Tax Relief and Income Support) Across the Income Distribution and by Education Groups.

Income Quintile	% of Tot. Income	% of Programs	Education	% of Tot. Population	% of Programs
1	1.7	12.7			
2	6.2	18.7	<HS	13.6	13.3
3	11.1	21.8	HS	31.8	34.6
4	22.2	25.2	Coll.	26.4	28.0
5	58.6	21.5	BA+	28.2	24.1

Source: Council of Economic Advisers, 2010b.
Note: Items may not add to 100% due to rounding. HS – high school; Coll – Some college; BA+ – Bachelor's degree or more.

of income growth will only have a negligible effect on the shares of aggregate income entering each quintile, hence suggesting that the overall effect of ARRA on income inequality will be negligible.

This is confirmed to some extent by the CEA estimates, which show that almost half of the more direct financial benefits from the ARRA such as tax relief and income support will go to those with a high school education or less, but less than a third to the bottom two quintiles of the income distribution (see Table 7).

7. CONCLUSIONS

This chapter measures worker inflows and outflows into unemployment in the United States between 1948 and 2009 and between 1976 and 2009 for several demographic groups. The focus of the chapter are the experiences of the most vulnerable groups during the last recession and a comparison with previous recessions.

We find that during the most recent recession the job finding probability exhibited its biggest drop from peak to trough since official measurement began (57%). In addition, the job separation probability also exhibited one of the largest increases in the postwar period. The decline in the job finding probability seems to be explaining a larger share of the fluctuations in the unemployment rate, although the separation rate also played a noticeable (although relatively smaller) role. We also find that when comparing unemployment rate or flows across time, it is important to keep in mind the changing composition of the labor force. When ageing of the labor force is taken into account, the unemployment rate reached during this recession is the highest in the postwar period.

This recession has also been accompanied by a large gender gap in unemployment with men driving the unemployment rate upward (particularly at older ages). Further insight shows that men currently have one of the highest unemployment rates in history due to very low job finding probability rates. The increase in separation probabilities has not been so dramatic. Gender differences though seem to be driven by the higher separation probabilities for men compared to women and not by the historically low finding probabilities for men and women.

We find that the race gap has also increased being driven by the gap for males as the differences in unemployment rates for black and white females have actually decreased. In terms of job finding probabilities, historically they have been higher for whites, and during this recession both white women and men have exhibited less of a decline in these probabilities than their black counterparts. Overall, the increase in the race unemployment gap for males seems to be driven by differences in job separation probabilities as job separation probability for blacks jumped noticeably above that for whites during the recent recession. Yet again, the job separation rate seems to be playing an important role in explaining the differences between unemployment rates across demographic groups.

In terms of the ARRA stimulus package and its effect on job creation, the research is only beginning. For the moment, we find that based on the distribution of ARRA created jobs by industries the nonwhites will benefit slightly more than whites and prime-age adults relatively more than the young. Industries that have been hit the hardest (trade and professional and manufacturing) and employ a majority of men will benefit the most. It is also worth noting that there is evidence that ARRA prevented acceleration of job losses in state and local government (Council of Economic Advisers, 2010a). Those suffering the most will be the low educated and the young, although alternative plans to recovery are suggested. For example, Antonopoulos et al. (2010) suggest that a fixed investment in construction infrastructure and social care can generate twice as many jobs. In terms of the income distribution of the ARRA stimulus package, the average income gain of those in the lower quantiles will be relatively greater than for those in the higher quantiles, but the effect on overall income inequality will be negligible. Almost half of the direct financial benefits from the ARRA will go to those with a high school diploma or less.

We believe that going forward, it will be important to keep the gendered perspective on job losses. It seems likely that although men suffered relatively more than women during the depth of the downturn, the job losses that are yet to come might affect women disproportionately more. State and local governments are faced with large revenue declines and increased demand for public services, while federal support is winding down over the next two years. Women represent a large share of this state and federal public sector. In other words, the situation is expected to deteriorate further before it improves (Wilson & Gerst, 2010), which means that job losses are on the horizon. Thus, while the Great Recession impacted male employment relatively more, the Hard to See Recovery might yet turn out more painful for women.

NOTES

1. See Bernanke, 2010 – http://www.federalreserve.gov/newsevents/speech/bernanke20100103a.htm.
2. See Yellen, 2009 – http://www.frbsf.org/news/speeches/2009/0728.html.
3. Both demand- and supply-side explanations for employment segregation have been advanced. On the demand side, employer discrimination against women, including the perception that women are on average less qualified, could result in a greater willingness to hire men and a greater willingness to lay off women first during economic downturns. On the supply side, one explanation is that women self-select into occupations that require smaller human capital investment, due to lower penalties for career breaks. This could be attributed to "societal discrimination" whereby women are expected to bear the burden of raising children, thus requiring more flexible jobs.
4. For example, Bonnie Erbe – http://www.cbsnews.com/stories/2009/04/14/usnews/whispers/main4944750.shtml; Dave Opton – http://blogs.jobdig.com/wwds/2009/03/11/age-discrimination-is-the-new-reality-in-job-market-says-guest-expert-dave-opton/
5. The 1994 redesign of the CPS survey introduces a discontinuity in the measurement of unemployment duration and other labor force variables. To make the series consistent over time, we apply the adjustment factors described in Elsby, Michaels, & Solon (2009). Other adjustment methods include Polivka and Miller, 1998 or Shimer, 2007, for example.
6. *Probabilities* summarize the concentration of spells at each instant along the time axis, while *rates* summarize the same concentration at each point of time, but conditional on survival in that state up to that instant.
7. An alternative approach to correct the CPS data for the time aggregation bias would be to impute discrete weekly hazard rates. Elsby et al. (2009) show that both types of correction yield broadly similar results.
8. We assume people in the sample are 16–65 years old, hence the share at each age is 1/48.
9. Although the choice of base year is irrelevant, we prefer this "year independent" formulation as it provides us with a clear picture of the changing

demographics throughout the sample period, which is more intuitive and not relative with respect to the chosen base year.

10. Note that here we focus on quarterly (rather than monthly data) to smooth some of the noise.

11. Please note that our choice of dates is different than in Elsby et al. (2009) because we choose the minimum rather than *the most recent* prerecession minimum unemployment rate.

12. Note that in this and all subsequent figures grey bars designate recession periods with dates determined by NBER.

13. Another is an increase in the share of adults with higher education, which we do not consider explicitly in this chapter.

14. Traditionally, part of the explanation for low rates of unemployment for older workers were exits from the labor force. During the past two recessions, older workers are not exiting but in fact reentering the labor force. This also seems to be correlated with stock market performance, which affects the value of their defined contribution plans and hence ability to finance current consumption. In the downturn of 2007, the massive losses of housing wealth have also contributed.

15. We also looked at a five-year average of each group's composition in the labor force, and the shares are very similar to those shown in the table. Thus, we only show shares as of December 2007.

16. Looking at the age-adjusted unemployment rate gaps only strengthens this conclusion. Age-adjusted unemployment rates are available form the authors upon request.

17. The gender-specific changes in inflow and outflow rates for the two races are not presented in this chapter, but are available from the authors upon request.

18. Our most recent calculations based on Dec 2007–Nov 2009 data indicate women lost about 35% of the jobs (see Table 6).

19. In both of these, the midpoint of "high" and "low" multipliers for transfers, taxes, and subsidies provided by the Congressional Budget Office is used. The difference lies in the further assumption regarding the industrial distribution of final demand generated by government purchases. The "government" scenario assumes it is distributed among government industries, and the "private" scenario assumes most of the final demand increase is captured by private industries.

20. As an alternative to the ARRA focus on job creation with a bias in construction infrastructure, Antonopoulos, Kim, Masterson, and Zacharias (2010) compared the job creation potential of a fixed investment in construction infrastructure and in social care. They find that the social care provision can generate twice as many jobs. The distribution of jobs would then be more equally distributed across races and be geared toward those with lower education levels and the lower part of the income distribution.

ACKNOWLEDGMENTS

The authors would like to thank Ian Hathaway for excellent research assistance; the participants of the IZA/OECD Workshop, Mary Daly, Bart Hobijn, Joyce Kwok, Rob Valletta, Philippe Van Kerm, Kathryn Wilson,

Gary Zimmerman, two anonymous referees, and the participants of the International Association for Research in Income and Wealth 31st General Conference for their helpful suggestions and comments.

REFERENCES

Antonopoulos, R. (2009). *The current economic and financial crisis: A gender perspective.* Working Paper no. 562. The Levy Economics Institute of Bard College, Annandale-on-Hudson, New York.

Antonopoulos, R., Kim, K., Masterson, T., & Zacharias, A. (2010). *Investing in care: A strategy for effective and equitable job creation.* Economics Working Paper Archive 610. The Levy Economics Institute of Bard College, Annandale-on-Hudson, New York.

Azmat, G., Guell, M., & Manning, A. (2006). Gender gaps in unemployment rates in OECD countries. *Journal of Labor Economics, 24*(1), 1–37.

Bardasi, E., & Gornick, J. (2008). Working for less? Women's part-time wage penalties across countries. *Feminist Economics, 14*(1), 37–72.

Blanchard, O. (1995). Macroeconomic implications of shifts in the relative demand for skills. *Economic Policy Review, 1*(1), 48–53.

Blank, R. (1998). Labor market dynamics and part-time work. *Research in labor economics, 17,* 59–93.

Booth, A. L., Francesconi, M., & Garcia-Serrano, C. (1999). Job tenure and job mobility in Britain. *Industrial and Labor Relations Review, 53*(1), 43–70.

Buddelmeyer, H., Mourre, G., & Ward, M. (2004a). *Recent developments in part-time work in EU-15 Countries: Trends and policy.* IZA Discussion Paper no. 1415. Institute for the Study of Labor, Bonn, Germany.

Buddelmeyer, H., Mourre, G., & Ward, M. (2004b). *The determinants of part-time work in EU countries: Empirical investigations with macropanel data.* IZA Discussion Paper no. 1361. Institute for the Study of Labor, Bonn, Germany.

Council of Economic Advisers. (2009). *The Economic Impact of the American Recovery and Reinvestment Act of 2009.* First Quarterly Report. The White House, Washington, DC. Available at http://www.whitehouse.gov/administration/eop/cea

Council of Economic Advisers. (2010a). *The Economic Impact of the American Recovery and Reinvestment Act of 2009.* Second Quarterly Report. The White House, Washington, DC. Available at http://www.whitehouse.gov/administration/eop/cea

Council of Economic Advisers. (2010b). *The Economic Impact of the American Recovery and Reinvestment Act of 2009.* Third Quarterly Report. The White House, Washington, DC. Available at http://www.whitehouse.gov/administration/eop/cea

Daly, M., Hobijn, B., & Kwok, J. (2009a). Jobless recovery redux? *FRBSF Economic Letter, 18,* 1–4.

Daly, M., Kwok, J., & Hobijn, B. (2009b). Labor supply responses to changes in wealth and credit. *FRBSF Economic Letter, 5,* 1–4.

Darby, M.R., Haltiwanger, J.C., & Plant, M.W. (1986). The ins and outs of unemployment: The ins win. NBER Working Papers 1997. National Bureau of Economic Research, Inc, Cambridge, MA.

Dolado, J., Felgueroso, F., & Jimeno, J.E. (2002). *Recent trends in occupational segregation by gender: A look across the Atlantic.* IZA Discussion Paper no. 524. Institute for the Study of Labor, Bonn, Germany.

Elsby, M. W. L., Michaels, R., & Solon, G. (2009). The ins and outs of cyclical unemployment. *American Economic Journal: Macroeconomics, 1*(1), 84–110.

Elsby, M., Hobijn, B., & Sahin, A. (2010). The labor market in the Great Recession. Brookings Papers on Economic Activity (Spring), 1-48.

Engemann, K., & Wall, H. (2009). *The effects of recessions across demographic groups.* Research Division Federal Reserve Bank of St. Louis Working Paper Series St. Louis, Missouri.

Frazis, H. J., & Ilg, R. E. (2009). Trends in labor force flows during recent recessions. *Monthly Labor Review Online, 132*(4), 3–18.

Hall, R. E. (2005a). Employment efficiency and sticky wages: Evidence from flows in the labor market. *The Review of Economics and Statistics, 87*(3), 397–407.

Hall, R.E. (2005b). *Job loss, job finding, and unemployment in the U.S. economy over the past fifty years.* NBER Working Paper no. 11678, National Bureau of Economic Research, Inc, Cambridge, MA.

Hegewisch, A., Liepmann, H., Haves, J., & Hartmann, H. (2010). Separate and not equal? Gender segregation in the labor market and the gender wage gap. Briefing Paper IWPR C3777. Institute for Women's Policy Research, Washington, DC.

Humphries, J. (1988). Women's employment in restructuring America: The changing experience of women in three recessions. (Chap. 1 pp. 15–47.) London: Routledge & Kegan Paul.

Joint Economic Committee Majority Staff. (2010). Working mothers in a Great Recession. Technical report. U.S. Congress' Joint Economic Committee, Washington, DC.

Mishel, L., Burnstein, J., & Allegretto, S. (2007). *The state of working America 2006/2007.* Cornell University Press, Ithaca, NY and London, UK.

Mumford, K., & Smith, P. N. (2003). Determinants of current job tenure: A cross-country comparison. *Australian Journal of Labour Economics, 6*(3), 435–451.

Munasinghe, L., & Reif, T. (2008). The gender gap in wage returns on job tenure and experience. *Labour Economics, 15*(6), 1296–1316.

Perry, G. (1970). Changing labor markets and ination. *Brookings Papers on Economic Activity, 1970*(3), 411–448.

Polivka, A. E., & Miller, S. M. (1998). The CPS after the redesign: Refocusing the economic lens. In: *J. Haltiwanger, M. E. Manser & R. Topel (Eds.), Labor statistics measurement issues: Studies in income and wealth* (Chap. 7, Vol. 60, 1970(3) 249–289). Chicago: University of Chicago Press.

Queneau, H. (2005). Changes in occupational segregation by race and ethnicity in the USA. *Applied Economic Letters, 12*, 781–784.

Rives, J., & Sosin, K. (2002). Occupations and the cyclical behavior of gender unemployment rates. *The Journal of Socio-Economics, 31*, 287–299.

Romer, C., & Bernstein, J. (2009). *The job impact of the American Recovery and Reinvestment Plan.* Unpublished Manuscript. January.

Ruhm, C. J. (1987). Job tenure and cyclical changes in the labor market. *Review of Economics and Statistics, 69*(2), 372–378.

Sahin, A., Song, J., & Hobijn, B. (2010). The unemployment gender gap during the 2007 recession. *Current Issues in Econnomics and Finance, 16*(2), 1–7.

Seguino, S. (2003). Why are women in the caribbean so much more likely than men to be unemployed? *Social and Economic Studies, 52*(4), 83–120.

Shimer, R. (1998). Why is U.S. unemployment rate so much lower? *NBER Macroeconomics Annual, 13*, 11–61.

Shimer, R. (2001). The impact of young workers on the aggregate labor market. *Quarterly Journal of Economics, 116*, 969–1008.

Shimer, R. (2005). The cyclicality of hires, separations, and job-to-job transitions. *Review* (July), 493–508.

Shimer, R. (2007). *Reassessing the ins and outs of unemployment.* NBER Working Paper no. 13421, NBER, Cambridge, MA.

Singh, A., & Zammit, A. (2002). Gender effects of the financial crisis in South Korea. Paper presented at New Directions in Research on Gender-Aware Macroeconomics and International Economies: An International Symposium. Levy Economics Institute of Bard College, Annandale-on-Hudson, New York.

Smeeding, T., & Thompson, J. (2011). Recent trends in income inequality: Labor, wealth and more complete measures of income. *Research in Labor Economics* (this volume).

Smith, M. (2009). Analysis note: Gender equality and recession: Grenoble: Ecole de Management.

Valletta, R., & Hodges, J. (2005). Age and education effects on the unemployment rate. *FRBSF Economic Letter, 15*, 1–4.

Wilson, D., & Gerst, J. (2010). Fiscal crises of the states: Causes and consequences. *FRBSF Economic Letter, 20*, 1–4.

Zacharias, A., Masterson, T., & Kim, K. (2009). *Distributional impact of the American Recovery and Reinvestment Act: A microsimulation approach.* Working Paper no. 568. The Levy Economics Institute of Bard College.

THE IMPACT OF THE GREAT RECESSION ON THE ITALIAN LABOUR MARKET

Francesco D'Amuri

ABSTRACT

This chapter provides an assessment of the effects of the Great Recession on the Italian labour market. Two-thirds of the decrease in employment taking place during the 2008:4 to 2009:4 period were due to the fall in job-finding probabilities, while transitions out of employment significantly increased only for employees with flexible contracts. According to micro-level multiple stochastic imputations coherent with the evolution of the employment rate, income losses related to job terminations will be partially offset by the highly fragmented income support safety nets available. A stress test shows that income stabilization offered is pro-cyclical, while labour income inequality is driven by changes in employment: inequality among the employed seems to be rather insensitive to the composition of employment.

Keywords: Great recession; labour market dynamics; unemployment benefits' system; income distribution

JEL Classifications: J64; J65; J82

Who Loses in the Downturn? Economic Crisis, Employment and Income Distribution
Research in Labor Economics, Volume 32, 155–180
ISSN: 0147-9121/doi:10.1108/S0147-9121(2011)0000032008

1. INTRODUCTION

Italy has been, together with Germany, one of the European countries experiencing the mildest increases in the official unemployment rate during the *Great Recession*[1] (Arpaia & Curci, 2010). This result could be partly explained by the intense use of government schemes providing wage subsidies to employees working at reduced hours (Cassa Integrazione Guadagni, CIG), preventing firms from shedding workers to reduce labour input in response to adverse demand shocks, and by the rise of discouragement among job-seekers dropping the labour force, particularly in the South, where participation rates were already lower than in the rest of the country (Cingano, Torrini, & Viviano, 2010).

Nevertheless, employment fell by 2.4% in the 2008–2009 interval, the greatest contraction since the 1992 crisis. In Italy, as in the rest of Europe (Arpaia & Curci, 2010) and the United States (Elsby, Hobijn, & Sahin, 2010), men and young workers were the hardest hit by the labour market downturn. This chapter analyses the labour market flows generated by such an unprecedented reduction in labour input.

Changes in unemployment rates are usually believed as being determined by an increase in transitions both into and out of employment.[2] Recent articles have somewhat questioned this view. According to both Hall (2005) and Shimer (2007), changes in the probabilities of transitions into employment have had an increasing role in determining unemployment variations: Shimer (2007) finds for example that "movements in the job finding probability account for 75% of fluctuations in the unemployment rate since 1948, rising to 95% during the last two decades".[3] Also Elsby et al. (2010) find that exits from employment were relatively more modest during the recessions started in 1990 and 2001, but do not interpret this as a secular change in the way recessions impact labour market flows. Indeed, they find that the recession started in 2007, as other severe recessions of the past, has been characterized by a substantial increase in out of employment transitions, driven by layoffs. Also Sierminska and Takhtamanova (2011) find *both* a significant decrease in job finding and an increase in job separation probabilities for the United States during the Great Recession. The analysis of yearly transitions in and out of employment carried out in this chapter shows that the probabilities of experiencing both transitions changed between the last quarter of 2008 and the same period of 2009 in Italy. Yearly job destruction probabilities increased by 0.4 percentage points (p.p.), arriving at 7.4%. Also job-finding probabilities were affected, having a substantial decrease (−1.4 points to 9.8%), accounting for two-thirds of the decrease in employment. Changes in job termination probabilities varied substantially with the type of contract. The brunt of the adjustment was borne by employees on temporary contracts (a result in line with Arpaia & Curci, 2010): the biggest increases concerned employees on flexible work arrangements including fixed term contracts and quasi-employees (+3.5 to 19.4 p.p.), 12% of total employment. The remaining 88%, employees on open-ended contracts and self-employed, did not experience major changes in the probability of having this type of transition.

After having identified the changes in labour market flows taking place during the *Great Recession*, the estimated probabilities for transitions in and out of employment are used to simulate, coherently with employment rate dynamics defined ex-ante, the likely evolution of labour income and its distribution in 2010. The analysis focuses exclusively on the labour market, while other sources of income are not taken into consideration.[4] According to our baseline simulations (assuming a 0.6 drop in employment between 2009 and 2010 and constant participation rate), gross labour income inequality among active individuals is expected to rise, with a Gini index increasing to 25.4 in 2010 from 24.7 in 2009 as a result of the increase in the number of unemployed, while labour income distribution among those remaining employed will barely change. We also simulate what would happen to labour income distribution assuming a zero job-finding rate during 2010, thus focussing on job destruction and unemployment benefits. In this case, Gini index would increase 3.3 points to 28.1, an increase only partly cushioned by unemployment benefits: accounting for income support schemes,[5] the increase in the Gini index (1.8 points) is less pronounced but still substantial. According to the simulations, standard income support schemes are able to absorb around 35% of income lost due to job separations. Beyond averages, unemployment benefits and wage subsidies' replacement rates vary considerably across sectors and working arrangements and quickly decrease with duration. At the fourth quarter of continuous unemployment, they are as low as 6%, with more than 70% of the displaced completely uncovered by labour market–related income support schemes.

Finally, a stress test of the unemployment benefits system is proposed, assuming different employment rates' dynamics obtained modifying the baseline scenario adding +1 and −1 standard deviation of the unemployment rate (1.7 p.p.) for a given participation rate. One year projections show that average replacement rates are pro-cyclical. We also find a clear impact of employment variations on labour income distribution: adding a standard deviation increase in the unemployment rate to the baseline scenario (bringing the unemployment rate in 2010 to 10.9 from 9.1) substantially increases the Gini index of active individual's gross labour income (+ 2.7 points to 27.1).

This chapter is organized as follows: Section 2 introduces the dataset employed and data refinements, Section 3 describes labour market related income support schemes. An analysis of transitions both into and out of employment is provided in Section 4, while Section 5 defines the multiple stochastic imputation method employed for simulating the distributional impacts of different labour market states. Results are provided in Section 6, while Section 7 concludes.

2. DATA

The Italian Labour Force Survey (ILFS), the official dataset used for estimating labour market conditions in Italy, provides the statistical basis for this study. It contains full information on labour market status and other socio economic characteristics of a large sample representative of the Italian population on a quarterly basis (for a description, see Ceccarelli, Discenza, & Loriga, 2006). We use data on respondents' labour market status relative to the 2006–2009 period, including the net wage earned by employees (available for year 2009 only). By means of standard mincerian regressions, we impute net labour income to self-employed workers as well.[6] Using the longitudinal version of the dataset, we are able to identify with high precision transitions in and out of employment on a 12-month interval. We prefer to impute labour status based on the longitudinal dataset rather than to use the recall questions to avoid mis-classifications due to recall error (Bowers & Horvath, 1984; D'Amuri, 2010; Poterba & Summers, 1986).

Gross labour incomes are predicted by an auxiliary regression estimated on a tax-form-based dataset.[7]

To correct for mis-reporting, wages are multiplied by a constant factor equalling the estimated total gross wage bill with the corresponding value taken from the national accounts. The same factor is also used for self-employment income, since in this case there is no external source available for validation.

3. THE ITALIAN UNEMPLOYMENT BENEFIT AND WAGE SUPPLEMENTATION SYSTEM

Average Labour Market Policy (LMP) expenditure per unemployed as a share of GDP per capita was 11% lower in Italy than in the EU27 average in 2007, according to Eurostat (2009) data (Table 1). Expenditure was

Table 1. Labour Market Policy (LMP) Expenditure.

Column	1	2	3	4	5	6
	LMP Services[a]	LMP Measures[b]	Out of work income support	Early retirement	Total LMP supports (3+4)	Total LMP experience (1+2+5)
EU-27	100	100	100	100	100	100
AT	133	167	167	403	187	175
BE	116	236	137	901	201	201
DE	108	84	131	53	125	112
DK	127	367	177	1036	248	268
ES	39	111	125	41	118	107
FI	64	146	111	438	138	132
FR	106	134	117	45	111	117
IE	159	145	131	111	130	137
IT	25	106	90	139	94	89
NL	432	291	300	-	275	298
PT	51	66	85	98	86	77
SE	92	203	75	-	69	109
UK	181	13	22	-	20	36

See Eurostat (2009, pp. 6–7), for further details.
Source: Spending per unemployed/GDP per capita: EU27 = 100.
Note: Author's calculations based on Eurostat (2009, 2010).
[a]LMP services include all publicly funded services for job seekers. These include advice, provision of information and guidance about jobs or training opportunities.
[b]LMP measures include training, job sharing, employment incentives, direct job creation, start-up incentives.

relatively higher (6% more than the EU27 average) in LMP measures (training, job sharing, employment incentives) and early retirement (39% more than the EU27 average), while being lower in public employment services providing advice and information on jobs and training. All the other main western European countries, with the exception of the United Kingdom, spent more than Italy on LMPs: Germany, France and Spain spent respectively 12%, 17% and 7% more than the EU27 average. The safety net for individuals experiencing transitions to non-employment is fragmented, lacking a basic framework common to different types of workers and working arrangements.

The main non-discretionary schemes for income support are unemployment benefits (ordinary or with reduced requirements), wage supplementation (ordinary or extraordinary) and long-term unemployment assistance [for further details see Anastasia, Mancini, and Trivellato (2009) and European Commission (2009)].

Ordinary unemployment benefits (indennità di disoccupazione) are the main source of support for individuals who have been laid off, or whose contract expired. Maximum duration is eight months (12 for workers older than 50), while replacement rates, equal to 60% in the first month of unemployment, are decreasing in the length of the treatment. To be eligible, the individual needs to have paid social security contributions for at least 52 weeks in the last two years. Individuals who do not meet this eligibility criterion, but who paid social security contributions for at least 78 days in the last two years, can apply for unemployment benefits with reduced requirements, characterized by lower replacement rates.

Ordinary wage supplementation is a wage subsidy for employees in manufacturing and construction, providing 80% of the wage for a maximum of 13 weeks in which the worker is temporarily not involved in production due to lower demand.[8] Actual replacement rates tend to be lower since the maximum payable amount is equal to 893 euros in 2010 (1,073 when gross monthly wage is above 1,932 euros). Trainees are excluded. Extraordinary wage supplementation provides similar replacement rates for a maximum of 36 months, but is available only for employees working in manufacturing or services firms undergoing closure, bankruptcy or a major restructuring. Eligibility depends on the size of the firm, at least 15 employees in manufacturing, 50 in the services sector.

Finally, the *long-term unemployment assistance* (indennità di mobilità) is an income support scheme reserved to employees enjoying open-ended contracts, having a tenure of at least one year in a firm that has exploited the extraordinary wage supplementation fund, or is undergoing closure or a major restructuring. Duration, increasing with the age of the worker, is up to three years and can be extended for another 12 months when the firm is located in the South of the country (where the economy is weaker).

In 2008 the Italian government (Decreto legge of the 29th of November 2008, n. 185) has extended income support schemes to some categories of previously uncovered individuals, introducing three-month unemployment benefits with a 60% replacement rate for individuals whose contract is temporarily suspended, provided they have paid social security contributions for at least 52 weeks in the previous three years and are not covered by the ordinary wage supplementation scheme. A one-off payment equal to 20% of last year labour income was also introduced for quasi-employees, a category including formally self-employed individuals actually working as employees mainly for tax reasons and for reducing Employment Protection Legislation (EPL). Moreover, wage supplementation income support schemes on a discretionary basis (Cassa Integrazione in Deroga) became available for those workers employed in firms not eligible for standard treatments.

4. TRANSITIONS IN AND OUT OF EMPLOYMENT

As a starting point we estimate with a linear probability model (LMP) individual probabilities of transition from employment (E) to non-employment (NE) and viceversa at one-year intervals. We include in estimation both a pre-crisis interval (2006:1 to 2008:3) and an interval including the crisis (2008:4 to 2009:4). For the E to NE (and viceversa) transition equations we estimate the following expression on the full interval:

$$y_{it_{|y_{it-4}=1}} = \alpha + \beta X_{it} + \lambda_{\text{Crisis}} + \varepsilon_{it} \qquad (1)$$

where y_{it} for individual i at time t is missing if the individual was non-employed in $t-4$, it is equal to 1 if the individual is non-employed in t and 0 otherwise, in the E to NE equation (opposite definition in the NE to E one). The equation for job terminations is estimated separately for four groups of workers: employees with open ended contracts (OEC), employees with fixed term contracts (FTC), quasi-employees[9] and self-employed workers. The job creation one is estimated instead on the non-employed. The dummy λ_{Crisis}, equal to 1 for five quarters (2008:4 to 2009:4 interval) and 0 for the remaining 11 quarters (2006:1 to 2008:3), identifies the change in transition probabilities taking place during the crisis. Finally, the matrix X_{it} includes usual controls for socio-demographic characteristics (in both equations) and job-related characteristics (only in the job termination one).[10]

According to our estimates, the probability of having a transition out of employment is higher for women, blue collar workers and in the South, while tenure has the expected negative sign on the linear term and positive on the quadratic one. During the crisis, the probability of experiencing a transition out of employment increased significantly for employees with fixed term contracts and for quasi-employees (Table 2), respectively by 3.8 p.p. and 2.4 p.p. The impact of the downturn is not statistically significant when considering the self-employed and workers with open ended contracts.

Turning to transitions into employment, Table 3 shows that the probability of finding a job for those not in employment is lower for

Table 2.   Transitions Out of Employment.

	OEC	FTC	Quasi-Employees	Self-Employed
Crisis	0.002	0.038***	0.024*	−0.003
	[1.08]	[5.78]	[1.82]	[1.25]
Female	0.031***	0.063***	0.048***	0.062***
	[19.05]	[9.70]	[3.64]	[19.42]
Intermediate education	−0.013***	−0.028***	−0.050***	−0.023***
	[6.90]	[3.48]	[2.77]	[8.41]
High education	−0.019***	−0.055***	−0.086***	−0.040***
	[7.50]	[4.78]	[4.33]	[10.00]
Centre	0.007***	0	0.023	0.016***
	[3.25]	[0.03]	[1.40]	[4.30]
South	0.027***	0.083***	0.083***	0.032***
	[15.20]	[11.55]	[5.24]	[11.55]
Aged 25–34	−0.044***	−0.067***	−0.157***	−0.094***
	[9.21]	[6.88]	[5.84]	[7.86]
Aged 35–44	−0.047***	−0.108***	−0.220***	−0.105***
	[9.55]	[9.19]	[8.02]	[8.87]
Aged 45–54	−0.046***	−0.082***	−0.204***	−0.102***
	[9.18]	[6.27]	[6.91]	[8.59]
Aged 55–64	0.069***	−0.003	−0.065*	−0.017
	[11.17]	[0.14]	[1.93]	[1.36]
Blue collar	0.017***	0.020**		
	[8.30]	[2.34]		
Foreigner	−0.014***	0.002	−0.029	0.011
	[3.98]	[0.13]	[1.13]	[1.38]
Tenure	−0.007***	−0.016***		
	[21.19]	[11.65]		
$(Tenure^2)/100$	0.020***	0.045***		
	[19.39]	[8.17]		
Constant	0.126***	0.280***	0.298***	0.154***
	[14.72]	[14.71]	[5.76]	[12.60]
Observations	194,234	30,363	6,062	70,902
R-squared	0.06	0.06	0.05	0.04

* Significant at 10%; ** Significant at 5%; *** Significant at 1%.
Notes: OEC stands for open ended contract, FTC stands for fixed term contract.
Weighted LPM regression for the probability of transition from employment to non-employment. T-statistics in squared brackets based on standard errors clustered at the individual level. Estimated on the 2006:1 to 2009:4 period. The "crisis" dummy is equal to 1 from 2008:4 to 2009:4, 0 otherwise. Additional controls: marital status, industry, firm size, quarter.

women and in the South, while it increases with the educational level. Time out of employment significantly reduces the probability of getting a job: it is 8.2 p.p. lower for individuals with a spell between 7 and 12 months compared to workers out of employment for less than six months. It is 24.8

Table 3.   Transitions into Employment.

Crisis	−0.016***
	[9.08]
NE for 7–12 months	−0.082***
	[7.90]
NE for more than 12 months	−0.187***
	[19.61]
No work experience	−0.248***
	[25.95]
Benefit receipt	−0.025*
	[1.82]
Female	−0.037***
	[17.71]
Intermediate education	0.030***
	[14.70]
High education	0.111***
	[20.28]
Married	−0.034***
	[13.45]
Centre	0.001
	[0.13]
South	−0.024***
	[11.68]
Aged 25–34	0.072***
	[17.10]
Aged 35–44	0.049***
	[11.63]
Aged 45–54	0.005
	[1.35]
Aged 55–64	−0.079***
	[24.27]
Constant	0.354***
	[35.98]
Observations	231180
R-squared	0.11

*Significant at 10%; **Significant at 5%; ***Significant at 1%.
Notes: NE stands for not in employment.
Weighted LPM regression for the probability of transition from non-employment to employment. Estimated on the 2006:1 to 2009:4 period. T-statistics in squared brackets based on standard errors clustered at the individual level. Additional controls: quarter. The "crisis" dummy is equal to 1 from 2008:4 to 2009:4, 0 otherwise.

p.p. lower when there is no previous work experience. Also benefit receipt has a negative, albeit significant only at the 10%, impact on the probability of finding a job (−2.5 p.p.). During the crisis, the probability of getting a job decreased significantly by 1.6 p.p., a result significant at the 1% level.

According to our estimates, during the 5 "crisis" quarters analysed here, the overall probability of experiencing a transition out of employment has been equal to 5.6% and 5.8% respectively for employees on OEC and for self-employed (Table 4). This probability is much higher for employees on FTC and quasi-employees (19.7% and 18.3%). The latter are also the ones experiencing a substantive increase in the likelihood of remaining out of employment during the crisis (+ 3.6 p.p. and + 2.4 p.p. respectively), while the probability of moving from non-employment to employment falls from 11.2% to 9.8% (−1.4 p.p., Table 5). These results underline the fact that changes both in the probabilities of transition out and into employment determined the adjustment in employment levels during the crisis, and in particular that variations in flows out of employment are non negligible, a

Table 4.   Transitions Out of Employment: 2008:4 to 2009:4 Interval.

Variable	Percentage Points			
	Share on employment	Crisis	No crisis	Variation during crisis
OEC	65.8	5.6	5.5	0.1
FTC	9.9	19.7	16.0	3.6
Quasi-employees	2.3	18.3	15.9	2.4
Self-employed	22.0	5.8	6.1	−0.3
Total	100.0	7.4	6.9	0.4

Notes: Out of employment (crisis) is the real flow (in percentage points) from employment in quarter t to non-employment in quarter $t+4$ during the 2008:4 to 2009:4 period. Out of employment (no crisis) is the same flow simulated based on the LPM regressions of Table 2 setting the *Crisis* dummy equal to 0. OEC stands for open ended contract, FTC for fixed term contract. Quasi-employees are a category including formally self-employed individuals actually working as employees mainly for tax reasons and for reducing EPL.

Table 5.   Transitions into Employment: 2008:4 to 2009:4 Interval.

	Percentage points
Crisis	9.8
No crisis	11.2
Variation during crisis	−1.4

Notes: Into employment (crisis), is the real flow (in percentage points) from non-employment in quarter t to employment in quarter $t+4$ during the 2008:4 to 2009:4 period. Into employment (no crisis) is the same flow simulated based on the LPM regressions of Table 3 setting the *Crisis* dummy equal to 0.

result in line with Elsby et al. (2010) and Sierminska and Takhtamanova (2011). Nevertheless, transitions out of employment are prevalent, accounting for two-thirds of the drop in employment levels.

5. MULTIPLE STOCHASTIC IMPUTATION AND SIMULATIONS

On the basis of the specifications of Section 4, estimated on the 2008:1 to 2009:4 interval, we assign to each worker employed in quarter t a probability of not being employed in quarter $t+4$ and viceversa, under the assumption that the parameters estimated in Eq. (1) remain constant during the $t,t+4$ period. Similar LPM models estimate the probability of benefiting from the wage-supplementation fund or of experiencing a temporary suspension of the work contract in quarter t for individuals employed in quarter t (for a definition of the relevant income support schemes see Section 3).

After active individuals are assigned a probability for each of these four events, we simulate the evolution of main labour market variables during the $t,t+4$ period for four different scenarios, assuming a constant participation rate and different patterns for the employment rate. These include a *baseline scenario* in which employment decreases 0.6% in the $t,t+4$ period, a scenario with constant employment and two more scenarios based on the *baseline* one, plus/minus one standard deviation[11] in the unemployment rate (1.7 points), bringing the change in employment respectively to −2.7% and 1.1%. Simulations are based on the probabilities estimated in Section 4 and a *multiple stochastic imputation* (Rubin, 1996).[12]

In the simulation assuming that the employment level remains constant in each of the four quarters of the $t,t+4$ period total gross labour income, its distribution and unemployment benefits paid might still change: even for a constant employment rate, individuals are still experiencing transitions into and out of employment, and their labour income and unemployment benefit entitlements might be different. Moreover, there is a continuum of probabilities of experiencing the employment to non-employment and non-employment to employment transitions for a given employment rate. We assume that these probabilities remain unchanged as estimated on the $(t,t-4)$ interval in Eq. (1). From those yearly probabilities, we numerically derive quarterly probabilities of transition that match the four scenarios for the employment rate for the period $(t,t+4)$. To impute labour market state in each of the four $t, t + 4$ quarters, a random draw is made from a uniform distribution [0,1]. If the realization of the draw is lower than the quarterly probability of experiencing the event, based on the estimate of Eq. (1) and the numerical approximation, the individual changes its state. For example, suppose a worker has been assigned a 0.1 probability of an employment to non-employment transition between t and $t + 1$, given she is employed in t. If the random draw gives a value smaller than 0.1, the individual becomes non-employed. In the same quarter, this process is repeated for non-employment to employment transitions (conditional on not being employed in the previous quarter) and for being on wage supplementation or suspension (conditional on being employed in the same quarter).

Conditional on imputed labour market status in $t + 1$, this exercise is repeated for transitions occurring between $t + 1$ and $t + 2$ and so on, until $t + 4$. It is important to recover the labour market conditions in each of the quarters of the simulation, and not only at yearly intervals, since unemployment benefits and transfers from the wage supplementation fund crucially depend on the duration of the event at study. In the simulation we assume 100% take up, while eligibility criteria for these transfers follow those described in Section 3.

Moreover, to assess the robustness of the results, we repeat the simulation 40 times with 40 different randomly generated draws from the uniform distribution. This multiple imputation exercise assesses the variability of the imputation; a more general assessment of total variance should also include the variability due to the sampling nature of the estimators, but this would be out of the scope of this chapter. In Fig. 1 we show the distribution of the estimates for the overall employment level in $t + 4$ resulting from the multiple imputation over the $t, t + 4$ period following the baseline scenario. Estimates show some variability, clustering at a value slightly below 22.8 million. Mean and median of the 40 estimates are very close (22,776 and 22,780 thousand of employed people), while the 10th and 90th percentile are in an interval of −0.3% and +0.3% with respect to the mean/median.

In the other three simulations, we assume different scenarios for the evolution of the employment rate. The starting point is common for all the simulations, and it is equal to actual labour market conditions for 2009:4 (employment and unemployment rates respectively equal to 57.1% and 8.6%). In the *baseline scenario*, employment decreases 0.6% in the 2009:4 to 2010:4 period, bringing the unemployment rate from 8.6% to 9.1%. The two remaining scenarios are simulated assuming the unemployment rate in 2010:4 is higher/lower than the *baseline scenario* by one standard deviation (1.7 p.p.). Again, we derive numerically the quarterly NE to E and E to NE

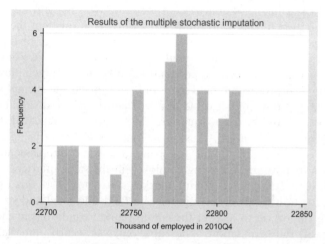

Fig. 1. Results of the Multiple Stochastic Imputation: Employment. *Notes*: Results of the multiple stochastic imputation for the baseline scenario, 40 iterations, see Section 5 for details. The histogram reports the distribution of simulated employment levels in 2010:4 for 40 different realizations of the random draws from the uniform distribution and a common starting point for 2009:4.

probabilities coherent with these labour market developments. To focus on the impact of changes in the level and composition of employment, simulations are carried out assuming zero growth in nominal wages.

6. RESULTS

6.1. Aggregate Projections

According to the simulation assuming a 0.6% drop in employment in the 2009:4 to 2010:4 period (*baseline scenario*, panel 1 of Table 6), total gross income is expected to drop in a similar fashion (−0.7%). As a consequence, the drop in the number of workers resulting from flows into and out of employment does not alter average wages much. Under the hypothesis of a constant participation rate, the drop in employment would entail a 0.6 p.p. increase in the unemployment rate, at 9.1%. To focus on the role of unemployment benefits in cushioning wage losses, we carry out an

Table 6. Labour Market Simulator Macro Projections.

Panel	(1)				(2)			
Scenario	Baseline (0.6% drop in employment)				Constant employment			
	Mean	Median	10th percentile	90th percentile	Mean	Median	10th percentile	90th percentile
Thousands								
Employed in 2009	22,922	22,922	22,922	22,922	22,922	22,922	22,922	22,922
Employed in 2010	22,776	22,780	22,723	22,814	22,929	22,923	22,897	22,968
2010/2009 variation	−0.6%	−0.6%	−0.9%	−0.5%	0.0%	0.0%	−0.1%	0.2%
Percentage points								
Unemployment rate, 2009	8.6	8.6	8.6	8.6	8.6	8.6	8.6	8.6
Unemployment rate, 2010	9.1	9.1	9.0	9.3	8.5	8.6	8.4	8.7
2010/2009 variation	0.6	0.6	0.4	0.8	0.0	0.0	−0.2	0.1
Euro$*10^9$								
Gross labour income, 2009	181.7	181.7	181.5	181.9	181.7	181.7	181.5	181.9
Gross labour income, 2010	180.4	180.5	180.0	180.8	181.5	181.5	181.2	181.7
2010/2009 variation	−0.7%	−0.7%	−0.9%	−0.6%	−0.1%	−0.2%	−0.2%	−0.1%
Gross labour income, 2010 (no NE to E transitions)	174.6	174.7	174.3	175.0	175.7	175.7	175.5	175.9
2010/2009 variation	−3.9%	−3.9%	−4.0%	−3.8%	−3.3%	−3.3%	−3.3%	−3.3%
Gross labour income +UB + WS, 2010 (no NE to E transitions)	177.3	177.3	177.0	177.5	178.1	178.1	177.9	178.3
2010/2009 variation	−2.5%	−2.4%	−2.5%	−2.4%	−2.0%	−2.0%	−2.0%	−2.0%

Notes: Macro level projections obtained from a multiple stochastic simulation at the individual level coherent with the evolution of employment rates and the individual probabilities of quitting or getting a job (for details, see Section 5). The simulation is repeated 40 times to test the robustness of the results to the stochastic imputation. The Table reports mean, median and percentiles of the distribution of the 40 estimates obtained for different random draws from a uniform distribution. Long-term unemployment assistance (indennità di mobilità) and discretionary wage supplementation (CIG in deroga) not included.

additional simulation, holding constant job separation probabilities and assuming no non-employment to employment transitions during the considered interval. In this case, gross labour income would decrease by 7.1 billion (−3.9%), with unemployment benefits making up for 38% of the loss (2.7 billion). Actual coverage of these income stabilizers would be higher, since some of the schemes (indennità di mobilità and cassa integrazione in deroga) are not included in the simulation.

When assuming a constant employment rate (panel 2 of Table 6), total gross income decreases by 0.1%. This is because even when the employment level is constant, average labour income slightly changes due to the recomposition of workers through flows into and out of employment and to the simulated changes in wage subsidies utilization. In this scenario, assuming no transitions from non-employment to employment, gross labour income would decrease by 6.0 billion, with unemployment benefits covering 40% of the loss. In a pessimistic scenario, adding one standard deviation in the unemployment rate to the *baseline scenario* (−2.7% in employment, panel 3 of Table 7), coverage would be lower (33%). On the contrary, when assuming an optimistic scenario (baseline minus one standard deviation in the unemployment rate) with a 1.1 growth in employment, 45% of the losses for the unemployed would be covered by the available safety nets.

All in all, apart from giving an assessment of the likely evolution of total labour income associated with changes in employment levels, simulation results show the pro-cyclical nature of the unemployment benefit system in place in Italy. This is because individuals on flexible work arrangements, who have higher job-separation probabilities, are also less protected by job-termination-related income losses. Finally, it is reassuring to note that all the results are virtually unchanged when considering alternatively the mean and the median of the estimates' distribution obtained through the multiple stochastic imputation. Even projections associated with the 10th or the 90th percentile of the distributions are not too far from these central values, always being in an interval including the mean/median of the distribution of the estimates ±0.2 p.p.

6.2. Unemployment Benefits and Labour Income Distribution

In the previous section, an assessment of the coverage offered by unemployment benefits was provided at the macro level, analysing how much of the gross labour income lost due to job termination would be covered by the available safety nets. In this section we take a different perspective, calculating

Table 7. Labour Market Simulator Macro Projections.

Panel	(3)				(4)			
Scenario	Baseline +1 sd of UR				Baseline −1 sd of UR			
	Mean	Median	10th percentile	90th percentile	Mean	Median	10th percentile	90th percentile
Thousands								
Employed in 2009	22,922	22,922	22,922	22,922	22,922	22,922	22,922	22,922
Employed in 2010	22,299	22,305	22,258	22,328	23,166	23,171	23,121	23,196
2010/2009 variation	−2.7%	−2.7%	−2.9%	−2.6%	1.1%	1.1%	0.9%	1.2%
Percentage points								
Unemployment rate, 2009	8.6	8.6	8.6	8.6	8.6	8.6	8.6	8.6
Unemployment rate, 2010	11.0	11.0	10.9	11.2	7.6	7.6	7.5	7.8
2010/2009 variation	2.5	2.5	2.4	2.6	−1.0	−1.0	−1.1	−0.8
Euro$^*10^9$								
Gross labour income, 2009	181.7	181.7	181.6	181.9	181.7	181.7	181.5	181.9
Gross labour income, 2010	177.1	177.1	176.8	177.4	183.1	183.1	182.8	183.4
2010/2009 variation	−2.5%	−2.5%	−2.6%	−2.4%	0.8%	0.8%	0.7%	0.8%
Gross labour income, 2010 (no NE to E transitions)	171.4	171.4	171.1	171.8	177.3	177.3	177.0	177.6
2010/2009 variation	−5.7%	−5.7%	−5.8%	−5.6%	−2.4%	−2.4%	−2.5%	−2.4%
Gross labour income +UB+WS, 2010 (no NE to E transitions)	174.8	174.9	174.6	175.1	179.3	179.3	179.1	179.6
2010/2009 variation	−3.8%	−3.8%	−3.9%	−3.7%	−1.3%	−1.3%	−1.3%	−1.3%

Notes: Macro level projections obtained from a multiple stochastic simulation at the individual level coherent with the evolution of employment rates and the individual probabilities of quitting or getting a job (for details, see Section 5). The simulation is repeated 40 times to test the robustness of the results to the stochastic imputation. The Table reports mean, median and percentiles of the distribution of the 40 estimates obtained for different random draws from a uniform distribution. Long term unemployment assistance (indennità di mobilità) and discretionary wage supplementation (CIG in deroga) not included 1sd. UR stands for one standard deviation of the unemployment rate (1.7 p.p., as calculated on the 1992–2009 period).

average workers' replacement rates for the duration of unemployment or suspension of the work contract. These indicators are more informative when focussing on individual conditions rather than on the coverage of income losses at the macro-level. Average individual replacement rates need not to be equal to the percentage of income loss covered by the benefits at the macro level, since replacement rates could be systematically different for individuals with different levels of labour income.

The stress testing of the unemployment benefits with different employment dynamics gives interesting results (Table 8): average workers' replacement rates start at 33% in the first quarter of unemployment/suspension, rapidly decreasing with the duration of the event (at the fourth quarter, the replacement rate is between 5.1 and 6.7 depending on the employment scenario considered). The percentage of uncovered displaced workers is sensitive to changes in labour market conditions: in the first quarter it is equal to 15.1% in the most optimistic projection (row 4) assuming a 1.1% increase in employment, while it is equal to 16.8% in the baseline scenario (0.6% drop in employment, row 1) and reaches its maximum (19.0%) in the pessimistic scenario (−2.7% in employment, row 3). Similar results emerge when considering the second quarter of continuous unemployment, while results are less clear for durations of three or more quarters, probably because the

Table 8.   UB Replacement Rates for Unemployment or Suspension Duration.

Scenario	Employment Variation 2010/2009	Quarters in Unemployment/Suspension							
		1st qtr in UE/S		2nd qtr in UE/S		3rd qtr in UE/S		4th qtr in UE/S	
		%RR	% at 0 RR	%RR	% at 0 RR	%RR	% at 0 RR	%RR	% at 0 RR
(1) Baseline	−0.6%	34.2	16.8	32.1	24.0	19.8	38.0	6.2	75.3
(2) Constant UR	0.0%	33.8	16.4	31.3	24.3	18.3	40.7	5.1	78.2
(3) Baseline + 1SD of UR	−2.7%	33.2	19.0	30.6	26.7	19.2	38.5	6.7	72.7
(4) Baseline − 1SD of UR	1.1%	34.4	15.1	31.9	23.7	18.3	42.0	5.7	79.5

Notes: UE: unemployment; S: suspension of work contract; RR: replacement rates (percentage points); % at 0 RR: percentage of displaced individuals with zero replacement rate. Long-term unemployment assistance (indennità di mobilità) not included. Each entry in the Table is the result of the simulation of the transfers obtained by each worker, obtained assuming 100% take up and following the institutional features described in Section 3.

underlying number of observations decreases with the spell length. Indeed, the simulation is carried out for four quarters, and only individuals who lost their job in the first quarter are at risk of being unemployed/suspended for four consecutive quarters.

The high fragmentation of the unemployment benefits, a well-known feature of the Italian income support system (Anastasia et al., 2009), is evident from the scatterplots of Fig. 2, in which the y axis reports the simulated replacement rates and the x axis the gross monthly labour income assuming a 0.6% drop in employment (baseline scenario). Coverage ranges between 0% and 80%, with higher replacement rates for lower paid individuals, provided they have coverage at all. Workers can be not-eligible for unemployment benefits either because they did not pay enough contributions to social security when working, or because they are uncovered (e.g., self-employed workers). Consequences of the lack of any

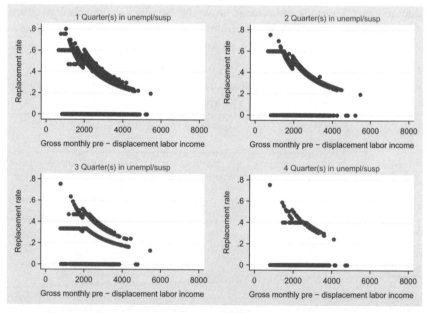

Fig. 2.   Individual Replacement Rates: Scatterplot. *Notes*: Replacement rates in the 2009:4 to 2010:4 period for individuals sampled in 2009:4. Long-term unemployment assistance (indennità di mobilità) and discretionary wage supplementation schemes (CIG in deroga) not included.

safety net for a broad category of workers are exacerbated by the fact that no basic income support is available in Italy.

Going back to the *baseline scenario*, Fig. 3 shows the changes of labour income distribution that occurred during the crisis. Density reductions are quite evenly distributed among workers earning between 700 and 4,000 thousand euros a month, with highest absolute decreases for workers earning 2000 euros.[13] Fig. 4 shows instead the simulated changes in income distribution during the 2009–2010 interval among workers employed in 2009, once UB and WS transfers are included. It is straightforward to see that in this case income losses are cushioned, but there is still a considerable increase in the density of displaced individuals with gross income lower than 1,000 euros per month, or no income altogether.

Always assuming the *baseline scenario*, labour income inequality increases in the 2009–2010 period, with a Gini index calculated on active individuals rising from 24.7 in 2009 to 25.4 in 2010 (Table 9). Following Atkinson and Brandolini (2006), we can decompose the increase in inequality in a component due to the rise in unemployed individuals, and a component due to the change in inequality among those who remain in the labour

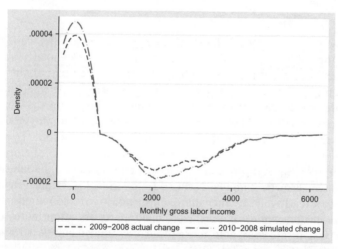

Fig. 3. Changes in the Gross Labour Income Distribution. *Notes*: Non-parametric estimates of the changes in gross labour income over the 2008:4 to 2010:4 period. Calculated on active individuals only, assuming a constant participation rate. Long-term unemployment assistance (indennità di mobilità) and discretionary wage supplementation schemes (CIG in deroga) not included.

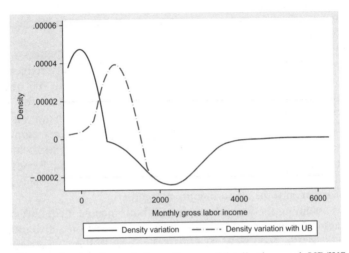

Fig. 4. Changes in the Gross Labour Income Distribution and UB/WS. *Notes:* Non-parametric estimates of the changes in gross labour income over the 2009:4 to 2010:4 period. Calculated only on individuals employed in 2009:4. Long-term unemployment assistance (indennità di mobilità) and discretionary wage supplementation schemes (CIG in deroga) not included.

force: $G_A = u + (1 - u)G_E$, where u is the unemployment rate, while G_A and G_E are the Gini indexes of gross labour income, calculated respectively among active and employed individuals. It can be noted that all the increase in inequality is due to the increase in unemployment, while wage inequality among those who stay employed barely changes. This means that changes in the composition of workers due to flows into and out of employment do not have a significant impact on labour income distribution. Even more interesting, this result holds true irrespective of the variation of employment levels: G_E remains basically constant assuming four different scenarios with employment growth ranging from -2.7% to 1.1%, while changes in inequality are driven by the share of unemployed individuals. With a common starting point for year 2009, a standard deviation increase in the unemployment rate compared to the baseline scenario entails a 1.8 increase in the overall Gini index for 2010.

To focus on the impact of job destruction on inequality, and on the role played by unemployment benefits, we also simulate the Gini index setting to zero NE to E transitions (lower panel of Table 9). In the baseline scenario, the overall Gini index in 2010 would be 3.3 points higher than in 2009,

Table 9. Crisis' Redistributive Impact: Gini Indexes (Individual Gross Labour Income).

	(1) Baseline scenario	(2) Constant UR	(3) Baseline + 1sd UR	(4) Baseline − 1sd UR
Employment variation 2010/2009	−0.6%	0.0	−2.7%	1.1%
Gini 2009	24.7	24.7	24.7	24.7
Share of employed 2009	91.4	91.4	91.4	91.4
Gini among employed 2009	17.7	17.7	17.7	17.7
Gini 2010	25.4	24.9	27.1	24.2
Share of employed 2010	90.7	91.3	88.7	92.3
Gini among employed 2010	17.7	17.7	17.8	17.8
2010/2009 variations				
Gini	0.6	0.2	2.4	−0.5
Share of employed	−0.7	−0.1	−2.8	0.8
Gini among employed	0.0	0.1	0.1	0.2
Gini 2010	28.1	27.6	29.7	26.9
(no NE to E transitions)				
2010/2009 variations	3.3	2.9	5.0	2.2
Gini 2010 + UB + WS	26.6	26.2	27.7	25.7
(no NE to E transitions)				
2010/2009 variations	1.8	1.5	3.0	1.0

Notes: Calculated on active individuals only, assuming a constant participation rate. UB: unemployment benefit; WS: wage supplementation (cassa integrazione). 1 SD of UR: one standard deviation of the unemployment rate (1.7 p.p.) calculated on the quarterly series starting with 1992. Long-term unemployment assistance (indennità di mobilità) and discretionary wage supplementation schemes (CIG in deroga) not included.

compared with a 0.6 points increase with non-zero NE to E transitions. Including UB and WS transfers, the increase in labour income inequality is less pronounced but still substantial (1.8 points to 26.6).

7. CONCLUSIONS

In this chapter, we estimate the changes in job finding and job termination probabilities occurred during the Great Recession. We then use these probabilities to simulate, by means of a micro level multiple stochastic imputation, the effects of changes in employment on the level and the distribution of gross labour income, taking into consideration the role played by the unemployment benefits system in cushioning the impact of job losses.

Our results show that two thirds of the decrease in employment taking place during the 2008:4 to 2009:4 period were due to the fall in job finding probabilities, while transitions out of employment significantly increased for employees on flexible contracts only. According to the projections, changes in labour income inequality between active individuals are driven by changes in employment, while inequality variations due to the changing composition of those remaining employed are negligible.

The income support system is able to reduce by 30–40% the short-term impact of job terminations on income, with coverage being pro-cyclical: higher when an optimistic employment scenario is assumed and lower otherwise. The safety net is highly fragmented, with actual replacement rates ranging between 0% and 80% and quickly decreasing over time: employees on flexible work arrangements, most hardly hit by the crisis, enjoy only partial coverage. Even for covered individuals, ordinary benefits' duration is short, while the absence of any universal basic income support scheme exacerbates the impact of job terminations on workers' income. A more efficient income support scheme should feature transfers whose duration is proportional to the amount of contributions paid before job-termination: the requirement of at least 53 weeks of social security contributions in the last two years to be eligible for ordinary unemployment benefits introduces completely different treatments for individuals around that threshold. Finally, a universal basic income support scheme, common to non-participants to the labour market, should be made available to otherwise uncovered workers.

NOTES

1. Strauss-Kahn (2009) was the first to refer in this way to the severe economic downturn started with Lehman Brothers' bankruptcy in September 2008.
2. See, among others, Blanchard and Diamond (1990) and Perry (1972).
3. The article uses data up to 2007.
4. For a more general assessment of the impact of the crisis and of the role of welfare systems in cushioning income losses for the unemployed, see Figari, Salvatori, and Sutherland (2011) and Dolls, Fuest, and Peichl (2011).
5. These include ordinary wage subsidies for workers on reduced hours and unemployment benefits (see Section 3 for a description of the Italian UB system).

Discretionary schemes (Cassa Integrazione in Deroga) and long term unemployment benefits (indennità di mobilità) not included.

6. Labour income from self-employment is not reported in the ILFS data. Self-employment income is imputed by means of six weighted mincerian regressions run separately for men and women and for three geographical areas (North, Centre and South), historically characterized by different labour market conditions. The dependent variable is the net average monthly labour income, while independent variables are: 103 province fixed effects, 12 dummies for maximum educational level attained and 7 age class dummies (identifying 10-year age intervals).

7. In particular, the auxiliary regression $Y_{\mathrm{Lgross}} = \alpha + \beta Y_{\mathrm{Lnet}} + \gamma Y_{\mathrm{Lnet}}^2$ is run on an administrative dataset (MEF, 2009) reporting gross labour income (Y_{Lgross}) and net labour income Y_{Lnet} earned in 2007 for discrete intervals of the former. Using the estimates for the parameters α, β and γ, a value of Y_{Lgross} is imputed at the micro level in the ILFS dataset based on the realizations of Y_{Lnet} in the same dataset (the tax code did not have any substantial change between fiscal year 2007 and 2009). The imputation gives a very good approximation of gross labour income. For employees, according to MEF (2009) data, labour income constituted 90.5% of total income subject to the personal income tax in the fiscal year 2007; as a consequence there is a close link between labour income, total income and thus tax rates. A more precise imputation would require a tax–benefit model and information on other sources of income, not available in the ILFS.

8. Extensions up to 12 months can be provided on a discretionary basis.

9. Quasi-employees are defined as formally self-employed workers, actually working as employees for tax reasons and for reducing EPL. They are defined as self-employed workers working for a single company, on the company's premises and with a non-flexible time schedule.

10. The socio-demographic characteristics are: gender, education, geographical area, age, citizenship; job-related ones are: tenure (linear and quadratic term), industry, firm size. The job-finding equation includes additional controls for the length of the time period spent out of employment and for benefit receipt. Quarter dummies are included to take seasonality into account.

11. Standard deviation is calculated on the 1993–2009 period.

12. See the Appendix for a brief description of the imputation procedure.

13. It has to be noted that wages are relative to the fourth quarter, a period including annual extra payments for Christmas.

ACKNOWLEDGEMENTS

I thank the editor and two anonymous referees for their helpful and constructive comments. A. Brandolini, M. Bryan, F. Faiella, F. Figari, C. Nicoletti and A. Rosolia also provided useful comments. I am grateful to R. Zizza for providing me the stata codes used to simulate Unemployment Benefits and Wage Supplementation Fund transfers and to the Economic and Social Research Council for financial support. *Opinions expressed here do not necessarily reflect those of the Bank of Italy.*

REFERENCES

Anastasia, B., Mancini, M., & Trivellato, U. (2009). Il sostegno del reddito dei disoccupati: note sullo stato dell'arte. Tra riformismo strisciante, inerzie dell'impianto categoriale e incerti orizzonti di flexicurity. ISAE Working Paper no. 112.

Arpaia, A., & Curci, N. (2010). EU labour market behaviour during the Great Recession. European Economy no. 405.

Atkinson, T., & Brandolini, A. (2006). From earnings dispersion to income inequality. In: F. Farina & E. Savaglio (Eds), Inequality and economic integration. London: Routledge.

Blanchard, O., & Diamond, P. (1990). The cyclical behavior of the gross flows of U.S. workers. Brookings Papers on Economic Activity, 1990(2), 85–155.

Bowers, N., & Horvath, F. W. (1984). Keeping time: An analysis of errors in the measurement of unemployment duration. Journal of Business & Economic Statistics, 2(2), 140–149.

Ceccarelli, C., Discenza, A. R., & Loriga, S. (2006). The impact of the new labour force survey on the employed classification. Data Analysis, Classification and the Forward Search, 359–367. Berlin: Springer.

Cingano, F., Torrini, R., & Viviano, E. (2010). Il mercato del lavoro italiano durante la crisi. Questioni di Economia e Finanza, No. 68, Bank of Italy.

D'Amuri, F. (2010). Recall errors and labor market dynamics: A comparative analysis. Mimeo, Bank of Italy.

Dolls, M., Fuest, C., & Peichl, A. (2011). Automatic stabilizers, economic crisis and income distribution in Europe. IZA Discussion paper no. 4917 (This Volume).

Elsby, M., Hobijn, B., & Sahin, A. (2010). The labor market in the great recession. Working Paper no. 2010-07. Federal Reserve Bank of San Francisco.

European Commission (2009). Italy. Labour market and wage developments in 2008, pp. 220–222.

Eurostat (2009). Labour market policy – expenditure and participants. Luxembourg: Publications Office of the European Union.

Eurostat (2010). Labour market statistics – Labour force survey. Available at http://epp.eurostat.ec.europa.eu/

Figari, F., Salvatori, A., & Sutherland, H. (2011). Economic downturn and Stress testing European welfare systems. ISER Working Paper no. 2010-18 (This Volume).

Hall, R.E. (2005). Job loss, job finding, and unemployment in the U.S. economy over the past fifty years. NBER Working Paper no. 11678.

MEF (2009). Analisi statistiche, Anno d'imposta 2007. Ministero dell'Economia e delle Finanze – Dipartimento delle Finanze.

Perry, G. L. (1972). Unemployment flows in the U. S. labor market. Brookings Papers on Economic Activity, 1990(2), 245–292.

Poterba, J. M., & Summers, L. H. (1986). Reporting errors and labor market dynamics. Econometrica, 54(6), 1319–1338.

Rubin, D. (1996). Multiple imputation after 18+ years. Journal of the American Statistical Association, 91, 473–489.

Shimer, R. (2007). Reassessing the ins and outs of unemployment. NBER Working Paper no. 13421.

Sierminska, E., & Takhtamanova, Y. (2011). Job flows, demographics and the financial crisis. Paper presented at the IZA/OECD workshop Economic Crisis, Rising Unemployment and Policy Responses: What does it mean for the Income Distribution? Paris, February, 8–9, 2010 (This Volume).

Strauss-Kahn, D. (2009). Crisis management and policy coordination: Do we need a new global framework? Speech at the Austrian Central Bank, May 15, 2009.

APPENDIX A. BRIEF DESCRIPTION OF THE LABOUR MARKET SIMULATOR

Stage 1

Probability Estimates

Hypothesis: no transitions out or in the labour force in the short period (12 months).

Estimate probabilities for:

- A transition to employment in the $[t-4, t]$ interval given non-employment at $t-4$
- A transition to non-employment in the $[t-4, t]$ interval given employment at $t-4$
- Use of work supplementation fund in t given employment in t
- Suspension of work contract in t given employment in t

Stage 2

Multiple Stochastic Imputation

On the basis of probabilities estimated in *Stage 1*, the model generates quarterly transitions for the period $[t + 1, t + 4]$ coherent with projections of the employment rate defined ex-ante. This is implemented through a quarterly stochastic imputation based on the individuals' labour market status in the current quarter and the comparison between drawings from a uniform distribution $[0,1]$ and quarterly individual probabilities of experiencing one of the four changes of state obtained through numerical approximation from the yearly ones introduced in *Stage 1*. Results of the stochastic imputation are sensitive to the actual realizations of the uniform drawings. To provide a robustness check, the stochastic imputation is repeated 40 times for independent realizations of the random drawings. Mean, median and percentiles of the distributions of the estimates provide an assessment of the variability introduced by the imputation.

Stage 3

Unemployment Benefits' Simulation and Aggregation
Once the exact quarterly labour market status of each individual is
recovered in *Stage 2*, unemployment benefits and wage subsidies are
estimated on the basis of the current institutional setting. Aggregate
projections are calculated based on the results of the multiple stochastic
imputation and on unemployment benefits simulation.

REVERSED ROLES? WAGE AND EMPLOYMENT EFFECTS OF THE CURRENT CRISIS

Lutz Bellmann and Hans-Dieter Gerner

ABSTRACT

In Germany, the economic crisis 2008/09 was restricted to export-oriented industries such as automotive, chemistry, and mechanical engineering and hence to industries with a high proportion of qualified employees. Therefore, we expect the most current crisis to have a reversed effect on the relative earnings position between more and less qualified in contrast to a development that favored the more qualified since the beginning of the 1980s. Our empirical study is based on the Institute for Employment Research (IAB) Establishment Panel, a representative German establishment level panel data set that surveys information from almost 16,000 personal interviews with high ranked managers.

Despite the "German Job Miracle," conditional difference-in-differences estimations to control for observed and unobserved heterogeneity reveal substantial employment reductions in establishments affected by the economic crisis. Falls in employment are strongest in plants with a relatively low proportion of qualified workers. Furthermore, our results indicate that the economic crisis is associated with a decline in wages, but only in those establishments that do not operate working time accounts. In sum, we do not find evidence for the current crisis having a reversed effect on

Who Loses in the Downturn? Economic Crisis, Employment and Income Distribution
Research in Labor Economics, Volume 32, 181–206
ISSN: 0147-9121/doi:10.1108/S0147-9121(2011)0000032009

the relative earnings position. Obviously once again, the higher qualified are better off than the lower qualified.

Keywords: Wage structure; turnover; layoffs; public policy

JEL Classifications: J31; J63; J68

1. INTRODUCTION

Since the middle of 2008, many countries all over the world, including Germany, are faced with the deepest recession since the Great Depression in 1929 (Stiglitz, 2009). In consideration of the severity of the crisis, economists have estimated a potential job loss of 3.2 million employees in the first half of 2008 compared to the first half of 2009 for Germany (cf. Möller & Walwei, 2009, p. 6). However, the actual increase in unemployment remained fairly moderate. Between March 2008 and March 2009 in Germany, the number of unemployed increased by only around 2% (form 3,507,383 to 3,585,784). The most prominent argument for this phenomenon is that firms affected by the current crisis are hoarding their labor force (Möller, 2010). It is shown for Germany that the firms most affected by the crisis tend to be in high-productivity exporting industries such as automotive and mechanical engineering. These firms also have higher than average investment in human capital and therefore have greater incentives to operate labor hoarding. In addition, because the crisis appears to have been so concentrated in a relatively small (albeit highly productive) sector of the economy, total job losses have been mitigated.

Although the increase of unemployment in Germany at an aggregate level until now is fairly moderate, the effect of the crisis on the relative income distribution between more and less qualified employees remains unclear. For example, do the employees partly co-finance the labor hoarding strategies of their employers by making wage concessions? For Germany, the most cited instruments for the implementation of labor hoarding strategies are working time accounts and short-time work (Möller & Walwei, 2009; Möller, 2010). But there is little detailed empirical evidence. Because mainly sectors with a high proportion of qualified workers and high wages are hit by the economic crisis, we expect the current downturn to have a reverse effect in contrast to the development observed during the past 30 years on the relative earnings position of more qualified in relation to less qualified employees (Atkinson, 2007; Dustmann, Ludsteck, & Schönberg, 2009).

In our empirical analysis, we focus on the first half of the years 2008 and 2009 using establishment level panel data. Basically, we compare the development in the number of employees and the development of wages between firms that are subject to the global crisis and those that are not by applying simple difference-in-difference estimators. Whether or not an establishment is subject to the global crisis, we are identifying by exploring the firms reported business expectations for the next year expressed in the first half of 2008 and 2009 respectively. All measures of firm performance, such as sales, refer to the previous calendar year. As 2009 is the most recent wave of data, this would not allow us to identify firms hit by the crisis. Instead, therefore, we use a measure based on the change in business expectations between 2008 and 2009. The survey asks, "How do you expect the business volume to develop in the current year compared to the previous?". The respondents can indicate whether they expect their business volume to remain constant, to increase, to decrease, or whether they have no idea in this regard.

A strong relationship between the reported business expectations (proportion of plants that report to expect the business volume to decrease) at the firm level and the gross domestic product (GDP) can be seen in Fig. 1. It shows the change in the proportion of German firms that report negative business expectations for the current year compared to the year before (dark bars). The white bars represent the difference of the current real GDP and the real GDP of the previous year. Obviously, there is a clear negative relationship between the development of the GDP and the development of the proportion of establishments, which report negative business expectations, except in those years shortly before a recession with a very low growth rate of the real GDP. To avoid confusion of structural problems with those caused by the current crisis and to pick up the very unexpectedness of the current crisis in the first half of 2008, finally, in our analysis, a plant is regarded to be hit by the global crisis if it reports negative business expectations in 2009 but not in 2008.

In our econometric analysis, we control potential confounders within a (ordinary least square (OLS)) regression framework and alternatively by using propensity score matching techniques. The latter is applied because the association between the change of the employment level and the incidence of the current crisis is likely to be interdependent. Hence, it is

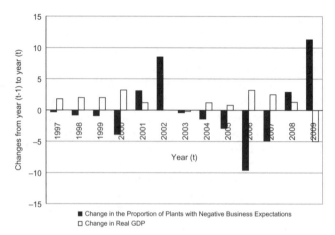

Fig. 1. Development of the Establishment Level Business Expectations and the Real GDP (1997–2009) *Source*: German Statistical Office and IAB Establishment Panel Surveys, own calculations.

essential to reduce the possible bias in the estimation caused by the endogeneity of the incidence of the crisis. The application of matching methods restricts the focus on comparable groups of crisis and noncrisis plants with respect to the confounding variables (Smith & Todd, 2005). Furthermore, no functional assumption for the connection between the confounders and the outcome variables is needed (Angrist & Pischke, 2009).

In particular, our empirical analysis is structured as follows. First of all, we investigate whether there are differences in the development of the number of employees and in the development of the wages between the plants that are affected by the global crisis and those that are not. To see whether establishments with a high proportion of qualified employees mainly adopt labor hoarding, we perform separate analyses for plants with a high and those with a low proportion of qualified workers. Finally, we study whether working time accounts and short-time work exert moderating effects on the development of wages and employment.

In the next section, we develop our hypotheses and review the relevant literature. Then, we describe the Institute for Employment Research (IAB) Establishment Panel Survey, the definition of our key variables, and present our empirical analysis. Our last section concludes.

2. HYPOTHESES

Since the advent of the recession in 2008, many companies have faced a dramatic decline in demand for their products and services. The way these companies respond depends on the severity of the recession as well as on their short-term and long-term expectations. Cost-cutting measures are of utmost importance for the firms (Heckmann, Kettner, Pausch, Szameitat, & Vogler-Ludwig, 2009 and for a European perspective, cf. European Foundation for the Improvement of Living and Working Conditions, 2009a, 71ff.). Strategies to reduce costs mainly consist of different measures to decrease the level of production with the consequence of reduced working time and measures to decrease wage costs. According to the study of Bell and Blanchflower (2009) using Organization for Economic Cooperation and Development (OECD) macroeconomic data, Germany was hit by the global crisis very hard in terms of the decline in gross national product (GNP); the overall employment effect, however, was relatively small between 2008 and 2009. As already mentioned, in the light of severity of the crisis, economists estimated for Germany a potential job loss of 3.2 million employees in the first half of 2008 compared to the first half of 2009 (Möller & Walwei, 2009, p. 6). One reason for this phenomenon may be the fact that in Germany, especially the export-oriented industries such as automotive or mechanical engineering are most badly affected. In these sectors, the proportion of qualified workers is high and hence the investments in human capital, which could explain labor hoarding at the firm level. Table 1 summarizes that the crisis is concentrated especially on the stars of the German economy such as automotive industry, chemistry, and mechanical engineering. Furthermore, Table 1 summarizes industries with less employment losses or even sound employment gains between 2008 and 2009, which could be an important reason for the "German Job Miracle."

In this context and moreover, the emerging shortage of skilled workers caused by the demographic change in many European countries gives firms incentives both to hoard their employees and to train them within the time period of low plant utilization rather than to fire them (Möller, 2010). Additionally, the industrial relations framework, in terms of both the objective rules and the spirit of cooperation, influences the possible outcome.

In general, there is on ongoing discussion about wage fluctuations over the business cycle (Devereux, 2001; Anger, 2007; Büttner, Jacobebbinghaus, & Ludsteck, 2010). For Germany, recent studies indicate such patterns are mainly driven by interfirm mobility of workers (Ludsteck, 2008). One

LUTZ BELLMANN AND HANS-DIETER GERNER

Table 1. Proportion of Establishments (Within Selected Industries) Affected by the Global Crisis and Employment Development (from 2008 to 2009).

	Proportion of Establishments Affected by the Global Crisis	Employment Development (between 2008 and 2009)
Manufacturing industry	0.45	−0.03
Automotive	0.52	−0.06
Chemistry	0.45	−0.03
Food Industry	0.19	+/− 0
Mechanical engineering	0.61	−0.03
Construction	0.24	−0.01
Hotels and restaurants	0.22	0.02
Banking and insurance	0.12	+/− 0
Wholesale and retail	0.24	+/− 0
Additional service activities	0.20	−0.01
Advertising and market research	0.37	+/− 0
Legal and tax consulting	0.14	+/− 0
Management consulting	0.22	−0.03
Research & development	0.35	0.03
Temporary employment agencies	0.66	−0.34
Total	0.27	−0.01

Source: IAB Establishment Panel Surveys 2008 and 2009.

explanation therefore may be the very centralized German wage setting system. Beside monthly wage reductions due to less paid overtime, it is very difficult to lower the wages for those workers who stay with the firm. In contrast, for new hires, wage adjustments can be easily achieved by sorting the new worker into lower paid slots of the sectoral-specific or firm-specific remuneration scheme (Ludsteck, 2008). The study of Büttner et al. (2010) reveals that the employers respond to excess supply of labor during downturns by increasing their hiring standards, which means it is more difficult for employees with lower qualification to find a job during the crisis.

Institutional settings such working time accounts or short-time work potentially play an important role in retaining sharp adjustments in employment and wages. Working time accounts can stabilize the firms' employment level, because adjustments in the time worked are accomplished over a certain period of time. Furthermore, temporary shifts in working time do not trigger wage adjustments. On the one hand, this means that establishments usually save overtime premia within an economic boom. On the other hand, for the employees, working time accounts act as an insurance against lower wages within an economic downturn (at least temporarily). In sum, working time accounts are smoothing the incomes of the employees over the business cycle (Carstensen, 2000).

In spring 2009, the European Foundation for the Improvement of Living and Working Conditions (2009b) conducted a large-scale representative survey addressed to managers and employee representatives. The focus of this survey was on the incidence of different forms of flexible working time arrangements. The proportion of companies with 10+ employees using working time accounts has reached 50% in Germany, which is the fourth position in the international ranking shown in Fig. 2. Furthermore, the possibility to accumulate credit hours for more than one year on long-term accounts is considerably less widespread in the other European Union countries than in Germany.

A second important institutional feature that serves as another possible stabilizer is the German short-time work allowance program, which was used by 64,000 establishment and 1,500,000 employees in June 2009

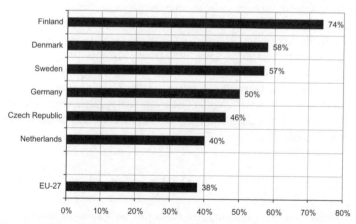

Fig. 2. Percentage of Companies with Working Time Accounts (2009).
Source: European Foundation for the Improvement of Living and Working Conditions (2009b) and own calculations.

(Crimmann, Wießner, & Bellmann, 2010). This very expensive measure was financed by the German federal government. Basically, there are three different types of short-time work (Crimmann et al., 2010). First of all, structural short-time work, which deals with permanent employment losses due to restructuring measures at the establishment level. Secondly, there is the so-called seasonal short-time work, which is mainly used in the construction sector or other outdoor professions. And finally, the most important type within the most current economic crisis, short-time work for economic reasons, if a plant is hit by an economic (demand) shock. Although at the moment the third type is the most important one, being affected by the economic crisis is not a necessary condition for applying short-time work schemes. Our further discussion concentrates on the third type, short-time work for economic reasons.

The basic idea of short-time work is that employers reduce the working time of their employees if they are faced with a strong negative demand shock. Simultaneously, weekly wages are reduced proportionately to the cut in hours worked. Employees are compensated for around 60% of the difference between the net income before and the net income after the working time reduction by the German Federal Employment Agency. Besides the gross earnings for the hours still worked, employers have to pay the full social security contribution for the employees' income before the cut in working time has taken place. The maximum duration of short-time work is 24 months. As some firms pay their employees a compensation for their income loss when applying short-time work, the income effect of this instrument is not always negative. In the current crisis, the program is innovative in the sense that incentives are introduced to combine short-time work with further training. This was done also in order to reach the international standards with respect to further training incidence and intensity. Until now Germany's rank in the respective league is in the midfield (Hoskins, Cartwright, & Schoof, 2010; Behringer, Moraal, & Schönfeld, 2008) although the demographic change will confront Germany with a major challenge.

3. DATA

For our analysis we use information from the IAB Establishment Panel (cf. Fischer, Janik, Müller, & Schmucker, 2009). The basis for its sampling is the establishment file of the Federal Employment Agency in Germany, where all German establishments are recorded, which have at least one employee covered by social security. The IAB Establishment Panel surveys approximately 16,000 establishments on an annual basis. The personal interviews are conducted with high-ranked managers of the firms by TNS Infratest Social Research Munich on behalf of the IAB. The annual questionnaire (2009: 94 questions) covers, for example, information about the development and the structure of the workforce, the business development, and the sum of the earnings. As we study the development of the average wages and the number of the employees on the firm level, we use a balanced panel for the survey years 2008 and 2009. Descriptive statistics for key variables can be found in Table 2. For a detailed definition of all variables used in our empirical investigations, see Table A1 (appendix).

Table 2 notes clear differences with respect to the employment structure and the main characteristics of establishments, which are subject to the global crisis and the others. The typical establishments affected by the crisis as defined in our analysis are larger, more export-oriented, more productive, more often with sectoral and firm-level collective bargaining, more often located in Western Germany, and have more often works councils. The

Table 2.   Descriptive Statistics for the Estimation Sample.

	Not Subject to the Global Crisis		Subject to the Global Crisis	
	2008	2009	2008	2009
ln(N), N: Number of employees	2.985	2.988	3.629	3.575
Ln(w/N), w: Sum of wages at the plant level	7.249	7.257	7.503	7.484
Exporting firm	0.187	0.202	0.390	0.406
Eastern German	0.442		0.409	
Sectoral collective bargaining	0.369	0.361	0.392	0.389
Firm-level collective bargaining	0.063	0.066	0.072	0.078
Works council	0.233	0.233	0.316	0.316
% Qualified	0.669	0.669	0.703	0.702
% Part-time	0.232	0.215	0.143	0.136
Weekly working time	39.387	39.329	39.188	39.113
Working time accounts	0.489		0.626	
Short-time work	0.085		0.323	
Number of observations	4,640		1,955	

Source: IAB Establishment Panel Surveys 2008 and 2009.
Note: Information for working time accounts and short-time work is taken from 2009.

employees of the crisis establishments are better qualified and work less often as part-timers or on a temporary basis. The crisis establishments are more likely to use working time accounts and short-time work, but these instruments are adopted not only by them. Another important issue, as already mentioned, is the fact that the economic crisis is not equally distributed over the industries.

4. MULTIVARIATE ANALYSIS

4.1. Methodology

In the first step of our multivariate analysis, we compare the change in the wages per employee and the number of employees from the first half 2008 to the first half 2009 between firms, which are subject to the global economic crisis and those which are not. This is done by applying a simple difference-in-difference estimator of the following form (Meyer, 1995):

$$\log(Y_{it}) = \beta_0 + \beta_1 C_i + \beta_2 T_{2009} + \beta_3 C_i T_{2009} + x'_{it}\gamma + \varepsilon_{it} \quad t : 2008, 2009 \quad (1)$$

Y_{it} is the outcome variable (average wages and number of employees) in firm i, year t. C_i is a dummy, which is one if the firm is subject to the crisis in 2009. T_{2009} is a time dummy for the year 2009. Furthermore, $C_i T_{2009}$ is an interaction term of the crisis dummy and the time dummy. Therefore, β_3 gives the difference in the development of the outcome variables between crisis plants and noncrisis plants. Finally, x_{it} is a vector of control variables (see Table A1, appendix, for detailed definitions) and ε_{it} is an error term. In our application, the notion difference-in-differences does not mean that we claim to identify the causal effect the crisis had on our two outcomes. We come back to this point when we discuss our results (see Section 4.2). Instead, we use this term in a pure technical manner, that is, it is a double before after estimator, which compares the development of our outcome variables, before and after some event, between two groups. The estimation of Eq. (1) is done by OLS. Standard errors are adjusted using a modified sandwich estimator, which takes into account correlated observations within firms (White, 1980; Rogers, 1993).

Alternatively, we control the potential confounders in x_{it} from Eq. (1) by applying propensity score matching techniques. One advantage of a resulting conditional difference-in-differences matching estimator over the simple difference-in-differences estimator within an OLS framework is that there is no functional assumption between the confounders and the outcome variables needed (Angrist & Pischke, 2009). However, if we restrict our analysis to the common support region, which helps to overcome selectivity problems, the interpretation of the results should also be restricted to this region (Smith & Todd, 2005; Gelman & Hill, 2009). Our basic matching approach is a 1:1 nearest neighbor algorithm with a caliper of 0.01 without replacement. The calculation of the propensity scores is based on the logit estimation reported in the appendix. This gives a suitable balancing quality measured by a mean standardized bias of, for example, 1.479 (Caliendo, 2006).[1]

In this context, it should be stressed furthermore that our results are not sensitive with respect to the matching algorithm we have chosen. This means that if we apply other matching techniques such as radius matching or nearest neighbor matching with more than only one neighbor and so on, the basic pattern of the results does not change. After we have selected a subsample of treatment and control plants through our basic matching approach, we regress the outcome variables again on the crisis dummy, the year dummy, the corresponding interaction term, and an intercept (Gelman & Hill, 2009, p. 206). Again, we are adjusting the standard errors for correlated observations within firms.

4.2. Results

To start with the discussion of the effects the crisis had on the development of the average wages, we consider the difference-in-differences estimates for the unmatched and the matched samples. Table 3 (first and second column) indicate no significant differences in the development of average wages between crisis and noncrisis establishments. One reason for this result may be that crisis firms first of all lay off low-skilled (less-productive) workers. These workers usually earn less than their high-skilled colleges. Therefore, a change in the composition of the pool of workers could entail a negative counteracting effect, which may lead in sum to an insignificant crisis effect on average wages. To find some empirical evidence for this argument, we compared the development of the proportion of qualified workers between 2008 and 2009 in crisis and noncrisis plants within a multivariate framework, that is, we estimated a further difference-in-difference regression similar to Eq. (1) for the proportion of qualified workers (see Table A2, appendix). The results reveal no shifts in the composition of the workforce from low-qualified to qualified workers. However, our proportion of

Table 3. Estimated Effects on the Average Wages and the Number of Employees.

	Dependent Variable			
	ln(Wages/employee)		ln(Number of employees)	
Method	Un-matched	Matched	Un-matched	Matched
Crisis	0.032***	0.037	0.175***	−0.004
Year 2009	−0.007	−0.001	−0.004	−0.003
Crisis* year 2009	−0.014	−0.008	−0.060***	−0.040***
% Qualified	0.644***	–	0.698***	–
% Part-time	−0.771***	–	0.045	–
Weekly working time	0.004	–	−0.007	–
Exporting firm	0.112***	–	0.664***	–
Eastern Germany	−0.243***	–	−0.249***	–
Sectoral collective bargaining	0.076***	–	0.382***	–
Firm-level collective bargaining	0.076***	–	0.452***	–
Works council	0.180***	–	1.880***	–
Nine establishment size dummies	***	–	–	–
39 sector dummies	***	–	***	–
Number of observations	13,190	6,380	13,190	6,380
R^2	0.591	–	0.523	–

Source: IAB Establishment Panel Surveys 2008 and 2009.
***Significant at the 1% level.
**Significant at the 5% level.
*Significant at the 10% level.

qualified workers is a rather vague measure for the composition of the workforce, although the only one available for our analysis. Our measure distinguishes between less qualified and qualified (vocational training or university graduates) only. Shifts within these broadly defined groups are not yet observable, but in future, employer–employee data can be used for additional investigations on this topic.

In contrast to the insignificant difference in the development of average wages, we find a significant difference in the development of the number of employees. Although the number of employees does not change significantly in noncrisis firms, in crisis plants, it decreases by around 6% on the basis of the unmatched sample (see Table 3, third column). The difference in the development of the number of employees between crisis and noncrisis plants based on the matched sample is still significant and negative, the amount however is smaller (−4%, see Table 3, fourth column). The results for the selection equation (logit model) and tests for the matching quality are presented in the appendix (Table A3). One reason for this smaller difference in the development of the number of employees is the higher proportion of manufacturing plants within the matched subsample, the proportion of plants from the production sector is higher. In particular, further regressions on the basis of the unmatched sample without plants from the service sector also show a lower difference of around 4 percent. Note finally that the significant negative fall in employment for the crisis firms does not arise because they were experiencing employment falls before the crisis hit. A comparison of employment changes between 2007 and 2008 reveals that the development in the number of the employees in crisis plants was even slightly better than in noncrisis plants, which is plausible with respect to the definition of our crisis indicator. Therefore, we refrain from a causal interpretation of our results.

To identify probable differences in the effect of the global crisis on the outcome variables between firms with a high and those with a low proportion of qualified workers, we divide our dataset into the quartiles of the proportion of qualified workers in 2008. The findings for the different outcome variables are listed in Tables 4 and 5 respectively.

First, according to Table 4, there is again no evidence that the development of the average wages differs between crisis and noncrisis establishments at all. Secondly, however, we can infer from Table 5 that the development of the number of employees differs not only between crisis and noncrisis establishments (Table 3) but also between those with a high and those with a low proportion of qualified workers. This is based on the unmatched sample the strongest decline (-13.2 percent, see column 1 Table 5) in those crisis firms with the lowest proportion of qualified workers. The same pattern holds on the basis of the matched subsample, but again, also in this case, the effects in general are lower (-6.3 percent, see column 2 Table 5) than those on identified on the basis of the unmatched sample. To see whether the differences between firms with a low and firms with a high proportion of qualified workers are significant, we apply a Hausman–White test (White, 1994) based on the Seemingly-Unrelated Cluster-Adjusted Sandwich Estimator, proposed by Weesie (1999). This procedure finally shows for the unmatched sample that the negative employment effect in plants with a proportion of qualified workers within the 25 percent quartile is significantly stronger than in the firms within the other quartiles. For the matched sample, this basic pattern remains. The only exception is the difference between the plants with the lowest proportion of qualified workers and those for the highest one which is not significant (with a p-value of 0.11).

Table 4. Estimated Effects on the Average Wages by Qualification Quantiles.

Proportion of Qualified	< 25% Quantile		> 25% Quantile < 50% Quantile		> 50% Quantile < 75% Quantile		> 75% Quantile	
			Dependent Variable: ln(Wages)					
Method	Un-matched	Matched	Un-matched	Matched	Un-matched	Matched	Un-matched	Matched
Crisis	0.102***	0.067	0.011	0.037	0.020	0.026	−0.003	0.012
Year 2009	−0.017	−0.012	−0.027***	−0.034	0.006	0.017	0.004	−0.015
Crisis* Year 2009	0.021	0.025	−0.027	−0.002	−0.022	−0.023	−0.025	−0.008
Number of observations	3,456	1,520	3,530	1,800	2,916	1,540	3,288	1,240
R^2	0.491	—	0.512	—	0.503	—	0.499	—

Source: IAB Establishment Panel Surveys 2008 and 2009.
Notes: The proportions of qualified workers are measured at firm level before the crisis. Also included are the same control variables as for the estimations presented in Table 3, with the exception of the proportion of qualified.
***Significant at the 1% level.
**Significant at the 5% level.
*Significant at the 10% level.

Table 5. Estimated Effects on the Number of Employees by Qualification Quantiles.

Proportion of qualified	< 25% Quantile		> 25% Quantile < 50% Quantile		> 50% Quantile < 75% Quantile		> 75% Quantile	
			Dependent Variable: ln(Number of Employees)					
Method	Un-matched	Matched	Un-matched	Matched	Un-matched	Matched	Un-matched	Matched
Crisis	0.361***	−0.037	0.120**	0.075	0.144**	0.134	0.101	0.126
Year 2009	0.016	−0.020	−0.007	−0.005	−0.019**	−0.010	−0.000	0.020
Crisis* Year 2009	−0.132***	−0.062***	−0.048***	−0.020*	−0.031**	−0.033***	−0.042***	−0.037**
Number of observations	3,456	1,520	3,530	1,800	2,916	1,540	3,288	1,240
R^2	0.491	–	0.512	–	0.503	–	0.499	–

Source: IAB Establishment Panel Surveys 2008 and 2009.
Notes: The proportions of qualified workers are measured at firm level before the crisis. Also included are the same control variables as for the estimations presented in Table 3, with the exception of the proportion of qualified.
***Significant at the 1% level.
**Significant at the 5% level.
*Significant at the 10% level.

We now turn to the role of working time accounts or short-time work in moderating the impact of the crisis on the development of the outcome variables. To do so, we firstly estimate the crisis effect in firms with working time accounts and in firms without working time accounts. Afterwards, we compare the estimated effects again by applying a Hausman–White test. For short-time work we follow the same estimation strategy. Tables 6 and 7 summarize the results for the two outcome variables. Again, we find no significant effects with respect to differences in the development of the average wages between crisis plants and noncrisis plants on the basis of the unmatched sample. The estimations based on the matched sample reveal a weak significant negative wage effect of the crisis for plants without working time accounts. In contrast, this effect is insignificant for plants with working time accounts. Moreover, the difference of the crisis effects between establishments with and those without working time accounts is statistically significant (with a p-value of 0.02). This result corroborates the hypothesis of intertemporal smoothed earnings achieved by the adoption of working time accounts (Carstensen, 2000). Thus, our results are compatible with the idea that working time accounts act as an implicit insurance against earnings variation. For firms without short-time work, we do not find significant changes in average wages over time (Table 6, sixth and seventh columns), whereas plants that adopted this instrument show a significant negative development in average wages between 2008 and 2009 irrespective of whether they are subject to the economic crisis or not.

When we look at the development in the number of employees within our unmatched sample, firms with working time accounts seem to suffer from a stronger crisis effect than those without this instrument (see Table 7, first and third columns). First of all, an explanation for this counterintuitive result may be that firms without working time accounts are hit by the economic crisis less seriously, so perhaps we are identifying some kind of selection effect. Second, a Hausman–White test reveals equal crisis effects in firms with and those without working time accounts. On the basis of our matched sample, we find the expected difference between plants with and those without working time accounts (see column 2 and column 4, Table 7), whereby this difference is also not significant at any conventional level. Hence, we can conclude that we only find weak evidence for working time accounts playing a moderating role in employment adjustment to the arising economic crisis between the first half 2008 and the first half 2009 (within the matched sample).

Finally, firms that apply short-time work exhibit no significant crisis effects for the development in the number of employees, whereas firms, which do not

Table 6. Estimated Effects on of the Average Wages by Working time Accounts and Short-Time Work (2009).

	Dependent Variable: ln(Wages)							
	Without Working Time Accounts		With Working Time Accounts		Without Short-Time Workers		With Short-Time Workers	
Method	Un-matched	Matched	Un-matched	Matched	Un-matched	Matched	Un-matched	Matched
Crisis	0.042**	0.054	0.022	0.025	0.035***	0.047*	0.011	0.008
Year 2009	−0.018**	−0.003	0.006	−0.008	−0.004	0.005	−0.039***	−0.047***
Crisis* Year 2009	−0.018	−0.035*	−0.018	0.013	0.006	−0.001	−0.033	−0.020
Number of observations	6,206	2,600	6,984	3,756	11,138	5,172	2,052	1,160
R^2	0.535	—	0.562	—	0.584	—	0.570	—

Source: IAB Establishment Panel Surveys 2008 and 2009.
Note: Also included are the same variables as for the estimations presented in Table 3.
***Significant at the 1% level.
**Significant at the 5% level.
*Significant at the 10% level.

Table 7. Estimated Effects on the Number of Employees by Working Time Accounts and Short-Time Work (2009).

	Dependent Variable: ln(Number of Employees)							
	Without Working Time Accounts		With Working Time Accounts		Without Short-Time Workers		With Short-Time Workers	
Method	Un-matched	Matched	Un-matched	Matched	Un-matched	Matched	Un-matched	Matched
Crisis	0.171***	0.053	0.140***	-0.003	0.117***	0.021	0.109	-0.041
Year 2009	-0.002	0.004	-0.003	-0.010	0.004	0.016	-0.089***	-0.073***
Crisis* year 2009	-0.049***	-0.043***	-0.068***	-0.035***	-0.057***	-0.051***	-0.011	0.001
Number of observations	6,206	2,600	6,984	3,756	11,138	5,172	2,052	1,160
R^2	0.391	–	0.501	–	0.477	–	0.609	–

Source: IAB Establishment Panel Surveys 2008 and 2009.
Note: Also included are the same control variables as for the estimations presented in Table 3.
***Significant at the 1% level.
**Significant at the 5% level.
*Significant at the 10% level.

use this instrument, reveal a significant negative crisis effect. Moreover, a Hausman–White test indicates that this difference is significant. It may be also of interest that short-time work plants show strong time effects, which could be interpreted as a strong selection effect of firms that apply short-time work in comparison to firms without short-time work schemes (for those firms we identify no significant time effect). This holds for the matched as well as for the unmatched sample. Therefore, we can summarize: We only find weak evidence for working time accounts (only in the matched sample) and short-time work playing a moderating role in the employment adjustment within the current crisis. Plants that apply short-time work reduce their employment between the first half 2008 and the first half 2009, irrespective of whether they are subject to the current economic crisis or not. This result makes sense, because firms that are using short-time work are required to demonstrate that they are in a bad economic situation to be subsidized by a short-time work allowance. The identification of a causal effect of working time accounts and short-time work finally is left for further research.

4.3. Robustness Checks

In our analysis, we define crisis plants to exhibit non-negative business expectations in 2008 and negative business expectations in 2009. To check the robustness of our results, we combine this crisis indicator with information regarding the industries, that is, we use the common knowledge that especially firms within industries such as automotive, chemistry, and mechanical engineering are hit by the economic crisis, whereas within the service sector, this holds for a few firms only (Möller, 2010). Therefore, the most straightforward extension to the estimations above is to restrict our analysis to the typical crisis sectors, that is, crisis firms within automotive, chemistry, or mechanical engineering, and the typical noncrisis sectors, that is, noncrisis firms within the service sector (without temporary employment agencies). The results are reported in Table 8.

The estimations again show no significant wage effects and a highly significant employment effect, which is higher than the employment effect identified above (6 percent, see Table 3), whereas the difference is hardly significant (p-value 0.100). Hence, our basic results with respect to a stricter definition of crisis and noncrisis plants that also takes into account industry information are robust. Moreover, we adopt a weaker crisis indicator by dropping the first condition, that is, non-negative business expectations in 2008. The results are reported in Table 9.

Table 8. Estimated Effects on the Development of Average Wages and the Number of Employees, Alternative Crisis Indicator A.

	Dependent Variable	
	ln(Wages/employee)	ln(Number of employees)
Crisis_A	0.544***	0.804***
Year 2009	−0.012	0.036***
Crisis_A* year 2009	−0.007	−0.091***
R^2	0.547	0.548
Number of observations	3,108	3,108

Source: IAB Establishment Panel Surveys 2008 and 2009.
Notes: Crisis plants within crisis industries (i.e., automotive, chemistry or mechanical engineering) and noncrisis plants within noncrisis industries (service sector without temporary employment agencies). Also included are the same control variables as for the estimations presented in Table 3.
***Significant at the 1% level.
**Significant at the 5% level.
*Significant at the 10% level.

Table 9. Estimated Effects on the Development of Average Wages and the Number of Employees, Alternative Crisis Indicator B.

	Dependent Variable	
	ln(Wages/employee)	ln(Number of employees)
Crisis_B	0.034***	0.163***
Year 2009	−0.006	0.007
Crisis_B* year 2009	−0.013	−0.078***
R^2	0.547	0.548
Number of observations	3,108	3,108

Source: IAB Establishment Panel Surveys 2008 and 2009.
Notes: Crisis plants are alternatively defined as those plants with negative business expectations in 2009 irrespective of the business expectations in 2008. Also included are the same control variables as for the estimations presented in Table 3.
***Significant at the 1% level.
**Significant at the 5% level.
*Significant at the 10% level.

Again, we see no significant wage effects and a highly significant slightly higher employment effect than the employment effect identified above (6 percent, Table 3), but the difference is obviously not significant. As we drop the first condition for a plant being categorized as a crisis plant (non-negative business expectations in 2008), we shift bad firms (firms that had already bad business expectations in 2008) from the group of noncrisis plants to the group of crisis plants, and therefore, the employment effects get larger. Finally, we conducted further robustness checks not reported here. They include, for example, definitions for crisis and noncrisis establishments that rely on the information about the industry affiliation only and again exhibit the same basic findings. Therefore, we conclude that our basic results are not sensitive to different (plausible) categorizations for crisis and noncrisis plants.

5. CONCLUSIONS

Despite the "German Job Miracle," our empirical study reveals substantial employment reductions in establishments affected by the global crisis. Falls in employment are strong in establishments affected by the crisis and vary with respect to the proportion of qualified employees in the establishment. In our estimations based on the full sample, firms that are faced with the economic crisis reduce their number of employees from the first half 2008 to the first half 2009 by around 6 percent, whereas there is no employment adjustment in noncrisis firms for the same time. Furthermore, the largest negative employment effects are in plants with relatively low proportions of qualified workers. The same pattern is found on the basis of the matched sample, although differences in employment reductions are smaller. Altogether, our results indicate that although the crisis hit establishments with a relatively high proportion of qualified workers more often, the higher qualified are better off than the lower qualified, because the establishments affected by the crisis tend to hoard their qualified employees.

Finally, we find only weak evidence for working time accounts (only in the matched sample) playing a moderating role in employment adjustment to the current situation and also only weak evidence for effects of short-time work. We find evidence (at least in the matched sample) that the economic crisis is associated with a decline in wages, but only in those establishments that do not operate working time accounts. This result corroborates with the hypothesis that working time accounts tend to smooth earnings.

We have shown, in Germany, the decline in employment has been concentrated in only a minority of firms, and in fact, those firms are concentrated in the high-productivity manufacturing sector. Among those firms affected, firms with a higher proportion of less qualified workers reduced employment by a greater amount. Therefore, an obvious empirical extension to our work will be to examine the effects of job loss on those workers affected. Additional studies are needed to assess the associated permanent income costs. These effects could be mitigated through either generous unemployment benefit systems or strict labor market regulations (cf. Gangl, 2006, for an international perspective). The incidence of rising unemployment on earnings losses and the associated decline in household incomes as well as the effectiveness of the existing income safety net in Germany are investigated by Bargain, Immervoll, Peichl, and Siegloch (2010).

NOTE

1. The mean standardized bias is a common measure for the matching quality. It is calculated by the differences in the relevant variables between the treatment group (crisis plants) and the control group (noncrisis plants), standardized by the corresponding variances. A mean standardized bias, lower than 3–5 (after matching), is seen as sufficient. See Caliendo (2006) for further discussions.

ACKNOWLEDGMENTS

The authors would like to thank two anonymous referees, the editors of this volume, Christian Hohendanner (IAB), Richard Upward (University of Nottingham), Stefan Zagelmeyer (International University of Applied Sciences Bad Honnef-Bonn), the participants of the IZA/OECD Workshop "Economic Crisis, Rising Unemployment and Policy Responses", 8–9 February 2010 in Paris, of the Foundation for International Studies on Social Security (FISS), 16–18 June 2010 in Sigtuna, of the Symposium "The Impact of the Global Financial Crisis on Human Resources Management at the Company Level: International and Comparative Perspectives" at the European Congress of the International Industrial Relations Association (IIRA), 28 June–1 July 2010 in Copenhagen, of the National Meeting of the German Statistical Society, 14–17 September 2010 in Nuremberg and of the

ESPANET Italia Conference, 30 September–2 October 2010 in Naples for very helpful comments and discussions.

REFERENCES

Anger, S. (2007). *The cyclicality of effective wages within employer-employee matches – Evidence from the German panel data.* DIW Discussion Paper 719. Deutsches Institut für Wirtschaftsforschung, Berlin.

Angrist, J. D., & Pischke, J. S. (2009). *Mostly harmless econometrics.* Princeton, NJ: Princeton University Press.

Atkinson, A. B. (2007). The distribution of earnings in OECD countries. *International Labour Review, 146,* 41–60.

Bargain, O., Immervoll, H., Peichl, A., & Siegloch, S. (2010). *Who are the losers of the labour-market downturn? A scenario analysis for Germany.* IZA Discussion Paper 5220. Forschungsinstitut zur Zukunft der Arbeit, Bonn.

Behringer, F., Moraal, D., & Schönfeld, G. (2008). Betriebliche Weiterbildung in Europa: Deutschland weiterhin nur im Mittelfeld. *Bildung in Wissenschaft und Praxis, 37,* 9–14.

Bell, D. N. F., & Blanchflower, D. G. (2009). *What should be done about rising unemployment in the OECD.* IZA Discussion Paper 4455. Forschungsinstitut zur Zukunft der Arbeit, Bonn.

Büttner, T., Jacobebbinghaus, P., & Ludsteck, J. (2010). Occupational upgrading and the business cycle in West Germany. *Economics, 4,* E-Journal.

Caliendo, M. (2006). *Microeconometric evaluation of labour market policies.* Berlin und Heidelberg: Springer.

Carstensen, V. (2000). Arbeitsplatzsicherheit durch Arbeitszeitkonten? In: U. Backes-Gellner, M. Kräkel, B. Schauenberg & G. Steiner (Eds), *Flexibilisierungstendenzen in der betrieblichen Personalpolitik – Anreize Arbeitszeiten und Qualifikation* (pp. 307–332). München und Mering: Rainer Hampp.

Crimmann, A., Wießner, F., & Bellmann, L. (2010). *The German work-sharing scheme an instrument for the crisis. ILO, Conditions of work and employment series.* Discussion Paper 25. International Labour Organisation, Geneva.

Devereux, P. J. (2001). The cyclicality of real wages within employer-employee matches. *Industrial and Labor Relations Review, 54,* 835–850.

Dustmann, C., Ludsteck, J., & Schönberg, U. (2009). Revisiting the German wage structure. *The Quarterly Journal of Economics, 124,* 843–881.

European Foundation for the Improvement of Living and Working Conditions. (2009a). Restructuring in Recession. Dublin.

European Foundation for the Improvement of Living and Working Conditions. (2009b). The European Company Survey – First Findings. Dublin.

Fischer, G., Janik, F., Müller, D., & Schmucker, A. (2009). The IAB establishment panel – Things users should know. Schmollers Jahrbuch. *Journal of Applied Social Science Studies, 129,* 133–148.

Gangl, M. (2006). Scar effects of unemployment. An assessment of institutional complementarities. *American Sociological Review, 71,* 986–1013.

Gelman, A., & Hill, J. (2009). *Data analysis using regression and multilevel/hierarchical models.* Cambridge: Cambridge University Press.

Heckmann, M., Kettner, A., Pausch, S., Szameitat, J., & Vogler-Ludwig, K. (2009). Wie Betriebe in der Krise Beschäftigung stützen. IAB-Kurzbericht 18/2009.

Hoskins, B., Cartwright, F., & Schoof, U. (2010). *Making lifelong learning tangible! European lifelong learning indicators.* Gütersloh: Bertelsmann Stiftung.

Ludsteck, J. (2008). *Wage cyclicality and the wage curve under the microscope.* IAB Discussion Paper 11/2008. Institut für Arbeitsmarkt- und Berufsforschung, Nürnberg.

Meyer, B. D. (1995). Natural and quasi-experiments in economics. *Journal of Business & Economic Statistics, 13,* 151–161.

Möller, J. (2010). The German labor market response in the world recession – de-mystifying a miracle. *Journal for Labour Market Research, 42,* 325–336.

Möller, J., & Walwei, U. (2009). Das deutsche Arbeitsmarktwunder auf dem Prüfstand. *IAB-Forum Spezial,* 4–11.

Rogers, W. H. (1993). Regression standard errors in clustered samples. *Stata Technical Bulletin, 13,* 19–23.

Smith, J. A., & Todd, P. E. (2005). Does matching overcome LaLonde's critique of nonexperimental estimators? *Journal of Econometrics, 125,* 305–353.

Stiglitz, J. (2009). The global crisis, social protection and jobs. *International Labour Review, 148,* 1–14.

Weesie, J. (1999). Seemingly unrelated estimation and the cluster-adjusted estimator. *Stata Technical Bulletin, 52,* 230–257.

White, H. (1980). A heteroskedasticity-consistent covariance matrix estimator and a direct test for heteroskedasticity. *Econometrica, 48,* 817–838.

White, H. (1994). *Estimation, inference and specification analysis.* Cambridge: Cambridge University Press.

APPENDIX

Table A1. Definitions for the Key Variables.

Variable	Definition
$\ln(N)$, N: Number of employees	Logarithm of the number of employees
$\mathrm{Ln}(w/N)$, w: Sum of wages at the plant level	Logarithm of the wages per employee calculated as the total sum of wages divided by the number of employees
Exporting firm	Is the plant exporting at least some of their goods in other countries? Dummy variable $D = 1$, if yes, $D = 0$ otherwise
Eastern German	Is the plant located in Eastern Germany? Dummy variable $D = 1$, if yes, $D = 0$ otherwise
Sectoral collective bargaining	Is the plant subject to a sectoral collective bargaining agreement? Dummy variable $D = 1$, if yes, $D = 0$ otherwise

Table A1. (*Continued*)

Variable	Definition
Firm-level collective bargaining	Is the plant subject to a firm-level collective bargaining contract? Dummy variable $D = 1$, if yes, $D = 0$ otherwise
Works council	Does the plant have a works council? Dummy variable $D = 1$, if yes, $D = 0$ otherwise
% Qualified	Proportion of qualified workers calculated as the number of qualified workers divided by the total number of employees. Qualified workers are defined as vocational training or university graduates
% Part-time	Proportion of part-time workers calculated as the number of part-time workers divided by the total number of employees
Weekly working time	Contracted working time per week
Working time accounts	Does the plant adopt working time accounts? Dummy variable $D = 1$, if yes, $D = 0$ otherwise
Short-time work	Does the plant adopt short-time work? Dummy variable $D = 1$, if yes, $D = 0$ otherwise

Table A2. Estimated Effects on the Proportion of Qualified Workers.

Crisis	0.012*
Year 2009	−0.004
Crisis* year 2009	0.002
% Part-time	−0.172***
Weekly working time	0.000
Exporting firm	0.008
Eastern Germany	0.107***
Sectoral collective bargaining	0.024***
Firm-level collective bargaining	0.023***
Works council	0.065***
Nine establishment size dummies	***
39 sector dummies	***
Number of observations	13,190
R^2	0.235

Source: IAB Establishment Panel Surveys 2008 and 2009.
***Significant at the 1% level.
**Significant at the 5% level.
*Significant at the 10% level.

Table A3.   Results of the Logit Estimation (Dependent Variable: Crisis Dummy) and Mean Comparisons Before and After 1:1 Nearest Neighbour Matching Without Replacement[a].

	Logit Model (Coeff.)	Before Matching			After Matching		
		Mean, Crisis = 0	Mean, Crisis = 1	*p*-Value	Mean, Crisis = 0	Mean, Crisis = 1	*p*-Value
Employment expectations							
• Positive in 2008[b]	0.181**	0.145	0.213	0.000	0.169	0.179	0.427
• Negative in 2008[b]	−0.494***	0.084	0.061	0.002	0.072	0.069	0.730
• Uncertain in 2008[b]	0.184	0.037	0.043	0.208	0.044	0.043	0.931
% Qualified	0.248*	0.669	0.703	0.000	0.700	0.697	0.742
% Part-time	−0.589	0.232	0.143	0.000	0.167	0.162	0.502
Weekly working time	0.001	39.37	39.19	0.001	39.35	39.39	0.606
Exporting firm	0.191**	0.187	0.390	0.000	0.319	0.319	1.000
Eastern Germany	−0.309***	0.441	0.409	0.013	0.426	0.418	0.641
Sectoral bargaining	0.001	0.369	0.392	0.080	0.391	0.381	0.561
Firm-level bargaining	−0.105	0.064	0.072	0.192	0.066	0.069	0.724
Works council	−0.180*	0.234	0.316	0.000	0.277	0.270	0.634
Mean standardized bias (MSB)							1.479
Number of observations	6,586	4,633	1,953	–	1,595	1,595	–

Source: IAB Establishment Panel Survey 2008 and 2009.
Note: Also included are nine establishment size dummies and 39 sector dummies.
***Significant at the 1% level.
**Significant at the 5% level.
*Significant at the 10% level.
[a]The matching for the results in Tables 4–7 was done separately for the different columns. Table 8 reports the matching results for the whole sample (Table 3) only.
[b]In comparison to plants with neutral employment expectations.

THE ECONOMIC CRISIS, PUBLIC SECTOR PAY AND THE INCOME DISTRIBUTION[☆]

Tim Callan, Brian Nolan and John Walsh

ABSTRACT

An important aspect of the impact of the economic crisis is how pay in the public sector responds – in the face not only of the evolution of pay in the private sector but also extreme pressure on public spending (of which pay is a very large proportion) as fiscal deficits soar. What are the effects on the income distribution of cutting public sector pay rates or alternative strategies to reduce the public sector pay bill? This chapter investigates these issues using data and a tax–benefit simulation model for Ireland, a country which faces a particularly severe fiscal crisis and where innovative measures have already been implemented to claw back pay from public sector workers in the guise of a 'pension levy', followed by a significant cut in nominal pay rates. The SWITCH (Simulating Welfare and Income Tax Changes) tax–benefit model first allows the distributional effects of these measures, which achieved a substantial reduction in the net public sector pay bill, to be teased out. The overall impact on the income distribution is assessed. This provides empirical evidence relevant to policy choices in relation to a key aspect of household income over which

[☆]This chapter was originally presented at IZA/OECD Conference, Paris, February 2010.

Who Loses in the Downturn? Economic Crisis, Employment and Income Distribution
Research in Labor Economics, Volume 32, 207–225
ISSN: 0147-9121/doi:10.1108/S0147-9121(2011)0000032010

governments have direct influence, while at the same time illustrating methodologically how a tax–benefit model can serve as the base for such investigation.

Keywords: Earnings; public-private wages; tax/welfare reform; income inequality

JEL Classification: D31; H23; I38; J45

1. INTRODUCTION

The economic crisis is impacting most directly on the numbers employed in the private sector and how much they are paid. However, a critical issue is how pay in the public sector then responds, particularly when there is extreme pressure on public spending as fiscal deficits soar. What are the effects on the income distribution of cutting public sector pay rates or alternative strategies to reduce the public sector pay bill, and how do these vary depending on the evolution of pay in the private sector? This chapter investigates these issues using data and a tax–benefit simulation model for Ireland, a country which faces a particularly severe fiscal crisis and where pay for public sector workers has been reduced by a pension levy, followed by a significant cut in nominal pay rates. The economic crisis will clearly feed through to the distribution of income via a range of direct and indirect channels, with the most obvious 'losers' being the newly unemployed, and in Ireland the bursting of the bubble in house prices also has complex distributional implications. Rather than aiming at a comprehensive analysis of the distributional impact of the crisis, though, here our focus is the impact of policy responses to the crisis, and in particular on a key aspect of immediate policy relevance for countries facing the challenge of reducing large fiscal deficits, namely pay policy towards the public sector.

We begin by describing the exceptionally severe nature of the economic crisis for Ireland, which has led to these dramatic policy measures. We then outline the changes in tax and welfare policy implemented in response and report on their distributional impact using conventional tax–benefit simulation model analysis. We then focus on how the same Irish model, the SWITCH (Simulating Welfare and Income Tax Changes) tax–benefit model,[1] can be used to analyse the distributional effects of the measures aimed at reducing the public sector pay bill. We first discuss the various rationales advanced for cutting public service pay in the context of the crisis, and describe the structured way in which this was done via a 'pensions levy' followed by a graduated set of pay cuts. The overall impact on the income distribution, set against alternative scenarios for pay in the private sector, is assessed. Finally, we discuss the implications for public policy in responding to the crisis.

2. IRELAND'S EXCEPTIONALLY SEVERE ECONOMIC CRISIS

The rate of economic growth and the increase in numbers employed in Ireland during the so-called 'Celtic Tiger' years from 1994 to 2007 were dramatic by any standards. Growth in GNP from 1994 to 2000 was among the highest in the OECD, and while lower from 2001 to 2007, was still substantial; over the whole period it averaged 6% per annum. By 2007, Ireland's GNP per capita was among the highest in the EU. Jobs growth was also remarkable, with the total number in employment rising by 75%, from 1.2 million to 2.1 million. Unemployment declined very rapidly, from 16% in 1994 to 4% by 2000, staying at that level up to 2007. Immigration was very important in allowing growth to continue at a rapid pace, with a wave of return migration by Irish people who had left for Britain and the USA in the 1980s, followed by substantial numbers from other EU countries, an entirely new phenomenon for Ireland. By 2006–2007 net immigration had reached 70,000 per year.

Export growth and foreign direct investment were strong in the earlier part of the boom, but there was an important shift in the drivers of economic growth after about 2000. Exports slowed significantly, with a loss in competitiveness as inflation ran well ahead of the rest of the euro-zone. Domestic sources of demand predominated, the construction sector in particular, with the number of dwelling units being built reaching a peak of almost 90,000 in 2006 – about three times the more usual level. This left the economy highly vulnerable to a slowdown in construction and house-building in particular, in a context where house prices had continued rising very rapidly throughout the period despite the scale of building.

After the onset of the international financial crisis in late 2007, Irish GNP fell by 3% in volume terms in 2008 as the impact of declining global trade and economic activity was compounded by the bursting of the domestic property bubble. The decline in GNP accelerated to 10% in 2009, marking

Ireland out as one of the OECD countries worst hit by the global economic crisis. Unemployment rose rapidly to exceed 12% by end-2009, despite the fact that outward migration resumed with both Irish nationals and a significant proportion of recent immigrants from elsewhere leaving to seek work. Construction activity, having accounted for as much as 14% of employment at its peak, fell away dramatically as house prices collapsed and commercial construction also stalled.

The slump has had a profound impact on the government's fiscal position, not only due to the downturn in economic activity and increase in unemployment but also because of the calamitous effect of the property 'bust' on tax revenue. The tax base had become highly unbalanced during the boom years, with income tax being cut substantially and replaced by revenue from stamp duties and other taxes on property development and sales – revenue that virtually disappeared when the property market ground to a halt. The general government balance went from a position of surplus to a deficit of 7% of GNP in 2008, and in the absence of corrective measures was set to reach 14% or above in 2009. The debt to GDP ratio, having fallen to 25% by 2007, soared: by end-2008 it was 44% and on track to exceed 70% by end-2009.

Against this background, Irish policymakers had to try to bring the public finances under control, while at the same time addressing the severe liquidity and solvency problems facing the banking system – reflecting both the international liquidity 'crunch' and the exceptional exposure of Irish banks to property-based loans whose underlying assets had lost much of their value. The measures announced from late 2008 onwards for implementation in 2009 and 2010 include major changes in the tax and social welfare system, whose distributional effects can be readily analysed via what is now standard tax–benefit simulation modelling as we report in Section 3; they further entail changes in the pay of public servants, which also have significant distributional implications but pose new analytical challenges, as we discuss in the remainder of the chapter.

3. THE DISTRIBUTIONAL IMPACT OF THE TAX AND WELFARE RESPONSE

Changes to taxes and social transfers constituted one of the main planks in the Irish government's response to the economic and fiscal crisis. Tax and welfare changes are announced in the annual Budget statement, and the Irish government did not begin to seriously address the fiscal implications of the crisis until the Budget for 2009, brought forward from the usual December date to October 2008 because of the collapse in tax revenues. The principal component was the introduction of a new income levy to be applied at the rate of 1% to gross income up to €100,100 per annum and 2% to income in excess of that amount, with none of the allowances or reliefs that apply in the standard income tax system, with the only exception being that social welfare payments are not liable. Social welfare rates for pensioners, unemployed etc. were increased by a little over 3%, in a context where price inflation was falling away (and indeed would turn out to be negative in 2009). As we shall see, this combination implied a remarkably strong redistributive effect, with lower deciles gaining and middle and upper ones losing substantially.

As the scale of the collapse in government revenue became apparent, a further set of measures was announced in February 2009 intended to deliver €2 billion in savings in the year. A central element was a new pension-related payment from public sector workers, graduated to take account of different pay levels in the public service, which we discuss in detail in the next section. A special 'emergency' Budget was then announced in April 2009, with substantial further tax increases. The new income levy rates were doubled, to 2% from €15,028 to €75,036, 4% up to €174,980, and a 6% rate to income in excess of that figure. In addition, the long-standing health levy – similarly applying to gross income and separate from the income tax system – also had its rate doubled to 4% (5% over €75,036), and the ceiling below which pay-related social insurance contributions were payable was increased substantially, from €52,000 to €75,036.[2] Savings in social welfare spending were also sought by not having the usual double payment at Christmas, and by halving the universal Early Childcare Supplement payment for children under 6 from 1 May and abolishing it from end-2009. (A replacement scheme is currently being introduced to provide support for a single year of pre-schooling, much less costly to the State.) With the stated aim of incentivising job-seeking, the rate of income support for new claimants aged under 21 was also cut substantially.

The next set of tax and welfare responses to the crisis were contained in the Budget for 2010 presented in December 2009. The two key elements in this Budget related to expenditure, comprising – quite exceptionally in Irish and international experience – significant reductions in nominal rates of social welfare support and public service pay. The cuts in weekly social welfare rates, of the order of 4%, were confined to recipients of working age, with pensioners left untouched. (Unemployment payments for those aged 21–25 were also sharply reduced, following on the cuts for those aged 21 in the previous Budget). In addition, the rates of universal child benefit paid every month were cut by 10%, although those dependent on social welfare received a compensating increase in their weekly payment. There were also substantial cuts in nominal rates of pay to workers in the public sector, to be discussed in detail in the next section. On the taxation side, the main innovation was the introduction of a carbon tax on fossil fuels. There were no important changes to income tax or levies, though the intention to work towards a fundamental re-structuring of direct taxation by 2011 was announced, to comprise just two charges on income: income tax and a new universal social contribution (to replace employee PRSI, the Health Levy and the Income Levy). The universal social contribution will operate with a very wide base and a relatively low rate, while income tax will have a progressive rate structure as at present. (The recommendation of the 2009 Commission on Taxation to introduce a property tax was also accepted in principle, but considerable work was said to be required on the registration of ownership and the valuation of land before it could be implemented.)

The distributional impact of the tax and welfare changes implemented in this series of Budgets can be analysed using the SWITCH tax–benefit simulation model developed and employed in the ESRI (see for example Callan, Keane, & Walsh, 2009a). The aim is to assess the distributional impact of tax and welfare changes against a benchmark which is 'distributionally neutral', rather than against the non-neutral benchmark implicit in the common budgetary practice of measuring changes against a scenario in which tax and welfare parameters are frozen in nominal terms. A budget indexed to wage growth – or in current very unusual circumstances decline – has been shown to approximate a neutral benchmark against which policy changes can be measured (Callan, Coleman, & Walsh, 2006), and this is what we use here. The baseline distribution here is one in which

(a) the impact of the crisis on private sector employment has already been incorporated through reweighting. This takes account of a 12% fall in employment between 2008 and 2010, and unemployment more than doubling over the same period, to a rate close to 14%;
(b) the policy response indexes tax and welfare parameters to the general fall in wages, of about 4%.

We then examine the impact of actual tax and welfare policy changes against this backdrop.

Fig. 1 shows the results of such a distributional analysis for the two Budgets for 2009 and the recent Budget for 2010. The impact on those at lowest incomes differs depending on the unit of analysis, that is whether the

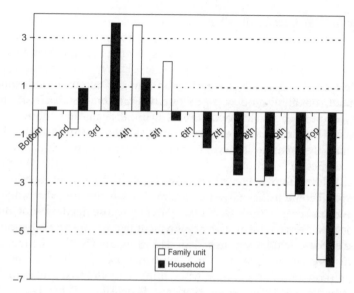

Fig. 1. Distributive Impact of Tax and Welfare Policy 2009–2010, Relative to Indexation in line with 4% Fall in Wages.

family or the broader household is taken to be the income sharing unit. The poorest family units see a drop in income of almost 5%, but the average income of the poorest decile of households does not fall. The main factor behind these results is the sharp reduction in the level of Jobseekers Allowance payable to the young unemployed, aged under 25. Many of these are living with their parents. On a family unit basis, they are assessed as separate units and have incomes placing them at the bottom of the distribution, so the falls of 25% and 50% in their payment rates have a sharp impact. On a household unit basis, incomes of their parents or other family members may place the household higher up the distribution, and the percentage impact of the reduction in unemployment payments is moderated by the presence of other incomes. The second decile saw a much smaller decline on a family unit basis and a 1 per cent rise on a household basis. On either family or household unit basis, there are gains of about 3% for deciles 3 and 4 – which includes substantial numbers of those on State pensions, which were maintained in nominal terms.

For the upper half of the distribution, results on a family unit and household basis are much closer. There have been substantial falls for the top end of the income distribution (about 6% for both households and family units) and for deciles 8 and 9 (losses of about 3%). These losses arise mainly from the income taxes and levies imposed in the Supplementary Budget of April 2009.

Table 1 gives a different perspective on how the burden of adjustment is distributed, distinguishing between family units on the basis of income source (employed, unemployed, retired, other), marital status (single, couples with one or two earners) and family status (with/without children). Once again the baseline scenario is policy adjusted in line with a 4% fall in average earnings.

Those with employment income lose between 2.5% and 3.5% of their disposable income if they have no children, and between 4.5% and 5.5% if they have children. Employed lone parents whose income would often combine a welfare payment with employment income are an exception, with average incomes falling by less than 1% compared with baseline of 4% negative indexation. The tax and levy increases are the main factors affecting those without children, while those with children are, in addition, affected by the 10% cut in universal child benefits.

Families depending mainly on social welfare incomes fared significantly better. This reflects the fact that welfare benefits were initially raised, and then cut, leaving them on balance close to their initial levels – as against a baseline of a 4% cut, in line with wage developments. For example, couples

Table 1.   Impact of Tax and Welfare Changes across Family Types.

Family Unit Type	Percentage Change in Disposable Income
Single employed without children	−2.5
Employed lone parent	−0.7
Single earner couple without children	−2.3
Single earner couple with children	−4.6
Dual earner couple without children	−3.5
Dual earner couple with children	−5.5
Single unemployed without children	−6.3
Non-earning lone parent	1.1
Unemployed couple without children	2.6
Unemployed couple with children	2.5
Single retired tax unit	5.3
Retired couple	3.3
All other tax units	0.8
All	−2.5

with an unemployed person, and no employee, have income changes about 2.5% above the baseline level. Retired couples have 3% above the benchmark provided by negative indexation, while single retired persons fare even better, with income changes at 5% above the benchmark. This reflects the fact that old-age benefits were raised by just over 3%, and not cut subsequently. Also, occupational pension incomes – in the public sector and elsewhere – typically did not fall.

4. THE FOCUS ON PUBLIC SECTOR PAY

As difficult decisions with respect to taxation and welfare were being made, the issue of public sector pay came centre-stage in the Irish public policy debate. At least four distinct strands of argument can usefully be distinguished in what became an exceptionally contentious debate that, as we shall see, culminated in an outcome that is unique for Ireland and quite exceptional across OECD countries: the implementation of substantial reductions in pay rates for public servants.

The first line of argument starts with the role of pay more generally in competitiveness, overall economic performance and growth. As already noted, concern about the competitiveness of Irish exports being eroded by relatively rapid wage and price increases had emerged well before the crisis hit. With domestic drivers of growth having collapsed and unemployment rising rapidly, the need to restore competitiveness came to the fore. As a member of the euro-zone devaluation is not an option, so squeezing down costs in general and pay costs in particular is a central plank in the government's macroeconomic strategy. Despite widespread reports of pay cuts in the private sector, there is considerable uncertainty about how deep and pervasive these have actually been. Depending on how one interprets the evidence in that respect, the competitiveness argument is then either (a) reductions in public sector pay should follow those in the private sector, both from an equity perspective and to reduce the costs to business associated with financing the public sector; or (b) private sector pay needs to fall more, but policymakers have few levers allowing them to directly influence it, so public pay cuts provide one way to lead private sector wages down via a demonstration effect and thus reduce wage costs for producers.[3]

A related argument is that public service pay has to be paid for by taxation, which raises the domestic cost base and cuts output and employment. In particular, taxes on labour tend to be passed on to employers (because of the elasticity of labour supply). This is the classic 'crowding out' of the private sector by the public sector argument,[4] which needs to be nuanced by consideration of the benefits that may flow from public expenditure (including capital spending), and has more relevance in some macroeconomic contexts than others.

The more specific argument currently advanced in the Irish case is that public sector pay had already got out of line with that in the private sector during the boom, due to the combination of the national pay agreements negotiated under the Ireland's Social Partnership process (in operation since 1987), together with special 'Benchmarking' and associated awards to public servants on the basis that their pay had lagged behind their private sector counterparts. The key *Public Service Benchmarking Body Report* (2002) provided no evidence that this was the case, and academic studies suggested that public sector workers enjoyed a wage premium at that time (Boyle, McElligott, & O'Leary, 2004). More recently, studies by Kelly, McGuinness, and O'Connell (2009a, 2009b) have been particularly influential in suggesting that the public sector premium for all employees rose sharply from 2003 to 2006, by 12 percentage points on average.[5] The Irish public sector premia are high compared with those estimated for other countries, as presented in for example Gregory and Borland (1999), Lucifora and Meurs (2006), and Bargain and Melly (2008). There has been some argument over the data and methodology employed,[6] and a heated public debate, but the notion that pay in the public sector was 'out of line' – particularly in the light of the generous pension arrangements they generally enjoyed at a time when private sector occupational pensions were under severe pressure due to the falls in asset values – was clearly an important part of the context in which the policy response to the fiscal crisis unfolded.

Quantile regression indicated that this premium was greatest for public sector employees at the lower end of the earnings distribution and also varied widely across sub-sectors and occupations – being lowest in the central Civil Service and local authorities and highest in education and for police and prison officers. International results find a gradient from highest premia at low earnings to small premia or discounts at the highest skill levels. Lucifora and Meurs (2006) state that 'In all countries the public sector is found to pay more to low skilled workers with respect to the private sector, whilst the reverse is true for high skilled workers'. The results of Kelly et al. (2009b) suggest that at the top of the distribution there was a small discount in 2003 but by 2006 this may have been eliminated or replaced with a small premium. However, the focus of the pay adjustment mechanisms on higher earnings would have altered this situation substantially, as we shall see.

A third, and in some sense the most straightforward, argument arises simply from that crisis. With wages and salaries one of the most important elements in public expenditure, it has been argued that the scale of the deterioration in the public finances left the government with no choice about reducing the public sector wage bill. If that is accepted – and even the trade unions ended up reluctantly doing so – then the next stage in the argument is that it would be preferable to achieve those reductions through cuts in pay rates rather than reductions in numbers, which would add to unemployment that was already rising sharply, as we saw earlier.

Finally, there is an argument that the value of guarantees of job security in the public sector increased as unemployment became a major threat to those in private sector employment. Public sector workers have faced cuts in their wages greater than those in the private sector, but private sector workers have, in addition, seen their risk of unemployment rise as numbers out of work have soared. Does this provide (another) valid justification in itself for reducing public sector wages – in other words, that it is a price public sector workers should be happy to pay for their job security? The first point to be made in this regard is that by no means all public sector workers do in fact have such security. A significant proportion would be on fixed term or temporary contracts, with the possibility – indeed likelihood – of non-renewal. Furthermore, outside the central administration (which constitutes a relatively small proportion of the overall public service) redundancies do occur. Even within the core civil service, various schemes aimed at reductions in staff complements lead to significant numbers of departures through early retirement etc., which while voluntary in nature may on occasion be 'encouraged' in various ways. On the other side of the equation, many private sector workers in fact face little real risk of losing their job, for example in protected sectors of the economy. So a contrast between a totally secure public sector and a totally exposed private one would be misleading.

In a broader context, it is to be expected that potential employees, in making career choices, take the perceived exposure to unemployment and its effect on lifetime earnings into account. The notion that the scale and expected duration of wage loss due to unemployment is a significant element in the compensating differentials paid to workers in different industries is a long-standing one. Hammermesh and Wolfe (1990), for example, used longitudinal data from the US Panel Study on Income Dynamics and brought out that it is the duration of unemployment – rather than just its incidence – that contributes to the compensating differentials across industrial sectors with varying exposure to substantial unemployment experience. Evidence from job-satisfaction questions for a range of countries shows that public sector jobs are indeed perceived as more secure and more insulated from labour market fluctuations (see for example Clark & Postel-Vinay, 2009). There is also evidence that more risk-averse individuals are indeed more likely to self-select into public sector employment, particularly those who are relatively averse more specifically to unemployment (see for example Pfeifer, 2011). This should clearly affect the market-clearing differential between public and private sector wages, although it will be only one of a variety of factors doing so.

While most of the extensive literature on the public–private sector wage premium has been cross-sectional in nature, there have been studies directly focusing on this long-term perspective and seeking to incorporate actual experience of job loss risks and unemployment. Postel-Vinay and Turon (2007), for example, use longitudinal data from the British Household Panel Survey to model income and employment dynamics and estimate lifetime values for jobs. Comparing these values for public and private sectors they find a positive public sector premium, which applies mostly to lower-employability workers.

Here our focus is on the distributional impact of reducing public sector pay in a context where private sector wages have been falling, rather than on the factors contributing to the pre-existing differential between public and private sector pay which recent studies suggest may have been particularly large in Ireland. The fact that, in addition to substantial wage falls on average, a significant number of private sector workers lost their jobs is certainly a central feature of the overall distributional impact of the economic crisis. Here, however, we are concerned specifically with the distributional impact of the reductions in public service pay; the extent to which greater job security in the public sector can be seen as 'justifying' those wage cuts depends on the extent to which that greater job security was already built into public sector wages, which is extremely difficult to assess. In any case, during Ireland's economic boom the argument that public sector wages should rise as private sector earnings soared was effectively employed: this made it difficult to resist the implication that when private sector wages fell those in the public sector should follow them down.

Some combination of these arguments led to two measures which had the effect of substantially reducing the take-home pay of public sector workers alone. The first was the introduction of a public sector pension levy[7] in March 2009, announced together with the fact that public sector pay rises due to be paid would not go ahead. Under the terms of the *Financial Emergency Measures in the Public Interest Bill 2009*, as amended in the April

2009 Budget, the first €15,000 of earnings was exempt from the levy, which was then charged at rates of:

- 5% on next €5,000 of earnings,
- 10% on earnings between €20,000 and €60,000 and
- 10.5% on earnings above €60,000.

The second measure directed at public sector workers, contained in the December 2009 Budget for 2010, announced that public service salaries would be reduced as follows:-

- 5% on the first €30,000 of salary,
- 7.5% on the next €40,000 of salary and
- 10% on the next €55,000 of salary.

This explicit pay cut produced overall reductions in salaries ranging from 5% to just under 8% in the case of salaries up to €125,000. Salaries above that level were adjusted in line with the recommendations of the Review Body on Higher Remuneration in the Public Sector, leading to reductions ranging from 8% on salaries of up to €165,000, 12% on salaries up to €200,000, 15% on salaries of €200,000 or more and 20% in the case of the Taoiseach/Prime Minister. These measures were expected to lead to annual savings of over €1 billion. Importantly, those retired from public sector employment and in receipt of pensions linked to current pay in the grade from which they retired – standard practice in the Irish public service – were not to see their pensions cut in line with that pay.

5. DISTRIBUTIONAL IMPACT OF PUBLIC SECTOR PAY CUTS

Both the public sector pension levy introduced in February 2009 and the pay cuts introduced in Budget 2010 were explicitly structured so as to have least impact at low pay levels and greatest impact at high pay levels. A flat percentage change in gross income would have had greatest impact on the net incomes of those with incomes too low to pay tax, a lesser impact on those paying some tax and a rising proportionate impact as incomes rose (Callan, Keane, & Walsh, 2009b). This arises essentially because of the progressive nature of the income tax system – it takes a higher proportion of income as income increases, so that when incomes are reduced, the net impact on take-home pay is not equal but shaped by the marginal rate structure. Looking at different parts of the overall income distribution, then, the impact of the pay cuts will be greatest in those parts where the reduction in the take-home pay for public sector employees is largest, and the proportion of households in the decile containing a public sector employee is greatest.

In Fig. 2 we look at the impact of these measures (pension levy and pay cuts) on net disposable incomes. We show there the proportionate impact on the total disposable income of all the households in a particular decile, and later will consider the impact on those affected only (i.e. households in the decile containing a public sector worker). We identify first of all the net impact of the pay cuts/pension levy against a 'no change' or frozen wage scenario. This is similar to the approach of Bozio and Johnson (2010) who analyse the impact on the household income distribution of a 5% flat rate pay cut in the UK public sector. One key difference is that the Irish policy measure involves a progressively structured pay cut, rather than a simple flat rate; another is that the size of the cut in pay is much greater. Our calculations, using the SWITCH tax–benefit model, indicate that in order to obtain an equivalent cost saving, a flat rate cut in pay of close to 13% would have been required. This gives a useful summary indication of the scale of the adjustment in public sector pay, for comparison with the 4% fall in private sector pay over the same period.

As there are few public sector employees in the bottom four deciles of family unit income, we aggregate over these and find that the net impact on these deciles is close to zero. The proportionate fall in disposable income

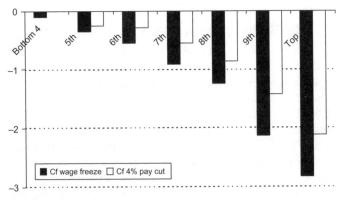

Fig. 2. Distributional Impact of Actual Public Sector Pay Cuts Relative to a Flat-Rate 4% Pay Cut.

rises gradually to about 1% for the eighth decile, 2% for the ninth decile and 3% for the top decile. (The 5% pay cut examined by Bozio and Johnson had a similar progressive pattern, but the maximum impact was a little over 1%, for the ninth decile.) Compared to a baseline with a 4% pay cut – approximating the estimated fall in the private sector – a similar pattern applies, but with the fall reaching 1.5% at the ninth decile and just over 2% for the top decile.

Above, we were interested in the impact of the changes on average decile income. It is also of interest to know the extent of the impact on those affected, classified by decile. We undertake this analysis against the counterfactual of a 4% cut in pay rates, in the public sector as well as the private sector. Analysis on this basis shows losses of 1–2.5% for the small number of family units containing a public sector worker and having disposable incomes in the lowest four deciles. Losses range from 2.5% to 4% for family units containing one or more affected workers in deciles 5–9, and to over 5.5% for those in the 10th decile. Recall, these losses come *on top of* the loss from a 4% flat rate cut in pay.

Three main factors contribute to the strongly progressive impact of the public sector pay cuts, over and above the fact that pay is itself a key driver of the income distribution:

1. The skill mix of the public sector means that public sector workers tend to have higher pay than private sector workers on average.
2. Growth in the public sector premium reinforces this tendency, so that public sector workers are more likely to be found in highly paid employment.
3. The pension levy and pay cut have each been structured in a way designed to give a progressive impact.

Work on the public sector premium has found that it tends to be greatest at low incomes, and least at high incomes (Kelly et al., 2009b; Lucifora & Meurs, 2006). The structure of pay cuts as implemented may help to reduce the premium at low pay, but could result in a negative premium at higher earnings levels. Even if in 2008 there were a public sector premium of, say, 10% at the 90th percentile of public sector earnings, it is clear that the highly progressively structured levy and pay cuts would have more than eliminated this by now, and probably reversed it into a 10% discount. This suggests that there are limits to the scope for further pay cuts structured along the lines of those already implemented.

6. CONCLUSIONS AND IMPLICATIONS

Cutting public service pay represent an instrument open to governments as they respond to the economic crisis, albeit one that would only be potentially feasible in such extreme circumstances. In addition to the fiscal and macroeconomic effects, the assessment of such a policy vis-a-vis alternatives should take distributional implications into account. The analysis of the distributional pattern associated with recent significant cuts in public service pay in Ireland provides empirical evidence relevant to policy choices in relation to a key aspect of household income over which governments have direct influence, while at the same time illustrates methodologically how a tax–benefit model can serve as the base for such investigation.

Given that public employees are predominantly located in the middle and upper parts of the income distribution, cutting their pay will generally have the immediate effect of reducing inequality. This might make it appear an attractive policy from a purely distributional perspective – certainly compared with welfare cuts. However, it is clearly important in the medium to longer term that pay rates in the public sector are of a sufficient level to attract and retain individuals with the qualifications and skills required to deliver good-quality public services. Furthermore, both the way in which pay cuts are structured – flat-rate or graduated – and the counterfactual against which they are assessed will be key to the conclusions reached about distributional impact.

In conclusion, it may be worth highlighting the distributional implications of the way in which pensions for public sector workers are treated if pay for current workers is constrained or reduced. Pensions of public sector retirees grew in line with the pay of public servants during Ireland's boom years. The latter part of that boom has proved unsustainable, and incomes of workers and social welfare recipients are adjusting to the changed circumstances. As 'pay parity' operated to the benefit of retirees in the boom times, one could argue that it should operate in a symmetrical fashion as the pay of those in public sector employment is reduced.

ACKNOWLEDGMENTS

This chapter was originally presented at the IZA/OECD Conference in Paris in February 2010, and comments from participants were very valuable.

Funding from the Irish Research Council for Humanity and Social Science is gratefully acknowledged.

NOTES

1. A description of the SWITCH model, focusing on the key features for the current analyses, is given in the appendix.
2. Other tax changes included ending mortgage interest relief for mortgages over 7 years, increasing the rates of capital gains and capital acquisitions tax from 22% to 25% and introducing a new levy on life assurance at the rate of 1% on premiums.
3. See for example the discussion in Bergin, Conefrey, FitzGerald, and Kearney (2009).
4. See for example FitzGerald et al. (2008), Chapter 2, and FitzGerald (2002).
5. Kelly et al. (2009a) show the premium increasing from 10% to 22%, while Kelly et al. (2009b) present estimates of 14% and 26% – both employ the same data but differ in the definition of what constitutes public sector and in the details of the analytical methods/specifications employed.
6. These focused in particular on the appropriateness of including controls for organizational size and trade union membership (see for example Central Statistics Office, 2009).
7. The formal name for the levy is the 'Pension-related Deduction' (PRD), but it is much more widely referred to as the public service pension levy.

REFERENCES

Bargain, O., & Melly, B. (2008), *Public sector pay gap in France: New evidence using panel data*, Discussion Paper no. 3427. Institute for Labour Economics (IZA), Bonn.

Bergin, A., Conefrey, T., FitzGerald, J., & Kearney, I. (2009) *The behaviour of the Irish economy: Insights from the HERMES macro-economic model*. ESRI Working Paper 287. Economic and Social Research Institute, Dublin.

Boyle, G. R., McElligott, R., & O'Leary, J. (2004). Public-private wage differentials in Ireland, 1994–2001. *ESRI Quarterly Economic Commentary*, Special Article, Summer. Economic and Social Research Institute, Dublin.

Bozio, A., & Johnson, P. (2010). Public sector pay and pensions. In: R. Chote, C. Emmerson & J. Shaw (Eds), *The IFS green budget*. London: Institute for Fiscal Studies.

Callan, T., Coleman, K., & Walsh, J. R. (2006). Assessing the impact of tax/transfer policy changes on poverty: Methodological issues and some European evidence. *Research in Labor Economics, 25*, 125–139.

Callan, T., Keane, C., & Walsh, J. R. (2009a). *Pension policy: New evidence on key issues*. Policy Research Series no. 14. The Economic and Social Research Institute, Dublin.

Callan, T., Keane, C., & Walsh, J. R. (2009b). Tax reform: Selected issues. In: T. Callan (Ed.), *Budget perspectives 2010*. Dublin: The Economic and Social Research Institute.

Central Statistics Office. (2009). *National employment survey 2007: Supplementary analysis*. Dublin: Stationery Office.

Clark, A., & Postel-Vinay, F. (2009). Job security and job protection. *Oxford Economic Papers*, *61*(2), 207–239.

Fitz Gerald, J. (2002). *The macro-economic implications of changes in public service pay rates*. Policy Discussion Forum. Quarterly Economic Commentary, Winter. The Economic and Social Research Institute, Dublin.

Fitz Gerald, J., Bergin, A., Conefrey, T., Diffney, S., Duffy, D., Kearney, I., Lyons, S., Malaguzzi Valeri, L., Mayor, K., & Tol, R. (2008). *Medium-term review 2008–2015, No. 11*. Dublin: The Economic and Social Research Institute.

Gregory, R. G., & Borland, J. (1999). Recent developments in public sector labor markets. In: O. Ashenfelter & D. Card (Eds), *Handbook of labor economics* (1st ed., Vol. 3, pp. 3573–3630). Amsterdam: Elsevier(chapter 53).

Hammermesh, D., & Wolfe, J. (1990). Compensating wage differentials and the duration of wage loss. *Journal of Labor Economics*, *8*(1, Part 2), S175–S197.

Kelly, E., McGuinness, S., & O'Connell, P. J. (2009a). Benchmarking, social partnership and higher remuneration: Wage settling institutions and the public–private sector wage gap in Ireland. *Economic and Social Review*, *40*(3), 339–370.

Kelly, E., McGuinness, S., & O'Connell, P. J. (2009b). *The public–private sector pay gap in Ireland: What lies Beneath?* Working Paper 321, The Economic and Social Research Institute (ESRI), Dublin.

Lucifora, C., & Meurs, D. (2006). The public sector pay gap in France, Great Britain and Italy. *Review of Income and Wealth*, *52*(1), 43–59.

Pfeifer, F. (2011). Risk aversion and sorting into public sector employment. *German Economic Review*, *12*(1), 85–99.

Postel-Vinay, F., & Turon, H. (2007). The public pay gap in Britain: Small differences that (don't) matter? *The Economic Journal*, *117*, 1460–1503.

APPENDIX. SWITCH, THE ESRI TAX–BENEFIT MODEL

SWITCH (Simulating Welfare and Income Tax Changes) is the static tax–benefit model used in this chapter to explore the distributional impact of recent tax and welfare policy changes, and also the impact of changes in public sector pay and pension-related deductions. The model has been widely used in distributional analyses of annual budgets and of particular policy proposals (e.g. changes to the tax treatment of pension contributions and the introduction of a property tax with income-related rebates).

The basic data for the version of the model used here comes from the 2005 Survey on Income and Living Conditions, conducted by the Central Statistics Office. The Survey gathered detailed information on 6,085 households containing 15,539 individuals. The weighting scheme used in that survey (which forms part of the wider EU SILC) is based on demographic variables. Cross-checks indicate a good representation of the population in receipt of social security and social welfare benefits and the information on welfare receipt is drawn for the most part from official registers, as respondents have opted to volunteer their registration numbers in order to supply this information. For tax–benefit modelling purposes, the initial weights are recalibrated to ensure a good representation of the income tax base, using information published by the Revenue authorities. Incomes are up-rated using separate factors for employment and self-employment income, in line with the forecasts underlying the Revenue budgetary model.

For social insurance schemes, the information gathered does not include details of contribution records, so receipt is taken as indicating entitlement, and the amounts payable are modelled using rules on payment rates and conditions governing additions in respect of dependants. For means-tested schemes, the conditions governing eligibility as well as payment rates are modelled.

On the income tax side, the model deals with the basic structure of the system (personal tax credits, the employee tax credit, tax rates and bands, the extent of transferability of bands between husband and wife etc.) and also includes simulation of the major income tax reliefs – reliefs on employer and employee pension contributions, and mortgage interest relief. Social insurance contributions and levies are also modelled. The new 'Pension-related deduction' has also been modelled.

For this chapter, the model has been extended to allow analysis of changes to public sector pay. The 2010 Budget introduced cuts in pay which vary by income level, as described above in the text, and routines implementing these cuts have been incorporated in the model.

AUTOMATIC STABILIZERS, ECONOMIC CRISIS AND INCOME DISTRIBUTION IN EUROPE

Mathias Dolls, Clemens Fuest and Andreas Peichl

ABSTRACT

This chapter investigates to what extent the tax and transfer systems in Europe protect households at different income levels against losses in current income caused by economic downturns like the present financial crisis. We use a multi-country microsimulation model to analyse how shocks on market income and employment are mitigated by taxes and transfers. We find that the aggregate redistributive effect of the tax and transfer systems increases in response to the shocks. But the extent to which households are protected differs across income levels and countries. In particular, there is little stabilization of disposable income for low-income groups in Eastern and Southern European countries.

Keywords: Automatic stabilization; crisis; inequality; redistribution

JEL Classifications: E32; E63; H2; H3

Who Loses in the Downturn? Economic Crisis, Employment and Income Distribution
Research in Labor Economics, Volume 32, 227–255
Copyright © 2011 by Emerald Group Publishing Limited
All rights of reproduction in any form reserved
ISSN: 0147-9121/doi:10.1108/S0147-9121(2011)0000032011

1. INTRODUCTION

Throughout Europe, the current economic and financial crisis has had a severe impact on incomes and employment. While the magnitude of the shocks is usually measured at the macro level, the resulting welfare effects depend not only on the total size of losses but also on their distribution across different groups of society and the cushioning effect of the tax–benefit system. This chapter investigates to what extent the tax and transfer system protects households at different income levels and in different European countries against income losses and unemployment.[1] As micro-data for an ex-post distributional analysis of the current crisis will only become available after a considerable time lag, it is interesting to explore the effects of stylized shocks on the income distribution ex-ante in order to assess the likely distribution of changes in market income and how they translate to changes in disposable income. While this is not a forecasting exercise, our approach does help to understand potential distributional implications of the current economic crisis.

What can we learn from past recessions in terms of distributional consequences? Heathcote et al. (2010) refer to the period from 1967 to 2006 and show for the United States that low-income households suffer the largest earnings declines in recessions. Households from top percentiles are much less affected which in turn leads to an increase in earnings equality. However, inequality in disposable income rises less than earnings inequality since government transfers, which constitute a large part of disposable income for households at the bottom of the earnings distribution, partly offset income losses. The cushioning role of the government in mitigating increases in earnings inequality can be substantial as is shown by Domeij and Floden (2010) for Sweden, a country with a larger government compared to the United States. In Sweden's severe 1992 recession, earnings inequality increased dramatically, whereas inequality in disposable income almost remained at its before-crisis level.

Given the experience from past recessions, the question is whether the current economic crisis will have similar distributional consequences. Heathcote et al. (2010), who use the latest US data, show that inequality in disposable income went up slightly in 2008. However, data for 2009 are not available yet, so it is too early for an overall ex-post evaluation of the current crisis. Other simulation studies provide a range of scenarios to assess likely distributional effects. Bargain, Immvervoll, Peichl, and Siegloch (2010) use matched employer–employee data to estimate labour demand in Germany and predict employment effects in response to output shocks. They find that low-skilled and part-time/irregular workers face higher risks of employment cuts. In some sectors, but not on average, the same is true for younger and older workers. Callan, Nolan, and Walsh (2011) analyse the distributional impact of recent public sector pay cuts in Ireland and conclude that they have an immediate inequality reducing effect, though further conclusions depend on the specific implementation.

It is the purpose of this chapter to analyse the effects of macro shocks on the income distribution and the role of the tax–benefit system to cushion these impacts. We focus on 19 European countries for which a European multi-country microsimulation model is available (EUROMOD). We run two controlled experiments of macro shocks to income and employment in a common microeconometric framework. The first shock is a proportional decline in household gross income by 5% (income shock, IS). This is the usual way of modelling shocks in simulation studies analyzing automatic stabilizers (Auerbach & Feenberg, 2000; Mabbett & Schelkle, 2007; Dolls et al., 2010). But economic downturns typically affect households asymmetrically, with some households losing their jobs and suffering a sharp decline in income and other households being much less affected, as wages are usually rigid in the short term. We therefore consider a second macro shock where the unemployment rate increases such that total household income decreases by 5% (unemployment shock).

It is important to note that all income sources from market activity (labour, business, capital, property and other income) are reduced by the same proportion. In principle, it would be possible to design scenarios which take into account the observed change in different income sources in the different countries to construct country-specific scenarios. However, as we do not aim at conducting an ex-post analysis of the actual development during the recent crisis but rather want to analyse stylized scenarios which are comparable across countries, we refrain from simulating country-specific scenarios. How would results change if the different income sources were affected asymmetrically? In the hypothetical case that, e.g. capital income, went down substantially, whereas one other income source, say labor income, did not change at all while the total income loss were equal to the scenario with a proportional reduction of all income sources by 5%, stabilization results would differ depending on the tax rates levied on capital and labor income. If capital income were taxed with a lower rate than labour income, automatic stabilization would be lower in this case. Furthermore, as capital incomes are concentrated more on the top of the income distribution, a decrease in capital incomes would, ceteris paribus, reduce income inequality.

For both scenarios, we compute measures of inequality, poverty and richness to assess the distributional impact of the macro shocks. This analysis enables us to explore diverse effects of the shock scenarios. Furthermore, we identify how much weight existing pre-crisis tax–benefit systems put on different income groups to protect them from income losses. In the next step, we compare the effects across countries in order to evaluate the cushioning effect of different welfare state regimes and to cluster the countries according to their stabilizing effect on the income distribution.

We find that the proportional IS leads to a reduction in inequality, whereas distributional implications of the asymmetric unemployment shock crucially depend on which income groups are affected by rising unemployment. Both shocks increase the headcount ratio for poverty and decrease the counterpart for richness. Turning next to subgroup decompositions, we conclude that European tax–benefit systems place unequal weights on the extent how different income groups are protected. In case of the unemployment shock, some Eastern and Southern European countries provide little income stabilization for low-income groups whereas the opposite is true for the majority of Nordic and continental European countries. With respect to the relationship between income stabilization and redistribution, we find that tax–benefit systems with high built-in automatic stabilizers are also those which are more effective in mitigating existing inequalities in market income.

The chapter is structured as follows. Section 2 describes the microsimulation model EUROMOD and the different shock scenarios we consider. In Section 3, we provide an institutional overview of tax and transfer systems in Europe and briefly show empirical evidence on pre- and post-tax inequality in European countries as was the case before the start of the current economic crisis. Section 4 presents the results of the distributional analysis and Section 5 concludes.

2. DATA AND METHODOLOGY

2.1. Microsimulation Using EUROMOD

We use microsimulation techniques to simulate taxes, benefits and disposable income under different scenarios for a representative micro-data sample of households. Simulation analysis allows conducting a controlled experiment by changing the parameters of interest while holding everything else constant (cf., Bourguignon & Spadaro, 2006). We therefore do not have to deal with endogeneity problems when identifying the effects of the policy reform under consideration.

Simulations are carried out using EUROMOD, a static tax–benefit model for 19 European Union (EU) countries,[2] which was designed for comparative analysis. EUROMOD is characterized by greater flexibility than typical national models, to accommodate a range of different tax–benefit systems. For instance, the model can easily handle different units of assessment, income definitions for tax bases and benefit means-tests, the order and structure of instruments. Overall, a common framework allows the comparison of countries in a consistent way. For further information on EUROMOD see Sutherland (2001, 2007).[3]

EUROMOD can simulate most direct taxes and benefits except those based on previous contributions as this information is usually not available from the cross-sectional survey data used as input datasets. Information on these instruments is taken directly from the original data sources. The model assumes full benefit take-up and tax compliance, focusing on the intended effects of tax–benefit systems. The main stages of the simulations are the following. First, a micro-data sample and tax–benefit rules for a given country are read into the model. Then for each tax and benefit instrument, the model constructs corresponding assessment units, ascertains which are eligible for that instrument and determines the amount of benefit or tax liability for each member of the unit based on the observed characteristics taken from the data. Finally, after all taxes and benefits in question are simulated, disposable income is calculated.

EUROMOD has been applied to analyse various questions of tax–benefit reforms and redistribution. In our analysis, we use EUROMOD to simulate the disposable incomes for the baseline as well as two different macro shock scenarios which are described in the next section. We then compare the changes in market and disposable incomes in order to construct our measure of automatic stabilization. Similar exercises have been conducted using EUROMOD before. Immvervoll, Levy, Lietz, Mantovani, and Sutherland (2006) analyse changes in poverty rates after changes in the income distribution or the employment rate for the EU-15 countries in 1998. Mabbett and Schelkle (2007) use the results from the income increase scenario in order to assess the extent of automatic stabilization in these countries. Recently, Figari, Salvatori, and Sutherland (2011) use EURO-MOD to "stress-test" the tax–benefit systems in several European countries when people are randomly selected to become unemployed.

2.2. Scenarios

The existing literature on income stabilization through the tax and transfer system has concentrated on increases in earnings or gross incomes to examine the stabilizing impact of tax–benefit systems (cf., Auerbach & Feenberg, 2000;

Mabbett & Schelkle, 2007). In the light of the current economic crisis, there is much more interest in a downturn scenario. Reinhart and Rogoff (2009) stress that recessions which follow a financial crisis have particularly severe effects on asset prices, output and unemployment. Therefore, we are interested not only in a scenario of a uniform decrease in incomes but also in an increase in the unemployment rate. We compare a scenario where gross incomes are proportionally decreased by 5% for all households (IS) to a scenario where some households are made unemployed and therefore lose all their labour earnings (unemployment shock). In the latter scenario, the unemployment rate increases such that total household income decreases by 5% as well in order to make both scenarios as comparable as possible.[4]

The increase in the unemployment rate is modelled through reweighting of our samples (cf., Figari et al. (2011)).[5] The weights of the unemployed are increased, while those of the employed with similar characteristics are decreased, that is, in effect, a fraction of employed households is made unemployed. With this reweighting approach, we control for several individual and household characteristics that determine the risk of becoming unemployed (see Appendix A.2). The implicit assumption behind this approach is that the socio-demographic characteristics of the unemployed – which are controlled for – remain constant (cf., Deville & Särndal, 1992; DiNardo et al., 1996).[6]

2.3. Automatic Stabilization

In order to explore the built-in automatic stabilizers of existing pre-crisis tax–benefit systems, in a companion paper (Dolls et al., 2010), we suggest the *income stabilization coefficient* τ^I which measures the sensitivity of disposable income, Y_i^D, with respect to market income, Y_i^M, as a measure for automatic stabilization. Market income Y_i^M of individual i is defined as the sum of all incomes from market activities:

$$Y_i^M = E_i + Q_i + I_i + P_i + O_i \qquad (1)$$

where E_i are earnings, Q_i business income, I_i capital income, P_i property income and O_i other income. Disposable income Y_i^D is defined as market income minus net government intervention $G_i = T_i + S_i - B_i$:

$$Y_i^D = Y_i^M - G_i = Y_i^M - (T_i + S_i - B_i) \qquad (2)$$

where T_i are direct taxes, S_i employee social insurance contributions (SIC) and B_i social cash benefits (i.e. negative taxes). We derive τ^I from a general functional relationship between disposable income and market income:

$$\tau^I = \tau^I(Y^M, T, S, B) \tag{3}$$

The derivation can be done either on the macro- or on the micro level. On the macro level, it holds that the aggregate change in market income (ΔY^M) is transmitted via τ^I into an aggregate change in disposable income (ΔY^D):

$$\Delta Y^D = (1 - \tau)\Delta Y^M \tag{4}$$

However, one problem when computing τ^I with macro-data is that this data includes behavioural and general equilibrium effects as well as active policy. Therefore, a measure of automatic stabilization based on macro-data captures all these effects. In order to single out the pure size of automatic stabilization, we compute τ^I using arithmetic changes (Δ) in total disposable income ($\sum_i \Delta Y_i^D$) and market income ($\sum_i \Delta Y_i^M$) based on micro-level information:

$$\sum_i \Delta Y_i^D = (1 - \tau^I)\sum_i \Delta Y_i^M$$

$$\tau^I = 1 - \frac{\sum_i \Delta Y_i^D}{\sum_i \Delta Y_i^M} = \frac{\sum_i(\Delta Y_i^M - \Delta Y_i^D)}{\sum_i \Delta Y_i^M} = \frac{\sum_i \Delta G_i}{\sum_i \Delta Y_i^M} \tag{5}$$

Thus, the coefficient can be decomposed into its components which include taxes, SIC and benefits:

$$\tau^I = \sum_f \tau_f^I = \tau_T^I + \tau_S^I + \tau_B^I = \frac{\sum_i \Delta G_i}{\sum_i \Delta Y_i^M} = \frac{\sum_i(\Delta T_i + \Delta S_i - \Delta B_i)}{\sum_i \Delta Y_i^M} \tag{6}$$

The main results of Dolls et al. (2010) are shown in Fig. 1.[7] In case of the IS (upper panel), approximately 38% of the shock would be absorbed by automatic stabilizers in the EU. Within the EU, there is considerable heterogeneity, and results for overall stabilization of disposable income range from a value of 25% for Estonia to 56% in Denmark. In general, automatic stabilizers in Eastern and Southern European countries are considerably lower than in Continental and Northern European countries.

In case of the unemployment shock (lower panel), automatic stabilizers absorb 47% of the shock in the EU, thus exceeding stabilization in case of the IS by 9 percentage points. The decomposition of overall stabilization into the components income taxes, SIC and benefits shows that benefits accounting for 40% of overall stabilization are a main driver of disposable

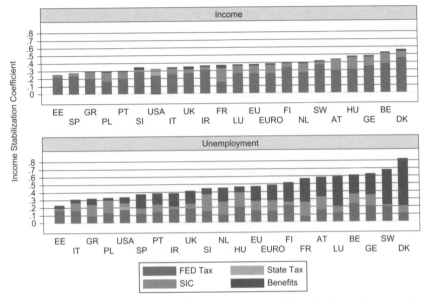

Fig. 1. Decomposition of Income Stabilization Coefficient in Both Scenarios for Different Countries. *Source:* Dolls et al. (2010).

income stabilization. Highest values for τ^I are again found in the Nordic countries Denmark and Sweden whereas automatic stabilizers in Estonia, Italy and Poland are at the lower end.

2.4. Inequality Measurement

Let an income distribution be a random variable $X = (x_1, x_2, \ldots, x_n)$, where $x_i \geqslant 0$ is the income of individual i, $i = 1, \ldots n$ and μ is the mean income. The Gini coefficient of inequality is defined as follows:

$$I_{\text{Gini}} = \frac{\sum_{i=1}^{n}\sum_{j=1}^{n}|x_i - x_j|}{2n^2\mu} \tag{7}$$

In case of maximum inequality, I_{Gini} corresponds to one, and in the case that all values are equal, I_{Gini} corresponds to zero.

We use disposable income defined as market income minus direct taxes and social contributions plus cash benefits (including pensions) for our distributional analyses. The unit of analysis is the individual. To compensate for different household structures and possible economies of scale in households, we use equivalent incomes throughout the analyses. For each person, the equivalent (per-capita) total disposable income is its household's total disposable income divided by the equivalent household size according to the modified OECD scale.[8]

3. TAX AND TRANSFER SYSTEMS IN EUROPE

3.1. Tax–Benefit Systems

The existing income tax systems in the 19 European countries under consideration offer considerable variety. As Table 1 shows, all Western European countries in our sample have graduated rate schedules with a number of brackets ranging from 2 (Ireland) to 16 (Luxembourg), with the top marginal income tax rate ranging from 38% (Luxembourg) to 59% in Denmark. There are also considerable differences across the Eastern European countries. Estonia has a flat tax system, with a single rate of 22% and a basic allowance of 1.304 euro, while the other Eastern European

Table 1. Income Tax Systems 2007.

	No of Brackets	Lowest Rate	Highest Rate	Form of Main Tax Relief
AT	4	38.3%	50.0%	0% bracket (10,000 EUR)
BE	5	25.0%	50.0%	Tax allowance (6,040 EUR)
DK	3	State 5.48%.	State 15%.	Tax allowance
		Local 24.6%	Local 24.6%	
EE	Flat tax	22.0%	22.0%	Basic allowance 1,304 EUR
FI	4	State 8.5%.	State 31.5%.	0% bracket (12,600 EUR).
		Local 16%	Local 21%	Tax allowance.
FR	4	5.5%	40.0%	0% bracket (5,614 EUR)
GE	Formula	15.8%	44.3%	0% bracket (7,664 EUR)
GR	3	15.0%	40.0%	0% bracket (12,000 EUR)
HU	2	18.0%	36.0%	Tax credit
IR	2	20.0%	41.0%	Tax allowance
IT	5	23.0%	43.0%	Tax credit
LU	16	8.0%	38.0%	0% bracket (10,335 EUR)
NL	4	33.6%	52.0%	Tax credit
PL	3	19.0%	40.0%	0% bracket (3,091 EUR)
PT	6	10.5%	40.0%	Tax credit
SI	3	16.0%	41.0%	Tax allowance (2,800 EUR)
SP	4	24.0%	43.0%	Tax allowance (5,151 EUR)
SW	2	State 20%.	State 25%.	Tax allowance
		Local 31.6%	Local 31.6%	
UK	3	10.0%	40.0%	Tax Allowance (5,225 EUR)

Source: Eurostat.

countries in our sample apply graduated tax schedules with a comparatively small number of brackets (2–3) and relatively low top marginal rates. Interestingly, Slovenia and Poland have very similar income tax schedules as the Western European countries, with highest rates around 40%, but with a lower amount belonging to the 0% bracket.

European countries do not only differ in their income tax schedules but also in the design of their system of social protection and redistribution. In each country, direct and indirect taxes as well as SIC are used to finance the welfare state (see Table 2 for an overview). The weight in the tax mix of these components depends on the structural design of the tax–benefit system in each country. For the Continental countries, it is evident that the SIC are more important to finance the welfare state than the direct taxes. This is also true for Eastern Europe, while in the Nordic countries the SIC play only a minor role. Denmark relies almost exclusively on taxes for financing the welfare state. In Southern European countries, indirect taxes tend to play the most important role. This is even more true for Eastern Europe. With

Table 2. Tax–Benefit Mix (as % of GDP) in 2005.

	Total Taxes	Indirect Taxes	Direct Taxes	Social Contribution	Direct Taxes + SIC/Indirect Taxes	Social Expenditure
AT	42.0	14.7	12.9	14.5	1.9	28.8
BE	45.5	13.9	17.8	13.9	2.3	29.7
DK	50.3	17.9	31.4	1.1	1.8	30.1
EE	30.9	13.5	7.1	10.4	1.3	12.5
FI	43.9	14.1	17.9	12.0	2.1	26.7
FR	44.0	15.8	11.9	16.4	1.8	31.5
GE	38.8	12.1	10.3	16.3	2.2	29.4
GR	34.4	12.9	9.5	12.1	1.7	24.2
HU	38.5	15.8	9.1	13.6	1.4	21.9
IR	30.8	13.6	12.4	4.8	1.3	18.2
IT	40.6	14.5	13.5	12.6	1.8	26.4
LU	38.2	13.4	14.1	10.7	1.9	21.9
NL	38.2	13.1	11.9	13.1	1.9	28.2
PL	34.2	13.9	7.0	13.7	1.5	19.6
PT	35.3	15.3	8.6[a]	11.3	1.3	24.7[a]
SI	40.5	16.4	9.3	14.8	1.5	23.4
SP	35.6	12.5	11.4	12.2	1.9	20.8
SW	51.3	17.3	20.1	13.8	2.0	32.0
UK	37.0	13.3	16.8	6.9	1.8	26.8

Source: Eurostat.
[a]Numbers for Portugal are from 2004.

few exceptions, there is a north-to-south and west-to-east decline with respect to the ratio of direct taxes and SIC to indirect taxes. The level of social protection (in terms of expenditures as % of GDP) is high in Nordic and Continental countries (an exception is Luxembourg) and particularly low in Eastern Europe as well as Ireland. A perhaps trivial but still interesting observation from Table 2 is that the level of social expenditures is correlated with the level of taxes and contributions.

3.2. Distribution and Redistribution

How do European countries differ in terms of pre-tax and post-tax inequality? The first column of Table 3 indicates that inequality in market income, Y_i^M, as measured by the Gini coefficient, displays huge disparities among the European countries of our sample. Coefficients range from 0.39 to 0.55, with values above 0.5 in some Southern and Eastern European countries (Estonia, Greece, Hungary, Poland, Portugal and Slovenia). At the lower end, the Netherlands is the only country with a Gini coefficient for equivalent market income which is below 0.4. Closest to the Netherlands are Sweden and Austria, both with values below 0.45.

Table 3. Distribution and Redistribution in the Baseline.

	$G_B^{Y^M}$	G_B^{YD}	$\Delta G_B^{Y^D - Y^M}$	$\Delta\% G_B^{Y^D - Y^M}$
AT	0.441	0.227	−0.214	−48.569
BE	0.491	0.247	−0.244	−49.704
DK	0.457	0.232	−0.226	−49.344
EE	0.509	0.324	−0.185	−36.403
FI	0.484	0.269	−0.215	−44.464
FR	0.487	0.260	−0.226	−46.523
GE	0.494	0.268	−0.225	−45.667
GR	0.502	0.323	−0.179	−35.590
HU	0.547	0.274	−0.273	−49.885
IR	0.459	0.309	−0.150	−32.642
IT	0.498	0.348	−0.149	−30.024
LU	0.472	0.243	−0.229	−48.459
NL	0.386	0.247	−0.139	−35.902
PL	0.545	0.332	−0.213	−39.102
PT	0.507	0.361	−0.146	−28.784
SI	0.504	0.270	−0.234	−46.353
SP	0.467	0.294	−0.172	−36.924
SW	0.437	0.234	−0.203	−46.523
UK	0.496	0.306	−0.190	−38.353

Source: Own calculations based on EUROMOD.

Column 2 shows that post-tax inequality, that is, the Gini coefficient based on disposable income, is substantially lower than pre-tax inequality in all countries. Thus, existing inequalities in market income are mitigated by European tax–benefit systems through a substantial degree of redistribution. Although there are significant differences in the size of redistribution, the overall inequality ranking of the countries basically remains the same.

Finally, the last two columns of Table 3 show the absolute and relative differences between the pre- and post-tax Gini coefficients as measures of redistribution (see also Fuest, Niehues, & Peichl, 2010). In countries such as Austria, Belgium, Denmark, Hungary or Luxembourg, tax–benefit systems reduce inequalities in market income by almost 50%. At the other end of the spectrum, we find lowest redistribution in Portugal and Italy with a reduction in inequality of approximately 30%.

4. EFFECTS OF SHOCKS ON INCOME DISTRIBUTION

4.1. Overall Distribution

What are the distributional consequences of the two macro shocks described above? Table 4 shows the percentage changes in the Gini coefficient and in the headcount ratios for being poor or rich, all based on equivalent disposable income.

While the proportional IS leads to a reduction the Gini coefficient in all countries, the asymmetric unemployment shock (US) increases inequality in 15 out of 19 countries. In the latter case, we find a reduction in the Gini coefficient only in Denmark, Luxembourg, Portugal and Sweden. In the case of the IS, the largest reductions in the Gini coefficient occur in Belgium, Denmark, Sweden and the United Kingdom (all $>2\%$), the smallest ones in Greece and Slovenia (each $<0.5\%$). In the case of the unemployment shock, distributional implications crucially depend on which income groups are hardest hit by unemployment and income losses. If low-income groups are the first who lose their jobs during a recession, one can expect an increase in inequality. However, if also middle-or upper- income groups are affected which seems to be relevant especially in long-lasting recessions such as the current one, distributional implications become more ambiguous. This ambiguity in terms of distributional effects of an asymmetric shock is reflected in the positive and negative signs of the Gini change.

Comparing the headcount ratios[9] for both shock scenarios, we can conclude that, not surprisingly, in case of the unemployment shock richness

Table 4. Effect of Shocks on Income Distribution.

	Income Shock			Unemployment Shock		
	Gini	Poor	Rich	Gini	Poor	Rich
AT	−1.297	4.760	−12.088	0.304	4.421	−3.619
BE	−2.270	2.673	−16.241	0.126	3.869	−4.322
DK	−2.064	3.838	−18.903	−0.218	1.176	−5.054
EE	−1.622	4.529	−11.508	0.914	6.542	−2.989
FI	−1.806	5.622	−13.981	0.347	7.104	−3.428
FR	−1.422	7.458	−9.947	0.210	4.083	−2.409
GE	−1.489	4.141	−12.982	0.445	6.245	−3.469
GR	−0.338	7.288	−11.355	0.166	2.509	−2.820
HU	−0.604	5.701	−9.241	0.518	5.612	−3.861
IR	−1.335	3.701	−12.591	1.154	10.295	−7.285
IT	−0.735	4.910	−5.857	0.507	3.567	−2.234
LU	−1.233	9.994	−14.276	−0.225	1.335	−3.843
NL	−1.232	10.629	−16.256	0.652	7.892	−3.985
PL	−0.923	6.749	−9.692	0.281	3.757	−2.639
PT	−0.611	4.693	−6.055	−0.709	1.528	−2.667
SI	−0.318	0.273	−1.290	0.327	4.354	−2.931
SP	−0.693	6.343	−13.806	0.590	3.545	−3.003
SW	−2.050	4.215	−15.446	−0.154	3.444	−3.774
UK	−2.219	3.753	−13.001	1.074	7.895	−2.873

Source: Own calculations based on EUROMOD.

is decreasing less than in the case of the proportional IS.[10] With the exception of Slovenia, the percentage reduction in rich people is substantially higher in the latter shock scenario. However, no such clear conclusion can be drawn considering the percentage change in poverty. In countries such as Ireland or the United Kingdom, the asymmetric unemployment shock leads to a much stronger increase in the headcount for the poor than the IS. However, the opposite is true for countries such as Greece, Luxembourg or the Netherlands. Here, distributional implications depend again crucially on which income groups are actually the first who become unemployed in a recession.

What is the effect of the two shock scenarios on market income inequality and the amount of redistribution achieved by the tax and the transfer system? Table 5 sheds further light on the implications for the overall income distribution. The first column shows the percentage change of the Gini coefficient based on equivalent market income between the unemployment shock scenario and the baseline $((G_{US}^{Y^M} - G_B^{Y^M})/G_B^{Y^M})$.[11] With the exception of Portugal, we find an increase in inequality which is highest in

Table 5. Change in Distribution and Redistribution.

	$\Delta\%G_{US-B}^{Y^M}$	$\Delta(G^{Y^D} - G^{Y^M})_{IS-B}$	$\Delta(G^{Y^D} - G^{Y^M})_{US-B}$
AT	1.564	−0.003	−0.006
BE	1.509	−0.006	−0.007
DK	2.673	−0.005	−0.013
EE	1.347	−0.005	−0.004
FI	1.737	−0.005	−0.007
FR	1.416	−0.004	−0.006
GE	1.827	−0.004	−0.008
GR	0.632	−0.001	−0.003
HU	0.836	−0.002	−0.003
IR	3.342	−0.003	−0.012
IT	0.798	−0.003	−0.002
LU	1.022	−0.003	−0.005
NL	1.766	−0.003	−0.005
PL	0.733	−0.003	−0.003
PT	−0.353	−0.002	−0.001
SI	0.810	−0.001	−0.003
SP	1.178	−0.002	−0.004
SW	2.176	−0.005	−0.010
UK	2.204	−0.006	−0.008

Source: Own calculations based on EUROMOD.

Ireland, Denmark, the United Kingdom and Sweden (all $>2\%$) and lowest in Greece, Hungary, Italy, Poland and Slovenia (all $<1\%$).

The last two columns of Table 5 show how the difference between the Gini coefficients based on equivalent disposable and market income has changed comparing the IS and the base scenario (column 3) and the unemployment shock and the base scenario (column 4), respectively $((G_{\text{Shock}}^{Y^D} - G_{\text{Shock}}^{Y^M}) - (G_B^{Y^D} - G_B^{Y^M}))$. The negative values indicate that both shocks lead to higher differences between the Gini coefficients based on equivalent disposable and market income. One conclusion of this finding is that post-shock inequalities in market income are even more reduced than in the base scenario, that is, the automatic stabilizers increase the redistributive effects of the tax–benefit systems in all countries in both scenarios.

4.2. Stabilization of Different Income Groups

In this section, we refer to the income stabilization coefficient from Section 2.3, but focus on the stabilization of disposable income for different income

Table 6. Stabilization of Income Groups – Proportional Income Shock.

	TAU	Q1	Q2	Q3	Q4	Q5
AT	0.439	0.023	0.045	0.072	0.107	0.192
BE	0.527	0.022	0.051	0.082	0.128	0.244
DK	0.558	0.017	0.046	0.088	0.135	0.273
EE	0.253	0.010	0.019	0.036	0.063	0.126
FI	0.396	0.010	0.031	0.063	0.099	0.192
FR	0.370	0.032	0.036	0.053	0.079	0.171
GE	0.481	0.019	0.045	0.072	0.116	0.228
GR	0.291	0.004	0.015	0.033	0.063	0.176
HU	0.476	0.029	0.041	0.056	0.097	0.254
IR	0.363	0.009	0.026	0.048	0.084	0.197
IT	0.346	0.010	0.035	0.051	0.077	0.173
LU	0.374	0.019	0.022	0.042	0.082	0.208
NL	0.397	0.020	0.040	0.062	0.093	0.182
PL	0.301	0.017	0.032	0.047	0.060	0.145
PT	0.303	0.012	0.013	0.029	0.055	0.194
SI	0.317	0.022	0.010	0.008	0.037	0.240
SP	0.277	0.006	0.020	0.036	0.062	0.153
SW	0.420	0.022	0.041	0.066	0.096	0.196
UK	0.352	0.010	0.034	0.047	0.079	0.182

Source: Own calculations based on EUROMOD.

groups. The income stabilization coefficient for quantile q based on equivalent disposable income becomes

$$\tau_q^I = 1 - \frac{\sum_{q,i} \Delta Y_{q,i}^D}{\sum_i \Delta Y_i^M} = \frac{\sum_{q,i} (\Delta Y_{q,i}^M - \Delta Y_{q,i}^D)}{\sum_i \Delta Y_i^M} = \frac{\sum_{q,i} \Delta G_{q,i}}{\sum_i \Delta Y_i^M} \qquad (8)$$

Note that in the denominator, changes in market income for the total population are added up – as in Eq. (5). Hence, the sum of the five quantile coefficients yields the overall income stabilization coefficient. Table 6 shows that in case of the proportional IS, the stabilization coefficients are an increasing function of the income quantiles. This result is due to higher changes between market and disposable income for high-income groups. It is worth mentioning that even a proportional tax would yield increasing coefficients for higher quantiles; that is, progressivity of the income tax is not required for this result.

In contrast to the increasing stabilization by income quantile for the IS, stabilization results for the unemployment shock follow a somewhat

Table 7.   Stabilization of Income Groups – Unemployment Shock.

	TAU	Q1	Q2	Q3	Q4	Q5
AT	0.585	0.111	0.094	0.069	0.130	0.181
BE	0.612	0.143	0.087	0.067	0.101	0.215
DK	0.823	0.095	0.189	0.166	0.196	0.177
EE	0.233	0.062	0.019	0.019	0.041	0.091
FI	0.519	0.118	0.057	0.074	0.093	0.176
FR	0.568	0.102	0.102	0.088	0.092	0.185
GE	0.624	0.144	0.078	0.090	0.118	0.193
GR	0.322	0.016	0.031	0.040	0.071	0.164
HU	0.467	0.091	0.045	0.048	0.071	0.212
IR	0.387	0.101	0.049	0.044	0.061	0.132
IT	0.311	0.011	0.021	0.047	0.081	0.151
LU	0.593	0.148	0.177	0.056	0.070	0.142
NL	0.452	0.123	0.048	0.054	0.088	0.140
PL	0.329	0.031	0.035	0.048	0.066	0.150
PT	0.386	0.014	0.005	0.040	0.075	0.252
SI	0.431	0.045	0.038	0.056	0.083	0.210
SP	0.376	0.038	0.049	0.065	0.076	0.148
SW	0.678	0.160	0.109	0.109	0.110	0.190
UK	0.415	0.142	0.034	0.030	0.060	0.150

Source: Own calculations based on EUROMOD.

different pattern as demonstrated in Table 7. Here, with the exception of some Eastern and Southern European countries, we find high stabilization also for the lowest income groups. As the unemployment shock is modelled through reweighting of our sample taking into account individual characteristics of the unemployed, a large part of the newly unemployed comes from lower income quantiles. The fact that tax and transfer systems in countries such as Estonia, Greece, Italy, Poland, Portugal, Slovenia or Spain provide only weak stabilization for low-income groups can be explained by rather low unemployment benefits in these countries.

To further investigate which components of the tax and transfer systems drive the results for the five income quantiles, we decompose the income stabilization coefficient τ_q^I into its components income taxes, SIC and benefits (Tables A.1 and A.2 in the Appendix A.1). First, consider Table 9 for the IS scenario. Clearly, taxes and, to a smaller extent, SIC play a large stabilizing role for higher income quantiles, whereas benefits are of minor importance for these income groups. This holds for all countries in our sample. Only in France, SIC are almost as important (fifth quantile) or even more important (fourth quantile) than taxes for stabilization of disposable

Table 8. Regressions on Income Stabilization Coefficient IS.

Dep. var.: TAU Income Shock	(1)	(2)	(3)	(4)
Redistribution	0.787***			0.441**
	(0.21)			(0.19)
Openness		0.109*		0.082*
		(0.06)		(0.04)
Ratio Direct to Indirect Taxes			0.203***	0.154***
			(0.06)	(0.05)
Constant	0.060	0.302***	0.004	−0.140
	(0.09)	(0.04)	(0.10)	(0.09)
Adjusted R^2	0.417	0.114	0.410	0.651
dof	17	17	17	15
F	13.9	3.3	13.5	12.2
N	19	19	19	19

Source: Own calculations based on EUROMOD.
Note: SE in parentheses. Significance level: * $p<0.01$, ** $p<0.05$, *** $p<0.10$.

income which can be explained with the progressive incidence of SIC. At the bottom of the distribution, stabilization of disposable income is rather low due to smaller changes in market income.

A different picture emerges again for the unemployment shock (Table 10). In this shock scenario, benefits play an important role, especially for low-income quantiles. The decomposition convincingly shows which component of the tax and transfer systems causes the difference between Southern and Eastern European countries on the one hand and its neighbours on the other. The former group of countries has a rather low level of income stabilization mainly because unemployment benefits are substantially less generous in these countries.[12]

4.3. Income Stabilization and Redistribution

It is interesting to explore the relationship between the degree of income stabilization and redistribution which is achieved by the respective tax and transfer systems. Are systems with high automatic stabilizers also those which provide significant redistribution? To answer this question, we relate the degree of redistribution measured by the percentage difference in

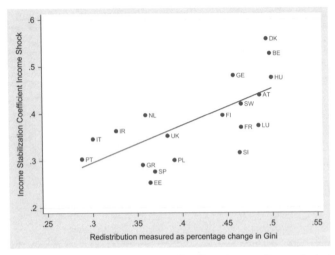

Fig. 2.   Income Stabilization IS and Redistribution. *Source:* Own calculations based
on EUROMOD.

the Gini coefficients based on market and disposable income to the income
stabilization coefficients for the IS (Fig. 2) and the unemployment shock
(Fig. A.1 in the Appendix A.1). The strong relationship between income
stabilization and redistribution is reflected in very high (population-
weighted) correlations of 0.67 (IS) and 0.86 (US).

Next, we consider the relationship between the income stabilization
coefficient and the ratio of direct to indirect taxes. We find a strong positive
correlation of 0.67 (Fig. 3). This is not surprising since the income
stabilization coefficient positively depends on the level of direct taxes. In
contrast, the mechanism how indirect taxes provide automatic stabilization
is different as discussed in Dolls et al., 2010. There, we assume that only
liquidity-constrained households will adjust their consumption to an IS and
indirect taxes contribute to demand rather to income stabilization. We also
find a positive relationship between the income stabilization and government size and openness of the economy[13], respectively, whereas no
correlation is found between automatic stabilizers and active fiscal policy
measures passed during the current economic crisis.

Table 8 shows the results of regressing the income stabilization coefficient
(of the IS) on our measure for redistribution, a measure for openness and
the ratio of direct to indirect taxes. Redistribution is again measured as the

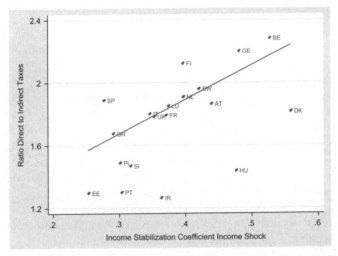

Fig. 3. Income Stabilization IS and Ratio Direct to Indirect Taxes. *Source:* Own calculations based on EUROMOD.

percentage difference in the Gini coefficients based on market and disposable income and openness as the average ratio of exports and imports to GDP from 2000 to 2004.

Because of the very small sample size ($N = 19$), this inference should be interpreted with caution. Having this in mind, the significant positive relationships between automatic stabilizers and each of the variables is also confirmed by this 'naïve' regression.

4.4. Cluster Analysis

In order to compare the clustering of countries with respect to the different measures of automatic stabilization and controlling for several variables, we conduct a hierarchical cluster analysis to group countries that have similar characteristics across a set of variables. When performing a CLUSTER analysis, a number of technical decisions have to be made. First, all variables have been standardized from 0 to 1 using z-scores, to prevent that the results are driven by large absolute values of some variables. Our method of grouping the countries is the common Ward's linkage, which combines such clusters which minimally increase the squared sum of errors.

Our results will be illustrated in a so-called dendrogram, which graphically presents the information concerning which observations are grouped together at various levels of (dis)similarity. At the bottom of the dendrogram, each observation is considered as its own cluster. Vertical lines extend up for each observation, and at various (dis)similarity values these lines are connected to the lines from other observations with a horizontal line. The observations continue to combine, until, at the top of the dendrogram, all observations are grouped together. The height of the vertical lines and the range of the (dis)similarity axis give visual clues about the strength of the clustering. In our case, the measure for the distance between cases is the common 'squared Euclidean'. Generally, long vertical lines indicate more distinct separation between groups, short lines more similarity, respectively.[14]

We perform a cluster analysis on the basis of the stabilization coefficients for the income and unemployment shock combined with inequality in market income and the ratio of direct to indirect taxes. The dendogram is illustrated in Fig. 4. In accordance with the classical typology of welfare state regimes (Esping-Andersen, 1990; Ferrera, 1996), the dendogram groups Continental and Nordic countries to the left and Anglo-Saxon, Southern and Eastern European countries to the right. The former group is characterized by a rather high level of income stabilization, modest

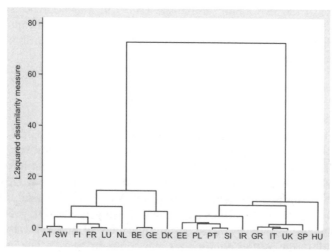

Fig. 4. Cluster Analysis. *Source*: Own calculations based on EUROMOD.

inequality in market income and an important role of direct taxes and SIC, whereas countries from the latter group tend to rank at the other end of the spectrum.

5. CONCLUSIONS

This chapter investigates the extent to which the tax and transfer system mitigates negative income and employment shocks at different income levels and in different countries. We have considered the distributional consequences of two types of shocks: a proportional shock on all incomes and an increase in unemployment which affects households asymmetrically. In both scenarios, post-shock inequalities in market income are even more reduced through the tax and transfer system than in the base scenario; that is, the redistributive effects of the tax benefit systems increase in all countries (Fig. 5).

Further, we investigate the degree of income stabilization for different income groups. In case of the proportional income shock, stabilization for higher income groups contributes relatively more to overall stabilization than stabilization for low-income groups, but this is due to the larger absolute shock on gross income for the former group. A different pattern emerges in case of the unemployment shock. With the exception of some Eastern and Southern European countries, we find relatively high income stabilization coefficients also for low-income groups. The stabilization for high-income groups is mainly driven by the income tax. A notable exception to this is France where (progressive) SIC are most important for stabilization. For low-income groups whose tax payments are negligible, benefits play a central role. As they are more generous in the Scandinavian and Western European countries, they contribute substantially more to stabilization of disposable income for lower income groups. We thus conclude that European tax–benefit systems put unequal weights on the extent different income groups are protected against macro shocks.

With respect to the relationship between income stabilization and redistribution, we find that tax–benefit systems with high automatic stabilizers are also those which are more effective in mitigating existing inequalities in market income. A simple regression of income stabilization on measures for openness, redistribution and the ratio of direct to indirect taxes confirms a significant positive relationship between the automatic stabilizers and each of the variables.

These results have to be interpreted in the light of various limitations of our analysis. Firstly, by modelling the unemployment shock through reweighting of the sample, we implicitly assume that the socio-demographic characteristics of the unemployed remain constant. Secondly, our analysis abstracts from automatic stabilization through other taxes, in particular corporate income taxes.[15] Thirdly, we have abstracted from the role of labour supply or other behavioural adjustments for the impact of automatic stabilizers. Furthermore, one should note, though, that our analysis is not a forecasting exercise. We do not aim at quantifying the exact effects of the current economic crisis but of stylized scenarios based on simulations in order to explore the built-in automatic stabilizers of existing pre-crisis tax–benefit systems. Conducting an ex-post analysis would include discretionary government reactions and behavioural responses (see, e.g., Aaberge, Björklund, Jäntti, Pedersen, Smith, & Wennemo (2000) for an empirical ex-post analysis of a previous crisis in the Nordic countries), and we would not be able to identify the role of automatic stabilization. We intend to pursue these issues in future research.

NOTES

1. Previous research has shown that European tax and transfer systems substantially vary in the degree of automatic income stabilization (Dolls, Fuest, & Peichl, 2010). But this literature focuses on aggregate automatic stabilization, whereas we are interested in income stabilization at different income levels.

2. These are Austria (AT), Belgium (BE), Denmark (DK), Estonia (EE), Finland (FI), France (FR), Germany (GE), Greece (GR), Hungary (HU), Ireland (IR), Italy (IT), Luxembourg (LU), the Netherlands (NL), Poland (PL), Portugal (PT), Slovenia (SI), Spain (SP), Sweden (SW) and the United Kingdom (UK).

3. There are also country reports available with detailed information on the input data, the modelling and validation of each tax–benefit system, see http://www.iser.essex.ac.uk/research/euromod. The tax–benefit systems included in the model have been validated against aggregated administrative statistics as well as national tax–benefit models (where available), and the robustness checked through numerous applications (see, e.g., Bargain, 2006).

4. Our scenarios can be seen as a conservative estimate of the expected impact of the current crisis (see Reinhart and Rogoff, 2009 for effects of previous crises). The (qualitative) results are robust with respect to different sizes of the shocks. The results for the unemployment shock do not change much when we model it as an increase in the unemployment rate by 5 percentage points for each country.

5. For the reweigthing procedure, we follow the approach of Immvervoll et al. (2006), who have also simulated an increase in unemployment through reweighting of the sample. Their analysis focuses on changes in absolute and relative poverty

rates after changes in the income distribution and the employment rate. A different approach would be to randomly select people who become unemployed.

6. This approach is equivalent (in terms of selecting the newly unemployed persons) to estimating probabilities of becoming unemployed (see, e.g., Bell & Blanchflower, 2009) and then selecting the individuals with the highest probabilities when controlling for the same characteristics in the reweighting estimation (see Herault, 2009). However, when it is not possible to control for all possible covariates, the reweighting procedure affects the structure of the population with respect to the characteristics not explicitly controlled for.

7. In this chapter, we also analyse the importance of liquidity constraints for demand stabilization.

8. The modified OECD scale assigns a weight of 1.0 to the head of household, 0.5 to every household member aged 14 or more and 0.3 to each child aged less than 14. Summing up the individual weights gives the household-specific equivalence factor.

9. People are classified as poor (rich) if their equivalent disposable income is less than 60% (more than twice) the median equivalent disposable income in the population.

10. The reweighting approach used for modelling an increase in unemployment is implicitly based on the assumption that the socio-demographic characteristics of the unemployed remain constant. A more in-depth description of the approach can be found in the Appendix A.

11. Note that the Gini coefficient of market income does not change in case of the proportional shock.

12. Note that the income stabilization coefficients in case of the unemployment shock depend on the coverage of the newly unemployed by unemployment benefits. Stabilization might be underestimated if the newly unemployed are eligible for unemployment benefits and if the unemployed whose weights are increased through the reweighting procedure are long-term unemployed with exhausted eligibility. However, the bias might have the opposite sign if the newly unemployed are mainly not eligible for unemployment benefits (e.g. school leavers).

13. Openness is measured as the ratio of imports and exports to GDP.

14. Note that the general clustering results presented here are robust to different linkage or dissimilarity measure specifications. We report the results for the most common combination found in the literature.

15. For an analysis of automatic stabilizers in the corporate tax system, see Devereux and Fuest (2009) and Buettner and Fuest (2010).

ACKNOWLEDGMENTS

This chapter uses EUROMOD version D21. EUROMOD is continually being improved and updated and the results presented here represent the best available at the time of writing. EUROMOD relies on micro-data from 17 different sources for 19 countries. These are the ECHP and EU-SILC by Eurostat, the Austrian version of the ECHP by Statistik Austria; the PSBH by the University of Liège and the University of Antwerp; the Estonian HBS by Statistics Estonia; the Income Distribution Survey by Statistics Finland; the EBF by INSEE; the GSOEP by DIW Berlin; the Greek HBS by the National Statistical Service of Greece; the Living in Ireland Survey by the Economic and Social Research Institute; the SHIW by the Bank of Italy; the PSELL-2 by CEPS/INSTEAD; the SEP by Statistics Netherlands; the Polish HBS by Warsaw University; the Slovenian HBS and Personal Income Tax database by the Statistical Office of Slovenia; the Income Distribution Survey by Statistics Sweden and the FES by the UK Office for National Statistics (ONS) through the Data Archive. Material from the FES is Crown Copyright and is used by permission. Neither the ONS nor the Data Archive bears any responsibility for the analysis or interpretation of the data reported here. An equivalent disclaimer applies for all other data sources and their respective providers.

    This chapter is partly based on work carried out during Andreas Peichl's visit to the European Centre for Analysis in the Social Sciences (ECASS) at the Institute for Social and Economic Research (ISER), University of Essex, supported by the Access to Research Infrastructures action under the EU Improving Human Potential Programme. Andreas Peichl is grateful for financial support by Deutsche Forschungsgemeinschaft DFG (PE1675). We would like to thank Cathal O'Donoghue, participants of the 2010 IZA/ OECD conference as well as seminar participants in Bonn, Cologne, and at the Worldbank for helpful comments and suggestions. We are indebted to all past and current members of the EUROMOD consortium for the construction and development of EUROMOD. The usual disclaimer applies.

REFERENCES

Aaberge, R., Björklund, A., Jäntti, M., Pedersen, P. J., Smith, N., & Wennemo, T. (2000). Unemployment shocks and income distribution: How did the Mordic countries fare during their crises? *Scandinavian Journal of Economics, 102*(1), 77–99.

Auerbach, A., & Feenberg, D. (2000). The significance of federal taxes as automatic stabilizers. *Journal of Economic Perspectives, 14*, 37–56.

Bargain, O. (2006). *Micro simulation in action: Policy analysis in Europe using EUROMOD, vol. 25 of the series Research in Labor Economics.* Amsterdam, NL: Elsevier.

Bargain, O., Immvervoll, H., Peichl, A., & Siegloch, S. (2010). Who are the losers of the labour-market downturn? A scenario analysis for Germany. Paper presented at IZA / OECD Workshop. Paris.

Bell, D., & Blanchflower, D. (2009). *What should be done about rising unemployment in the UK.* IZA DP No. 4040. IZA, Bonn, Germany.

Bourguignon, F., & Spadaro, A. (2006). Microsimulation as a tool for evaluating redistribution policies. *Journal of Economic Inequality*, *4*(1), 77–106.

Buettner, T., & Fuest, C. (2010). The role of the corporate income tax as an automatic stabilizer. *International Tax and Public Finance, 17*, 686–698.

Callan, T., Nolan, B., & Walsh, J. (2011). The economic crisis, public sector pay, and the income distribution. Paper presented at IZA / OECD Workshop. Paris. (This Volume)

Devereux, M., & Fuest, C. (2009). Is the corporation tax an effective automatic stabilizer? *National Tax Journal, LXII*, 429–437.

Deville, J.-F., & Särndal, C.-E. (1992). Calibration estimators in survey sampling. *Journal of the American Statistical Association, 87*, 376–382.

DiNardo, J., Fortin, N., & Lemieux, T. (1996). Labor market institutions and the distribution of wages, 1973–1992: A semiparametric approach. *Econometrica, 64*, 1001–1044.

Dolls, M., Fuest, C., & Peichl, A. (2010). *Automatic stabilizers and economic crisis: US vs. Europe.* NBER Working Paper no. 16275. NBER, Cambridge, MA, US.

Domeij, D., & Floden, M. (2010). Inequality trends in Sweden 1978–2004. *Review of Economic Dynamics, 13*(1), 179–208.

Esping-Andersen, G. (1990). *The three worlds of welfare capitalism.* Oxford: Blackwell Publishers.

Ferrera, M. (1996). The 'Southern Model' of welfare in social Europe. *Journal of European Social Policy, 6*(1), 17–37.

Figari, F., Salvatori, A., & Sutherland, H. (2011). Economic downturn and stress testing European welfare systems. Paper presented at IZA / OECD Workshop, Paris. (This Volume).

Fuest, C., Niehues, J., & Peichl, A. (2010). The redistributive effects of tax benefit systems in the Enlarged EU. *Public Finance Review, 38*(4), 473–500.

Heathcote, J., Perri, F., & Violante, G. (2010). Unequal we stand: An empirical analysis of economic inequality in the United States, 1967–2006. *Review of Economic Dynamics, 13*(1), 15–51.

Herault, N. (2009). *Sequential linking of computable general equilibrium and microsimulation models.* WP No. 2/09. Melbourne Institute of Applied Economic and Social Research, The University of Melbourne.

Immvervoll, H., Levy, H., Lietz, C., Mantovani, D., & Sutherland, H. (2006). The sensitivity of poverty rates to macro-level changes in the European Union. *Cambridge Journal of Economics, 30*, 181–199.

Mabbett, D., & Schelkle, W. (2007). Bringing macroeconomics back into the political economy of reform: The Lisbon Agenda and the 'fiscal philosophy' of the EU. *Journal of Common Market Studies, 45*, 81–104.

Reinhart, C., & Rogoff, K. (2009). The aftermath of financial crisis. *American Economic Review: Papers & Proceedings, 99*(2), 466–472.

Sutherland, H. (2001). *Final report – EUROMOD: An integrated European benefit-tax model.* EUROMOD Working Paper no. EM9/01. Institute for Social and Economic Research, University of Essex, Colchester, UK.

Sutherland, H. (2007). Euromod: The tax-benefit microsimulation model for the European Union. In: A. Gupta & A. Harding (Eds.), *Modelling our future: Population ageing, health and aged care (Vol. 16 of International Symposia in Economic Theory and Econometrics*, pp. 483–488). Amsterdam, NL: Elsevier.

APPENDIX A

A.1. Additional Results

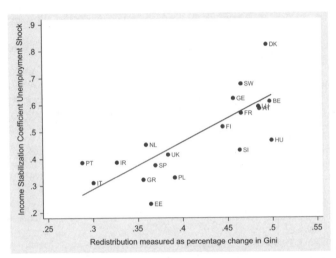

Fig. A.1.   Income Stabilization, US and Redistribution. *Source*: Own calculations based on EUROMOD.

A.2. Reweighting Procedure for Increasing Unemployment

In order to increase the unemployment rate while keeping the aggregate counts of other key individual and household characteristics constant, we follow the approach taken by Immvervoll et al. (2006). The increase in the unemployment rates is modelled through reweighting of our samples while controlling for several individual and household characteristics that determine the risk of becoming unemployed.

We follow Immvervoll et al. (2006) and define the unemployed as people aged 19–59 declaring themselves to be out of work and looking for a job. The within-database national 'unemployment rate' is calculated as the ratio of these unemployed to those in the labour force, defined as the unemployed plus people aged 19–59 who are (self)employed. The increased total number

Table A.1. Stabilization of Income Groups by Components–Income Shock.

	Q1			Q2			Q3			Q4			Q5		
	Tax	SIC	BEN	Tax	SIC	BEN	Tax	SIC	BEN	Tax	SIC	BEN	Tax	SIC	BEN
AT	0.010	0.009	0.004	0.025	0.019	0.001	0.044	0.028	0.001	0.069	0.037	0.001	0.146	0.045	0.000
BE	0.011	0.005	0.006	0.031	0.015	0.005	0.058	0.023	0.002	0.094	0.034	0.000	0.189	0.055	0.000
DK	0.012	0.003	0.001	0.033	0.007	0.006	0.068	0.015	0.005	0.108	0.022	0.005	0.234	0.039	0.000
EE	0.005	0.001	0.004	0.017	0.002	0.000	0.032	0.004	-0.000	0.058	0.005	0.000	0.117	0.010	-0.000
FI	0.006	0.001	0.003	0.024	0.004	0.002	0.054	0.009	0.001	0.086	0.013	0.000	0.170	0.022	0.000
FR	0.003	0.011	0.019	0.008	0.020	0.008	0.018	0.030	0.005	0.032	0.043	0.004	0.092	0.078	0.001
GE	0.004	0.008	0.007	0.024	0.018	0.003	0.045	0.027	0.000	0.081	0.035	0.000	0.197	0.030	0.001
GR	0.001	0.003	0.000	0.005	0.010	0.000	0.017	0.016	0.000	0.038	0.024	0.000	0.142	0.034	0.000
HU	0.008	0.013	0.008	0.021	0.018	0.001	0.034	0.021	0.000	0.065	0.031	0.000	0.177	0.076	-0.000
IR	0.004	0.001	0.004	0.016	0.004	0.006	0.039	0.007	0.002	0.072	0.011	0.001	0.179	0.017	0.001
IT	0.006	0.003	0.001	0.022	0.008	0.005	0.035	0.013	0.003	0.057	0.019	0.001	0.134	0.037	0.002
LU	0.002	0.007	0.011	0.008	0.013	0.001	0.024	0.017	0.002	0.059	0.024	-0.001	0.172	0.036	0.000
NL	0.004	0.011	0.005	0.015	0.021	0.004	0.033	0.028	0.001	0.060	0.032	0.000	0.158	0.024	0.000
PL	0.007	0.007	0.003	0.014	0.014	0.004	0.021	0.020	0.006	0.030	0.028	0.002	0.096	0.048	0.000
PT	0.001	0.003	0.009	0.005	0.007	0.001	0.015	0.014	0.000	0.036	0.019	0.000	0.145	0.048	0.000
SI	0.002	-0.000	0.019	0.007	0.007	0.003	0.008	0.000	0.000	0.034	0.010	0.003	0.238	0.014	0.002
SP	0.003	0.001	0.001	0.016	0.004	0.000	0.030	0.006	0.000	0.052	0.010	-0.000	0.139	0.014	-0.000
SW	0.013	0.002	0.007	0.031	0.006	0.004	0.055	0.010	0.001	0.083	0.012	0.000	0.186	0.009	0.000
UK	0.003	0.001	0.006	0.014	0.005	0.015	0.031	0.011	0.005	0.060	0.017	0.002	0.160	0.020	0.003

Source: Own calculations based on EUROMOD.

Table A.2. Stabilization of Income Groups by Components–Unemployment Shock.

	Q1			Q2			Q3			Q4			Q5		
	Tax	SIC	BEN	Tax	SIC	BEN	Tax	SIC	BEN	Tax	SIC	BEN	Tax	SIC	BEN
AT	0.002	0.005	0.104	0.008	0.017	0.068	0.016	0.027	0.026	0.033	0.043	0.053	0.103	0.078	0.000
BE	0.000	0.004	0.139	0.009	0.010	0.068	0.023	0.017	0.027	0.057	0.030	0.013	0.151	0.062	0.001
DK	−0.021	−0.003	0.120	−0.039	−0.002	0.230	0.019	0.015	0.132	0.059	0.028	0.109	0.098	0.055	0.024
EE	0.001	0.001	0.059	0.011	0.002	0.006	0.023	0.004	−0.007	0.045	0.006	−0.009	0.093	0.011	−0.013
FI	−0.017	−0.001	0.137	0.005	0.003	0.050	0.031	0.009	0.035	0.058	0.014	0.021	0.146	0.025	0.006
FR	−0.001	0.005	0.098	0.001	0.017	0.083	0.005	0.032	0.051	0.015	0.048	0.029	0.055	0.089	0.041
GE	0.001	0.005	0.137	0.010	0.018	0.051	0.023	0.029	0.037	0.047	0.042	0.029	0.128	0.050	0.015
GR	0.000	0.004	0.012	0.001	0.013	0.017	0.003	0.022	0.014	0.011	0.043	0.018	0.078	0.068	0.018
HU	0.006	0.016	0.069	0.010	0.019	0.016	0.014	0.024	0.011	0.034	0.038	−0.001	0.139	0.094	−0.022
IR	0.001	0.001	0.099	0.008	0.003	0.038	0.020	0.006	0.019	0.038	0.010	0.013	0.111	0.016	0.005
IT	0.003	0.002	0.006	0.010	0.010	0.001	0.019	0.018	0.010	0.037	0.026	0.018	0.094	0.049	0.007
LU	−0.000	−0.009	0.157	−0.000	−0.008	0.185	0.006	0.015	0.035	0.022	0.024	0.024	0.099	0.057	−0.014
NL	0.001	−0.011	0.133	0.004	0.025	0.019	0.011	0.038	0.005	0.021	0.049	0.017	0.067	0.070	0.003
PL	0.004	0.007	0.020	0.010	0.019	0.006	0.016	0.028	0.004	0.025	0.039	0.002	0.080	0.072	−0.002
PT	0.000	0.001	0.013	−0.008	0.005	0.008	0.005	0.010	0.026	0.016	0.019	0.041	0.133	0.063	0.055
SI	0.001	0.007	0.041	0.005	0.020	0.016	0.013	0.032	0.012	0.029	0.053	0.003	0.105	0.109	0.001
SP	0.001	0.005	0.032	0.004	0.008	0.037	0.010	0.011	0.044	0.021	0.016	0.039	0.088	0.028	0.033
SW	−0.040	−0.012	0.211	−0.003	−0.002	0.113	0.026	0.005	0.078	0.058	0.013	0.039	0.158	0.022	0.010
UK	−0.009	0.001	0.150	0.009	0.004	0.021	0.024	0.010	−0.004	0.044	0.017	−0.001	0.123	0.030	−0.003

Source: Own calculations based on EUROMOD.

of unemployed people is calculated such that total household income decreases by 5% within each country.

In EUROMOD, the baseline household weights supplied with the national databases have been calculated to adjust for sample design and/ or differential non-response (see Sutherland, 2001 for details). Weights are then recalculated using the existing weights as a starting point, but (a) using the increased (decreased) number of unemployed (employed) people as the control totals for them, and (b) also controlling for individual demographic and household composition variables using the existing grossed-up totals for these categories as control totals. The specific variables used as controls are as follows:

- employment status
- age (0–18, 19–24, 25–49, 50–59, 60 +)
- gender
- marital status and household size
- education
- region.

This method implies that the households without any unemployed people that are similar to households with unemployed people (according to the above variables) will have their weights reduced. In other words, these are the households who are 'made unemployed' in our exercise. In case of multiple solutions, the applied procedure ensures that the distance to the original sample weights is minimized.

ECONOMIC DOWNTURN AND STRESS TESTING EUROPEAN WELFARE SYSTEMS☆

Francesco Figari, Andrea Salvatori and Holly Sutherland

ABSTRACT

As unemployment rises across the European Union (EU), it is important to understand the extent to which the incomes of the new unemployed are protected by tax–benefit systems and to assess the cost pressures on the social protection systems of this increase in unemployment. This chapter uses the EU tax–benefit model EUROMOD to explore these issues, comparing effects in five EU countries. It provides evidence on the differing degrees of resilience of the household incomes of the newly unemployed due to the variations in the protection offered by the tax–benefit systems, according to whether unemployment benefit is payable, the household situation of the unemployed person and across countries.

☆A preliminary version of the paper has previously been circulated as Figari, F., Salvatori, A., & Sutherland, H. (2010). *Economic downturn and stress testing European welfare systems*. ISER WP 2010-18, University of Essex, Colchester.

Who Loses in the Downturn? Economic Crisis, Employment and Income Distribution
Research in Labor Economics, Volume 32, 257–286
ISSN: 0147-9121/doi:10.1108/S0147-9121(2011)0000032012

Keywords: unemployment; European Union; household income; microsimulation

JEL Classification: C81; H55; I3

1. INTRODUCTION AND MOTIVATION

The social impact of the economic downturn faced by European countries since the end of 2008 (OECD, 2009) is not easy to anticipate. The consequences of the crisis on the most vulnerable individuals depend on the interaction between their labour market participation, living arrangements and the capacity of the tax and benefit systems to absorb macro-economic shocks.

As unemployment rises, it is important to understand the extent to which the incomes of the new unemployed are protected by the tax–benefit system and to assess the cost pressures on the social protection system of this increase in unemployment.

Stress testing is a common practice applied to financial institutions (Jones, Hilbers, & Slack, 2004; Sorge & Virolainen, 2006). Applied to social protection schemes it offers the possibility of examining the impact of the loss of income on the living standards of the individuals and on the total cost to the government (Atkinson, 2009). Indeed the existence in all European countries of a welfare state (Schubert, Hegelich, & Bazant, 2009) that is intended to protect people and their families against economic crisis is one of the main differences between the crisis faced today and that which occurred in the 1930s. However, this in turn leads us to ask some crucial questions: how effective is today's welfare state in providing protection? Are those losing their jobs in fact cushioned against a catastrophic loss of income? Do income-tested benefits stabilise family incomes in the face of a downturn?

Our aim is not to predict what will happen, but to test the resilience of the welfare state with respect to unemployment and the consequent loss of income. The economic crisis may have impact on poverty and social exclusion, which current indicators will have serious difficulties in capturing (Nolan, 2009). Our analysis is not a forecasting exercise, which would require, at least, some macro–micro linkage modelling. However, it allows us to illustrate the variation in social impact of potential scenarios across countries and social protection systems (Atkinson, 2009).

In due course, survey data collected over the period of increasing unemployment will provide evidence of the evolution of the income distribution and the incomes of the unemployed (Aaberge, Bjorklund, & Jäntti, 2000). Analysis of panel data will show us how incomes change for the new unemployed (Jenkins, 2000). The approach taken here provides, in a timely fashion, an indication of these income changes, highlighting the direct cushioning effects of the tax–benefit system rather than those arising from adaptive changes that the unemployed or other members of their households may make.

The economic downturn affects many dimensions of the economic system. We provide evidence on one important aspect: the implications for the living standards of those most likely to become unemployed over the initial period of economic downturn, exploring the interactions between the circumstances of individual families and the policy instruments in operation. The cushioning effect of contributory and means-tested benefits for the unemployed are identified, along with the effects of other means-tested benefits and tax credits designed to protect families on low income. The role of other household incomes, in the form of earnings of those still in work as well as pensions and benefits received by other household members is considered.

We exploit the information from a representative sample of each national population using data from the European Union Statistics on Income and Living Conditions (EU-SILC) and the simulation of the tax–benefit instruments in place in each country. This is done using EUROMOD, the EU-wide tax–benefit microsimulation model, which is described in section 2. We consider the effects of tax–benefit systems in protecting the new unemployed in five countries of the European Union: Belgium, Italy, Lithuania, Spain and the United Kingdom. This selection of countries provides examples of cases with large increases in unemployment (as in Lithuania and Spain) and also a range of types of welfare states whose most relevant features are described in Section 3. The following section introduces the indicators adopted in the analysis, aiming to capture the resilience of the welfare system in both relative and absolute terms, as well as the budgetary cost implications. Cross-country evidence using these indicators is presented in Sections 5–7. Section 8 concludes.

2. METHODOLOGY

2.1. Data and Approach

Our analysis makes use of EUROMOD, which simulates tax liabilities and benefit entitlements for the household populations of EU Member States.

EUROMOD is a multi-country, Europe-wide tax–benefit microsimulation model that provides measures of direct taxes, social contributions and cash benefits as well as market incomes in a comparable way across countries. EUROMOD simulates non-contributory cash benefit entitlements and direct tax and social insurance contribution liabilities on the basis of the tax–benefit rules in place and information available in the underlying data sets. The components of the tax–benefit systems which are not simulated (e.g. benefits which depend on contribution history) are taken from the data, along with information on original incomes. See Sutherland (2007) for further information.[1]

Underlying micro data come from the 2006 EU-SILC[2] with the exception of the UK component which is based on the national 2003/2004 Family Resources Survey. The analysis in this chapter is based on the tax–benefit rules in place in the 2008 (as of 30th June) which is the most recent policy year currently covered by EUROMOD. Monetary values referring to 2005 (2003/2004 for the United Kingdom) have been updated to 2008 according to actual changes in prices and incomes over the relevant period.[3] No adjustment is made for changes in population composition between 2006 and 2008.

In this analysis, EUROMOD does not take account of any non-take-up of benefits or tax evasion. The only exception is Italy for which gross self-employed income has been calibrated in order to obtain an aggregate amount corresponding to that reported in fiscal data (Fiorio & D'Amuri, 2006). It is generally assumed, however, that the legal rules are universally respected and that the costs of compliance are zero. This can result in the over-estimation of taxes and benefits.[4] Our results can be interpreted as measuring the intended effects of the tax–benefit systems.

Baseline systems in EUROMOD have been validated at micro level (i.e. case-by-case validation) and macro level (Figari, Iacovou, Skew, & Sutherland, 2011) and the model has been tested in numerous applications (e.g. Bargain, 2006).

A microsimulation approach (Bourguignon & Spadaro, 2006) allows us to compute the household incomes of individuals under different scenarios, taking account of the operation of tax–benefit systems and the way they depend on the level of individual market income and personal/household characteristics. Income, after becoming unemployed, is calculated as an annual average assuming the person is unemployed for one year (or the number of months spent in work in the income reference period if these are less than 12). This captures some of the effects of the variation in duration of unemployment benefit eligibility across countries. However, it is also relevant to measure what would happen after unemployment benefit eligibility is exhausted, and in cases where there is no eligibility. For this reason, we make two alternative assumptions about the receipt of unemployment benefits.

First, we simulate the amount received as contributory unemployment benefit (based on reported earnings and under assumptions about contributions made in the past) and any additional income-tested benefits received by the family (i.e. housing benefits, social assistance, in-work benefits and other means-tested support) and reductions in income tax and social contributions; this is the net total support received in the short-term.

Second, we restrict the support to that which a family is likely to receive in the long-term (such as housing benefits, social assistance, in-work benefits), assuming the exhaustion of entitlement to unemployment insurance benefits.

2.2. Sample of Interest

We focus on a sub-sample of people who are identified from among the currently employed or self-employed in our data as most likely to lose their jobs at the time of the current economic crisis.

The people with the highest risk of becoming unemployed in the initial period of economic downturn are identified using published information from the European Labour Force Survey (EU-LFS) (Eurostat, 2010). The characteristics of the new unemployed are established by comparing the information on the stock of unemployed in the first quarter of 2008 (the last quarter with positive growth for the EU as a whole) with that of the stock in the third quarter of 2009 (the latest available at the time of writing). These changes are identifiable in published statistics by gender, age group (three categories) and education level (three categories), while other potentially relevant characteristics such occupation, sector of activity and region of residence are not available. The increase in numbers of unemployed with each combination of characteristics (i.e. within each cell) is calculated and cases selected randomly in the EUROMOD input databases conditioning on gender, age and education as well as currently being in work. The sample of people making the transition from employment to unemployment has the same combinations of characteristics as the new unemployed in the LFS statistics. As shown in Table 1 the increase in the unemployment rate given by the LFS varies widely from 1 percentage point in Belgium and Italy to 10 points in Lithuania. Once the EUROMOD data samples have been inflated, the sample size of new unemployed varies from 268 in Belgium to 1,452 in Spain.[5]

Table 1.   Characteristics of the New Unemployed.

	Belgium	Spain	Italy	Lithuania	United Kingdom
Increase in unemployment rate (ppt)	1.2	9.5	1.3	10.3	2.6
Sample size	268	1,452	436	872	959
% Male	53.2	65.3	78.1	71.2	65.9
Age groups (%)					
15–24	47.1	19.6	29.9	24.6	41.8
25–49	42.5	66.9	48.2	55.5	44.5
50–74	10.4	13.5	21.9	19.9	13.7
Education level (%)					
Lower secondary	1.1	60.0	29.0	9.0	25.9
Upper secondary	53.0	22.7	51.1	64.0	49.0
Tertiary	45.9	17.4	19.9	27.0	25.2
With children (%)	32.9	43.0	37.6	45.1	38.8
Household income quintile (%)					
Q1	5.5	11.9	13.3	11.5	7.3
Q2	13.2	17.3	16.4	11.1	13.8
Q3	16.7	23.3	21.1	21.2	23.9
Q4	26.6	26.0	21.3	26.5	28.2
Q5	38.1	21.5	27.8	29.7	26.8
Number of earners (%)					
1	19.9	23.5	29.1	26.7	26.6
2	57.6	47.7	46.9	50.1	49.6
3+	22.4	28.8	24.0	23.2	23.8
% with other new unemployed in household	6.3	13.1	1.1	14.4	6.3
% entitled to unemployment benefits	86.7	88.9	61.8	92.5	73.0

Notes: New unemployed are individuals who became unemployed between the first quarter of 2008 and the third quarter of 2009. Shaded cells show characteristics controlled using LFS information on changes.
Source: EUROMOD version F2.21.

An alternative approach would be to re-weight the data to take into account macro-economic changes such as an increase in unemployment rate (Immervoll, Levy, Lietz, Mantovani, & Sutherland, 2006; Dolls, Fuest, & Peichl, 2009). However, such a method has a major limitation related to the focus of this chapter. By increasing the weights of households containing unemployed people at the time the survey was collected and reducing the weights of other similar households, in order to keep demographic characteristics and household structures constant, this method implicitly assumes that the new unemployed are like those unemployed at the time of the survey. This can be particularly misleading for two reasons. First, the characteristics of those becoming unemployed at the beginning of the downturn might be different from those unemployed years before. Second, those recorded as unemployed in the data include the stock of long-term unemployed who have already exhausted the unemployment benefits to which the new unemployed might be entitled. In addition, the lack of enough information on how the original EU-SILC weights were constructed prevents us from being able to re-construct them without introducing unknown distortions into the weighted samples.

Table 1 shows the marginal distributions of the characteristics that are used to control the selection of the new unemployed (shaded area) and the differences across countries in other characteristics which might have a relevant impact on the results. Those most at risk of becoming unemployed are more likely to be male (especially in Italy where 78% of the new unemployed are men). In Belgium they are more likely than in the other countries to be younger but educated to a relatively high level. In Spain they are more likely to only have low-level educational qualifications, whereas in Lithuania the proportion of older workers is relatively high. The remainder of the table shows some other characteristics of those selected, including whether or not they have children, their household income quintile group before unemployment and the number of people with earnings in the pre-unemployment household.

3. WELFARE SYSTEMS FOR THE UNEMPLOYED

The countries covered in this chapter make use of very different policy packages to support individuals who suffer from unemployment and their families. Continental countries, like Belgium, have a Bismarkian tradition of contribution-financed unemployment benefits with social assistance safety nets. These are less important than in countries, such as the United Kingdom, with systems based on the principles of Beveridge and where unemployment insurance is less generous, especially for high earners. Southern European countries, such as Italy and Spain, tend to have a lower level of protection and rely more on informal family support. However, Spain resembles the Continental countries with quite generous unemployment benefits and regional social assistance (Bonoli, 1997). Eastern European countries, such as Lithuania, add even more heterogeneity to the European mix of systems. As a result, replacement rates, eligibility requirements, duration and benefit amounts differ considerably across countries (Bertola, Jimeno, Marimon, & Pissarides, 2000).

Table 2 shows the main characteristics of the unemployment protection schemes, as of 30th June 2008, which can be classified into unemployment

Table 2. Unemployment Benefit and Social Assistance Schemes as of 30th June 2008.

	Schemes		Contributions Conditions	Payment Rate	Duration (Months)	Tax and SICs
Belgium	Insurance	Earnings-related benefit (flat rate for young persons); amount depends on family situation	Between 45 weeks in 18 months and 89 weeks in 3 years	Single persons: 60% (from second year 53%). Cohabitants without dependants: 58% (from second year 40%). Lower and upper ceilings	No limit	Benefit is subject to income tax
	Assistance Social Assistance	None *Minimex*	Means-test			
Spain	Insurance	Earnings-related benefit	12 months in 6 years	70% for first 6 months; afterwards 60%. Lower and upper ceilings	From 4 months to 2 years	Benefit is subject to income tax, SICs and credited contributions
	Assistance	Flat-rate benefit	Generally none with the exception of some allowances	80% of the "Public Income Rate of Multiple Effects"	6 months with possible extension up to 18 months	
	Social Assistance	*Renta Activa de Inserción*	Means-test			

Italy	Insurance	Earnings-related benefit[a]	52 weeks in 2 years	60% (for the first 6 months, 50% for month 7 and 8 and 40% for the rest). Upper ceiling	8 months (12 months for the those aged >50)	Benefit is subject to income tax
	Assistance	None				
	Social Assistance	None				
Lithuania	Insurance	Earnings-related benefit	18 months in 3 years	Fixed component (€83) and variable component based on earnings	From 6 (<25 years in work) to 9 months (>35 years in work)	Benefit is not subject to income tax
	Assistance	None				
	Social Assistance	*Socialinė pašalpa*	Means-test			
United Kingdom	Insurance	Flat-rate benefit for all employed and some self-employed persons	Contributions paid in one of the 2 years on which the claim is based, with minimum level	From €46 to €80 per week	6 months	Benefit is subject to income tax
	Assistance	*Income-based Jobseeker's Allowance (JSA)*	Means-test		Unlimited, for those seeking work	
	Social Assistance	*Income support* (for those exempt from seeking work)	Means-test			

Notes: SICs: Social Insurance contributions paid by the unemployed. Credited contributions are paid by the social security agency on the unemployment benefit.
Source: MISSOC (2008) and EUROMOD country reports.
[a]Special schemes in the building sector and after the wage supplementation scheme (*mobilità*) are not simulated in EUROMOD.

insurance and unemployment assistance benefits. Unemployment insurance is usually the main scheme whose eligibility is based upon contributory history and whose amount depends on previous earnings. Unemployment assistance is not available in all countries and covers those who are not eligible to or have exhausted unemployment insurance on a means-tested basis. Means-testing is usually assessed at the family or household level, whereas entitlement to insurance benefits depends on individual contributions. Underpinning these schemes in some countries, Social Assistance schemes provide a guaranteed minimum level of income which is independent of employment status (although able bodied working age people are usually expected to be available for work).

Unemployment benefits are quite generous in Belgium and Spain, both in terms of replacement rate and duration. Belgium provides a replacement rate of around 60%, with minimum and maximum daily amounts and a family component with dependant's additions conditional on the dependant not receiving income in excess of a specified amount. After 12 months reduced amounts are still payable. Means-tested social assistance operates as an alternative to unemployment benefits for those not eligible and also as a top-up in cases where unemployment benefit is not sufficient to reach the levels of household income guaranteed by social assistance.

In Spain, the earnings-related unemployment benefit is paid at a rate of 70% of the previous earnings, with ceilings. It lasts for between 4 and 24 months, depending on contribution history. There is also a means-tested unemployment assistance scheme which lasts for 6 months, with the possibility of extension up to a maximum of 18 months. There is no national social assistance scheme, but instead, a series of widely varying regional schemes.

In Italy, only as a result of recent increases in the generosity of the unemployed benefits, the earnings-related benefit is paid at a rate of between 40% and 60%, with a ceiling, for up to 8 months or 12 months if aged 50 or more. There is no social assistance at the national level.

The UK system has a low flat amount of contributory benefit (i.e. contributory Jobseeker's Allowance (JSA)) that lasts for 6 months. It can be topped up by a means-tested benefit (i.e. income-based JSA) for those on low family incomes and this means-tested benefit is also an alternative for those not eligible for the contributory benefit or those who have exhausted entitlement. Low-income families who pay rent may also be entitled to Housing Benefit.

In Lithuania, the unemployment benefit is composed of a flat amount plus an earnings-related component (40% of insured income). A ceiling was introduced in 2008. The benefit lasts at this level for 6 months, which may be extended at a reduced level for 9 months, depending on contributory history. Means-tested social assistance acts as an alternative and as a top-up.

In all countries, unemployment insurance schemes are subject to income tax with the exception of Lithuania. In Spain, the unemployment benefit is also subject to social contributions paid mostly by the social security agency and only a residual part by the unemployed.

In Belgium and Italy, wage supplementation schemes provide an additional compensation for reduced hours of work. However, people brought onto wage supplementation schemes do not count as unemployed in the official statistics. In the simulations, we consider only those losing their jobs and not those retaining any wages and reducing hours of work.[6]

In the simulation of unemployment benefits, we faced a number of issues which need to be borne in mind when interpreting the results. First, the duration of unemployment is assumed to be equal to 12 months unless the duration in employment in the income reference period is less (in this case the calculation takes place for the months of employment). Second, the point in time at which the unemployment benefit entitlement is calculated is assumed to be 12 months after becoming unemployed.[7] Third, the contribution history before becoming unemployed is assumed to be equal to the duration of work as reported in the data.

As shown in Table 1, around 90% of the unemployed in Belgium, Spain and Lithuania are judged to qualify for contributory unemployment benefits. Generally, those that are older than the age limit, self-employed or have not worked long enough to receive the contributory unemployment benefits make up the remainder. The share is lower and equal to 73% in the United Kingdom (where a relatively large share of new unemployed has not worked long enough to qualify) and only equal to 62% in Italy (due to higher relevance of self-employed and restrictions to unemployment benefit entitlement for those on temporary contracts).

4. WELFARE RESILIENCE INDICATORS

We deploy a number of indicators, designed to capture different aspects of the protective effect of tax–benefit systems.

4.1. Relative Resilience

First, in order to assess the extent to which incomes are protected relative to the pre-shock baseline, we measure household disposable income after the shock as a proportion to that before the shock and call this the Relative Welfare Resilience Indicator (RWRI).

$$\text{RWRI} = \left(\frac{Y_{\text{post}}}{Y_{\text{pre}}} \right)$$

where Y is household disposable income made up of original income (which includes any form of market and private income, and even in the unemployment scenarios may be positive due to capital incomes, private pensions, inter-household transfers or the earnings of other household members) plus benefits minus taxes.[8] Savings could be seen as another channel of self-insurance but given the poor quality of the underlying data we treat them as one of the components of original income without highlighting their specific role.

In analysing the RWRI, we decompose the effect by income source and explore the composition of post-shock household income as a proportion of pre-shock household income:

$$\text{RWRI} = \left(\frac{O_{\text{pre}}}{Y_{\text{pre}}} + \frac{O_{\text{post}} - O_{\text{pre}}}{Y_{\text{pre}}} \right) + \left(\frac{B_{\text{pre}}}{Y_{\text{pre}}} + \frac{B_{\text{post}} - B_{\text{pre}}}{Y_{\text{pre}}} \right)$$
$$- \left(\frac{T_{\text{pre}}}{Y_{\text{pre}}} + \frac{T_{\text{post}} - T_{\text{pre}}}{Y_{\text{pre}}} \right)$$

where O is the original income, B is the sum of benefits and T includes income taxes and social insurance contributions paid by employees and the self-employed.

Benefits are further decomposed into

- Unemployment benefits, both insurance and assistance schemes;
- social assistance, including minimum income schemes, housing benefits, means-tested in-work benefits such as the Working Tax Credit in the United Kingdom and other residual social assistance benefits;
- Other benefits, including contributory old-age and survivors pensions, early retirement benefits, disability and invalidity benefits and family benefits due to the presence of children in the family.

The RWRI generally takes a value between zero (if a household does not have any income after the unemployment shock) and 1 (if household disposable income after the shock is equal to the income before the shock). Focusing on the new unemployed, the average RWRI is intended to provide a cross-country indication of the extent of protection of disposable income for those affected by the unemployment shock.[9] We make no judgement about a desirable level of RWRI. The positive and negative effects of generous income protection for the unemployed are the subjects of an extensive literature (Atkinson & Micklewright, 1991; Tatsiramos, 2009) but are beyond the scope of this chapter.

4.2. Absolute Resilience

The second indicator captures the protection offered in absolute terms, by looking at the extent to which the household income falls below a low absolute income threshold after the unemployment shock.

The Absolute Welfare Resilience Indicator (AWRI) is

$$AWRI = \frac{\tilde{Y}_{post}}{PovLine_{pre}}$$

where $\tilde{Y}_{post}$ is the equivalised disposable income, using the modified OECD scale, after the unemployment shock and $PovLine_{pre}$ is the poverty threshold at 60% of the median in the pre-shock baseline, used for convenience as a low absolute income threshold.

A value of the AWRI of less than 1 identifies people who are poor, as conventionally measured using a fixed poverty line. In analysing the AWRI, we also distinguish between those affected by an unemployment shock with income already below the threshold in the baseline before the shock ('poor in work'), those falling below as a result of the shock ('at risk') and those remaining above in spite of the shock ('protected').

As with the RWRI, we make no explicit judgement about a desired level of the AWRI. However, it is implicit, given the clear policy goal of reducing the numbers at risk of poverty, that household income should not fall below the poverty threshold.

4.3. Cost of Protection

The third indicator is a measure of the budgetary cost to the public budget per person affected by the shock. This includes any increase in net benefit payments and reduction in income taxes and social contributions. It also includes reductions in employer contributions and, where relevant, credited contributions paid for the unemployed. In order to make comparisons across countries, the cost per person is measured as a percentage of national per capita disposable income in the baseline.

5. RELATIVE RESILIENCE

The RWRI is shown in Table 3. The top panel shows the average value for all the new unemployed, both with unemployment benefit (if eligible) and without.

On average, with unemployment benefits, in Belgium and Spain household income falls to around 80% of its pre-unemployment level. The average RWRI is 68% in Italy, while in the United Kingdom and Lithuania it is just over and just under 60% respectively. As expected, without unemployment benefits the average RWRI is lower in all countries showing the role played by the unemployment benefits. In the United Kingdom, the contributory unemployment benefit does not offer a more generous protection than the social assistance and the drop is less than 2 percentage points. In the other countries, unemployment benefit makes a bigger difference. In particular, in Spain, on becoming unemployed without unemployment benefits, household income falls by a further 25 percentage points, while in Belgium, Italy and Lithuania the additional income loss is between 16 and 19 percentage points.

These averages can be unpicked in a number of ways. First, we consider how the protective effects vary according to the composition of the household, and in particular focus on the case where the person becoming unemployed is the sole earner in the household and no other earned income remains. Next we disaggregate the effects by income component and focus on the particular taxes and benefits providing cushioning effects. Finally, we explore how the relative replacement of income varies by household income level before unemployment.

Table 3. Average Relative Welfare Resilience Indicator (RWRI) With and Without Unemployment Benefits (UBs).

		Belgium	Spain	Italy	Lithuania	United Kingdom
All	With UBs	0.823	0.800	0.677	0.592	0.618
	Without UBs	0.664	0.544	0.490	0.430	0.603
Sole earner	With UBs	0.691	0.700	0.459	0.463	0.526
households	Without UBs	0.471	0.441	0.159	0.213	0.514

Notes: RWRI is the ratio of household disposable income after and before the unemployment shock.
Source: EUROMOD version F2.21.

Any earnings that remain in the household will play a major role in maintaining income relative to its pre-unemployment level. This is indicated by the lower values of the RWRI in the bottom panel of Table 3 referring to sole-earner households, which are always at least 10 percentage points lower than the corresponding values in the upper panel. The largest differences are found in Italy, where without unemployment benefits the average single-earner household RWRI is 30 points lower than for the unemployed as a whole. The opposite is true in the United Kingdom, where the tax–benefit system provides a household income level for those not qualifying for unemployment benefits equivalent to 51% of pre-unemployment income, only one percentage point lower than the average with unemployment benefits.

Once we disaggregate the RWRI according to income source, the protective role of other earnings is evident. Fig. 1 shows the components of post-unemployment household income as a proportion of pre-unemployment household disposable income, on average across all the new unemployed and for the sub-group for whom no earned income remains

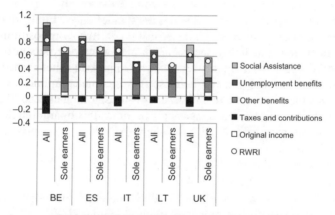

Fig. 1. Average Relative Welfare Resilience Indicator (RWRI) and Post-Unemployment Household Income Composition, With Unemployment Benefits. *Notes:* 'Taxes and contributions' include personal income tax, employee social insurance contributions and other direct taxes such as the UK Council Tax and property tax in Italy and Lithuania; 'other benefits' include pensions, family benefits, disability and invalidity benefits; 'social assistance' includes minimum income payments, housing benefits and means-tested in-work benefits. RWRI is the ratio of household disposable income after and before the unemployment shock. Bars show Average RWRI and income components as a percentage of pre-unemployment household disposable income. *Source:* EUROMOD version F2.21.

in the household (sole-earner households, before unemployment). This confirms the importance of other household original income (mostly earnings: shown as the white sections of the bars) on average for the group as a whole (shown in the first bar of each pair). This makes up at least half of post-unemployment household income in all five countries. Other benefits play a small role. In most cases these are pensions or other benefits received by other household members before and after the new unemployment, although in the United Kingdom this also includes means-tested family benefits that increase due to the loss of income on unemployment. Unemployment benefits play a large role in Belgium and Spain, making up 30% and 36% respectively of pre-unemployment household income. They are less important in Italy and Lithuania (21% and 15%). In these countries social assistance plays a small additional role, adding between 5% in Belgium and virtually nothing in Italy. In the United Kingdom, however, means-tested benefits are on average the larger source of support: 14% of pre-unemployment income compared with just 4% for contributory unemployment benefits.

For households without remaining earnings, the income replacement role of benefits becomes paramount. RWRIs are smaller on average and the effect of remaining original income becomes very small. In sole-earner households other benefits and unemployment benefits play a major role, although this is mainly because they make up a larger proportion of a lower pre-unemployment income and not because they are higher in absolute terms. Social assistance increases to fill some of the gap in Belgium, Spain and Lithuania and in the United Kingdom it becomes the major source of post-unemployment income (57%), equivalent to 30% of pre-unemployment household income.

The elements of income that have a protective effect vary across the pre-unemployment income distribution, as shown in Fig. 2 for all new unemployed (assuming contributory unemployment benefit is payable if entitled). In all countries other household earnings (net of taxes) are important at the top of the income distribution and unemployment benefits play a larger relative role at the bottom. The net effect is that the RWRI varies only slightly with pre-unemployment household income. Aside from the effects arising from the distribution of post-unemployment household original income across pre-unemployment household income quintiles, which shows marked differences across countries, we can make a number of further observations. First, the RWRI rises with income in Italy, with no substantial social assistance scheme protecting incomes at the bottom. It is quite flat in Belgium where the strongly earnings-related

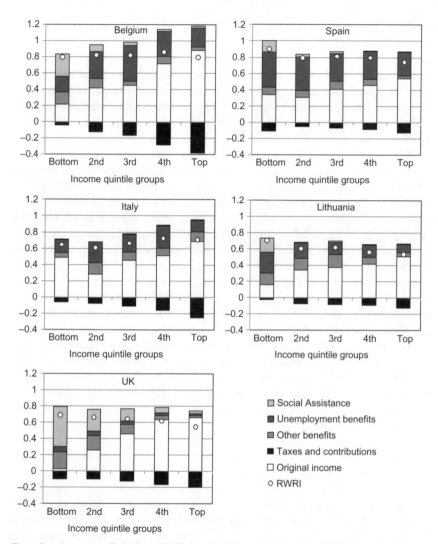

Fig. 2. Average Relative Welfare Resilience Indicator (RWRI) and Post-Unemployment Household Income Composition by Household Income Quintile Group, With Unemployment Benefits. *Notes*: Bars show Average RWRI and income components as a percentage of pre-unemployment household disposable income. *Source:* EUROMOD version F2.21.

unemployment benefits are complemented by social assistance at low income and relatively high taxes at high incomes. In Spain the gradient is also generally quite flat but the RWRI is higher at low pre-unemployment income levels due to regional social assistance schemes (combined with relatively high original incomes). In the United Kingdom and Lithuania, flat-rate unemployment benefits and social assistance combine to provide a lot of targeted support at the bottom resulting in profiles that fall gently with income.

However, the cross-country differences evident from Fig. 2 may be to some extent affected by differences in the composition of the income quintile groups. In order to control for this and to summarise the main socio-economic characteristics associated with variations in the RWRI, Table 4 shows the results from an OLS regression, where the RWRI of the new unemployed is regressed on their demographic characteristics (gender, age, education and being in receipt of unemployment benefit) and those of their household.

Controlling for other relevant characteristics (including the presence of a partner with positive earnings or other household members receiving old-age benefits), the RWRI has a negative association with the pre-unemployment household disposable income quintile group. Individuals living in better-off households are less protected in relative terms in particular in Spain, Lithuania and the United Kingdom, mainly due to the flat and the means-tested components of the unemployment benefits. In Belgium and Italy, where earnings-related unemployment benefits are dominant, the downward effects are less relevant and not significantly different across quintiles.

The number of children in the family has a positive association with the extent of protection in the United Kingdom, where there is a relatively generous income-responsive family benefit (the Child Tax Credit), which compensates to some extent for the loss of earned income.

The RWRI is significantly higher for the unemployed with an earning partner and there is an additional positive effect if the unemployed person is female (except in Italy). This is what might be expected, given the importance of original incomes as identified in Fig. 1, and the fact that the contribution of any remaining earnings is likely to be higher on average if it is the male partner that remains in employment.

Also as expected, being in receipt of unemployment benefit makes individuals better protected in relative terms with the exception of the United Kingdom, where the effect is not significant. In the United Kingdom, if an unemployed person is not eligible to receive the contributory JSA but

Table 4.   RWRI and Socio-Economic Characteristics.

	Belgium	Spain	Italy	Lithuania	United Kingdom
Male	−0.054***	−0.085***	−0.005	−0.041***	−0.068***
	(0.017)	(0.008)	(0.040)	(0.013)	(0.013)
Age (/10)	−0.291***	−0.040*	−0.337***	−0.252***	−0.190***
	(0.061)	(0.022)	(0.060)	(0.041)	(0.036)
Age square (/100)	0.033***	0.003	0.041***	0.031***	0.020***
	(0.008)	(0.003)	(0.008)	(0.005)	(0.005)
Lower secondary	−0.084	0.054***	−0.079*	0.064**	0.008
education	(0.072)	(0.011)	(0.043)	(0.029)	(0.017)
Upper secondary	0.040**	0.040***	−0.126***	0.033**	−0.023
education	(0.018)	(0.012)	(0.041)	(0.016)	(0.015)
2nd quintile	−0.083*	−0.121***	−0.016	−0.136***	−0.101***
	(0.044)	(0.013)	(0.039)	(0.026)	(0.026)
3rd quintile	−0.090**	−0.142***	−0.044	−0.172***	−0.176***
	(0.044)	(0.013)	(0.039)	(0.024)	(0.025)
4th quintile	−0.085*	−0.154***	−0.068*	−0.269***	−0.208***
	(0.044)	(0.013)	(0.040)	(0.024)	(0.026)
5th quintile	−0.116**	−0.188***	−0.083**	−0.248***	−0.255***
	(0.045)	(0.015)	(0.040)	(0.025)	(0.027)
Dual earner couple	0.135***	0.145***	0.296***	0.221***	0.157***
	(0.024)	(0.009)	(0.024)	(0.016)	(0.015)
Number of children	0.007	−0.006	−0.017	0.01	0.043***
	(0.011)	(0.005)	(0.014)	(0.008)	(0.006)
Households in receipt	0.067**	0.094***	0.172***	0.140***	0.068***
of old-age benefits	(0.027)	(0.010)	(0.024)	(0.014)	(0.018)
In receipt of UB	0.129***	0.172***	0.280***	0.241***	−0.002
	(0.026)	(0.012)	(0.021)	(0.024)	(0.015)
Constant	1.250***	0.765***	1.011***	0.820***	1.081***
	(0.104)	(0.044)	(0.117)	(0.083)	(0.063)
N	268	1,452	436	872	959
R^2	0.410	0.394	0.541	0.388	0.347

Notes: *$p<0.10$, **$p<0.05$, ***$p<0.01$. Standard errors in parenthesis. OLS regression. Dependent variable: Relative Welfare Resilience Indicator (RWRI), ratio of household disposable income after and before the unemployment shock. Sample: new unemployed.
Source: EUROMOD version F2.21.

their family incomes are low enough to be eligible for the means-tested benefit (known as income-related JSA but equivalent to the social assistance, Income Support), there is no effect on their disposable income at the family level. However, if their income is too high to qualify for social assistance the low flat amount of the JSA would not make any substantial difference to the household income.[10]

6. ABSOLUTE RESILIENCE

Absolute resilience, measured as the ratio of post-unemployment household income to the income level indicated by the poverty threshold is shown for all new unemployed and sole earners, both with and without unemployment benefit, in Table 5. This shows that in Belgium, for example, the household incomes of the new unemployed as a whole, with unemployment benefit, fall to a level that is on average 1.7 times the poverty threshold. The figure is much lower for unemployed without other household earnings and without unemployment benefits: for example 0.27 for Italy. The rankings of countries are largely similar to those shown in Table 3 for the RWRI.

These indicators are averages over all cases and it is relevant to also show how many of the people affected by unemployment fall below the poverty threshold and how many remain above it. Fig. 3 shows the proportion with household equivalised incomes below the threshold before unemployment ('poor in work'), those falling below as a result of becoming unemployed ('at risk') and those remaining above in spite of unemployment ('protected'). It shows the situation for all the new unemployed and for the sub-group of sole-earner households before unemployment, assuming unemployment benefits are received. First, it is worth noting that rates of in-work poverty for those vulnerable to unemployment are quite high in Spain, Italy and

Table 5. Average Absolute Welfare Resilience Indicator (AWRI) With and Without Unemployment Benefits (UBs).

		Belgium	Spain	Italy	Lithuania	United Kingdom
All	With UBs	1.716	1.562	1.471	1.404	1.383
	Without UBs	1.391	1.062	1.104	1.089	1.348
Sole earner	With UBs	1.134	1.050	0.781	0.663	0.833
households	Without UBs	0.732	0.617	0.269	0.315	0.809

Notes: AWRI is the ratio of post-unemployment household income to the income level corresponding to the poverty threshold, measured as 60% of median pre-unemployment equivalised household disposable income.
Source: EUROMOD version F2.21.

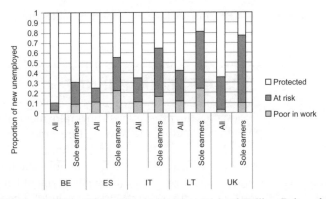

Fig. 3. The Proportion of New Unemployed at Risk of Falling Below the Poverty Threshold, With Unemployment Benefits. *Notes:* The poverty threshold is fixed at 60% of baseline median household disposable equivalised income. *Source:* EUROMOD version F2.21.

Lithuania (over 10%) but much lower in Belgium and the United Kingdom (under 4%). In-work poverty risk is higher in all countries for those in one-earner households before unemployment: over 20% in Spain and Lithuania and at least 9% in all five countries. Those at risk of falling below the poverty threshold on becoming unemployed make up between 7% (in Belgium) and 43% (in Italy) of the group as a whole. The figure is 13% in Spain and 31% in Lithuania and the United Kingdom. Those whose incomes do not fall below an absolute level equivalent to the poverty threshold are protected by a combination of other household earnings and benefits.

The bars in Fig. 3 indicating the effects in sole-earner households demonstrate the extent of protection offered by benefits alone (including benefits and pensions received by other household members). In all countries the proportion of this sub-group at risk is much higher. This is especially so in Italy, Lithuania and the United Kingdom, where the proportion of the group remaining protected is only 9%, 19% and 23% respectively. The situation is even worse if no unemployment benefit is payable (not shown) with proportions of sole earners protected from poverty falling to 9% in Italy and Spain and 5% in Lithuania. The figure is also much reduced in Belgium (21% compared with 69% with unemployment benefits). In the United Kingdom there is no difference in the

Table 6. AWRI and Socio-Economic Characteristics.

	Belgium	Spain	Italy	Lithuania	United Kingdom
Male	−0.018	−0.169***	−0.118	−0.089	−0.117***
	(0.057)	(0.022)	(0.128)	(0.059)	(0.038)
Age (/10)	−0.573***	−0.105*	−0.443**	−0.558***	−0.352***
	(0.201)	(0.061)	(0.193)	(0.182)	(0.108)
Age square (/100)	0.065**	0.01	0.052**	0.070***	0.036**
	(0.028)	(0.008)	(0.025)	(0.024)	(0.015)
Lower secondary	−0.114	0.039	−0.296**	−0.011	−0.127**
education	(0.237)	(0.031)	(0.138)	(0.127)	(0.052)
Upper secondary	0.019	0.006	−0.378***	0.01	−0.133***
education	(0.061)	(0.035)	(0.132)	(0.069)	(0.046)
2nd quintile	0.188	0.265***	0.304**	0.094	0.008
	(0.145)	(0.038)	(0.127)	(0.115)	(0.078)
3rd quintile	0.356**	0.535***	0.508***	0.264**	0.109
	(0.144)	(0.037)	(0.125)	(0.108)	(0.075)
4th quintile	0.630***	0.913***	0.857***	0.467***	0.364***
	(0.145)	(0.038)	(0.130)	(0.107)	(0.077)
5th quintile	1.163***	1.610***	1.683***	1.537***	0.902***
	(0.147)	(0.041)	(0.127)	(0.111)	(0.080)
Dual earner couple	0.368***	0.315***	0.625***	0.558***	0.406***
	(0.080)	(0.026)	(0.077)	(0.071)	(0.043)
Number of children	−0.018	−0.059***	0.044	−0.011	0.029
	(0.037)	(0.013)	(0.044)	(0.035)	(0.018)
Households in receipt	0.084	0.156***	0.363***	0.252***	0.107**
of old-age benefits	(0.089)	(0.027)	(0.077)	(0.063)	(0.053)
In receipt of UB	0.287***	0.342***	0.437***	0.463***	−0.041
	(0.087)	(0.033)	(0.066)	(0.108)	(0.043)
Constant	1.566***	0.577***	1.028***	0.935**	1.540***
	(0.342)	(0.125)	(0.377)	(0.369)	(0.188)
N	268	1,452	436	872	959
R^2	0.589	0.718	0.631	0.456	0.428

Notes: *$p<0.10$, **$p<0.05$, ***$p<0.01$. Standard errors in parenthesis. OLS regression. Dependent variable: Absolute Welfare Resilience Indicator (AWRI), ratio of post-unemployment household income to the income level corresponding to the poverty threshold, measured as 60% of median pre-unemployment equivalised household disposable income. Sample: new unemployed.
Source: EUROMOD version F2.21.

proportion protected: on the basis of our calculations which assume full take-up of social assistance, contributory unemployment benefits are too low in value to play a role in maintaining incomes above the poverty threshold.

Table 6 summarises the extent to which the socio-economic characteristics are associated with the AWRI. As expected, there is a positive gradient between income and AWRI, with the individuals living in better-off households being better protected in absolute terms and facing a smaller risk of falling below the poverty threshold as long as they belong, before unemployment, to the upper quintile groups. However, the risk is not significantly different between the first two quintiles in Belgium, Lithuania and the United Kingdom.

The composition of the household matters, both in terms of number of children and presence of household members with old-age benefits. Of course, the effects are due, by construction, to the equivalence scale used in the definition of the AWRI, but they are still informative in their association with the level of absolute protection.

The number of children (which reduces the equivalised income of the household) is expected to be associated with a lower absolute protection when the support to families with children has an implicit equivalence scale lower than the equivalence scale used in the definition of the AWRI. The effect is statistically significant in Spain, showing that the public support covers a smaller share of the needs of families with children, captured by the equivalence scale.

The effect of the presence of household members with old-age benefits depends on the amounts of these benefits relative to the equivalised household income: their contribution supports the absolute protection of the family as a whole in most of the countries.

The receipt of unemployment benefit guarantees a higher level of absolute protection in all countries, with the exception of the United Kingdom, given the absence of any substantial difference on average between the amount received as unemployment benefit or social assistance.

7. COST OF PROTECTION

The average cost of providing benefits for each new unemployed person (and their dependents) plus the revenue loss from reduced taxes and contributions on pre-unemployment earnings is shown, as a proportion of national household per capita income, in Fig. 4. Estimates are shown both without and with unemployment benefit. The difference in the height of the pairs of bars is largely accounted for by the cost of unemployment benefit (net of some social assistance that may substitute when unemployment benefit is not payable and any taxes on unemployment benefit). In Spain the

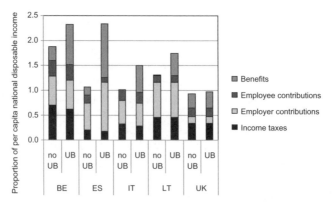

Fig. 4. Average Budgetary Cost per Unemployed Person (as a Proportion of Per-Capita National Disposable Income). *Source*: EUROMOD version F2.21.

cost of employer contributions increases because the government pays the employer contribution on behalf of the unemployed on benefits (this additional cost is added to the lost contributions paid by employers). In Belgium and Italy the cost related to the loss in revenue from income tax is lower when unemployment benefits are paid because they are taxed. The effect is negligible in Spain and the United Kingdom because, even if unemployment benefits are in principle taxable, they are lower than the tax-free allowance. Overall, the average tax–benefit cost of each person becoming unemployed ranges from 93% of national per capita disposable income in the United Kingdom (without unemployment benefits) to 234% in Spain (with unemployment benefits). Focussing on the estimates with unemployment benefits, in all countries the bulk of the cost is due to lost (or additional) contributions and taxes, rather than additional benefits. As a proportion of total costs, employer contributions are particularly large and employee contributions particularly small, in Spain and Lithuania. Taxes make the proportionately largest contribution in the United Kingdom and smallest in Spain. The cost of benefits is largest in Spain and smallest in the United Kingdom.

Fig. 5 shows how this average cost varies depending on the pre-unemployment position in the household income distribution, on average across all new unemployed. In all countries, the cost per unemployed person is highest at the top of the income distribution largely because lost revenue from taxes and contributions is highest there.

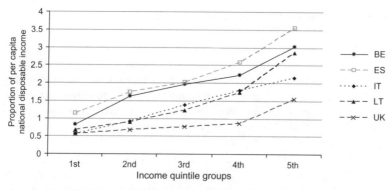

Fig. 5. Average Budgetary Cost Income quintile groups per Unemployed Person by Pre-Unemployment Income Quintile (as a Proportion of Per-Capita National Disposable Income), With Unemployment Benefits. *Source:* EUROMOD version F2.21.

8. CONCLUSIONS

We have provided evidence of the implications for the living standards of those most likely to become unemployed over the initial period of economic downturn, exploring the interactions between the circumstances of individual families and the policy instruments in operation. Across European countries there is a huge variety of systems of social protection for the unemployed, ranging from generous earnings-related benefits to flat-rate low-level amounts.

As expected, different countries provide a wide-ranging degree of protection of relative household income when a household member becomes unemployed. Assuming individuals are eligible for unemployment benefits, the highest average level of protection is provided in countries characterised by a Bismarkian tradition of contribution-financed unemployment benefits like Belgium and, to some extent, Spain.

However, the factor which plays the major role in protecting the household from a large drop in income is whether there are other people in the household with earnings. If this is not the case then household incomes fall much lower as a proportion of pre-unemployment income. Our analysis highlights the role for adequate minimum income schemes alongside unemployment benefits.

Individuals living in better-off households are less well protected in relative terms than those in lower income households where unemployment benefits are characterised or complemented by flat and means-tested components, as in Spain, Lithuania and the United Kingdom.

It could be argued that guaranteeing a reasonable minimum level of protection for all potentially unemployed people is of higher importance than relative income maintenance for a smaller (and generally higher income) group. On that basis we have shown that there is wide variation in the extent to which welfare systems protect the new unemployed from poverty-level incomes. In none of the countries are *all* new unemployed protected, but generally, the risk of falling below the threshold is much lower in Belgium and Spain and higher in Lithuania. Support for families with children in the United Kingdom helps to cushion the loss of income, but the absolute level of protection is lower than in the other countries. In the context of concern about growing child poverty in the recession, this points to a role for child-targeted support alongside adequate unemployment protection.

As expected, the effects on income (both absolute and relative) are correlated with the cost of benefits for the unemployed. However, our analysis highlights how the direct implications of unemployment for government budgets extend beyond benefit payments to lost taxes and social contributions. We have shown that not only is benefit expenditure a minor part of the total, but also that the cost per unemployed person rises with pre-unemployment income level, due to the increasing effect of income taxes and contributions especially.

Our assumptions as well as the methods employed have some implications for these findings in a number of respects. In particular the reference time period that is assumed for unemployment can have a large effect on the measured importance of unemployment benefits. Our assumptions have been common across countries but the result is to maximise the resilience measures in some countries (such as Belgium) but not in others (such as the United Kingdom and Lithuania), because of different durations of maximum unemployment benefit entitlement.

Furthermore, our calculations involve assumptions that conceal some further possible weaknesses in the welfare systems. First, we have assumed that all sources of income are shared equally within the household. Our analysis has not considered directly either the protective role of contributory unemployment benefits for unemployed people with earning partners or the implications for those who are unprotected of becoming dependent on others' incomes. Second, we have assumed that entitlements to benefits are always taken up. In the case of a newly unemployed person with access to no other resources, this may well be a realistic assumption. But in other cases, perhaps particularly if the household retains a substantial amount of income from other sources, this may be less realistic. In general, it means that the scenarios without unemployment benefit may appear artificially optimistic in terms of what happens to household income, relative to the scenarios with unemployment benefits. This is relevant to some extent on all countries except Italy and in particular it applies to Spain, where our estimates of the regional social assistance schemes are likely to be over-stated. It also applies in the case of the United Kingdom to both scenarios, because the means-tested benefit often acts as a top-up, even if there is entitlement to the (relatively small) unemployment benefit. However, one can interpret these results as being the best possible outcomes. In practice, to the extent that there is incomplete benefit take-up among the unemployed, the situation may be worse than that represented here.

Nevertheless, we believe that these calculations are informative about the differing degrees to which unemployment has the potential to reduce household incomes, and the extent of resilience of those incomes due to the protection offered by the tax–benefit systems, according to whether unemployment benefit is payable, the household situation of the unemployed person and across countries.

The analysis presented here can be seen as a first step in a larger research project. First, this chapter is the basis for a future comparison of ex-ante with ex-post analyses of the crisis which are very likely to appear as soon as longitudinal data for the relevant period become available. Second, a further extension of this chapter could consider the optimal degree of government protection during an economic crisis. This could borrow relevant insights from the optimal taxation literature which is usually focussed on a stable economic environment.

ACKNOWLEDGMENTS

We would like to thank Tony Atkinson, André Decoster, Horacio Levy, Eric Marlier, Alari Paulus, Alberto Tumino and two referees for their suggestions and comments. We are grateful for the comments received at the OECD/IZA workshop on *Economic Crisis, Rising Unemployment and Policy Responses: What Does it Mean for the Income Distribution?* in Paris, 8th to 9th February 2010, and at the *International Conference on Comparative EU statistics on Income and Living Conditions* in Warsaw, 25th to 26th March 2010, as well as for financial support from Eurostat's Net-SILC network. We are also indebted to all past and current members of the EUROMOD consortium. The usual disclaimers apply. The version of EUROMOD used here is in the process of being extended, and updated, financed by the Directorate General for Employment, Social Affairs and Equal Opportunities of the European Commission [Progress grant no. VS/2008/0318]. We make use of micro data from the EU Statistics on Incomes and Living Conditions (EU-SILC) made available by Eurostat under contract EU-SILC/2009/17 (EUROMOD) and EU-SILC/2009/09 (Net-SILC), the Italian version of the EU-SILC (IT-SILC XUDB 2006 – version April 2008) made available by ISTAT and the Family Resources Survey (FRS) made available by the UK Department of Work and Pensions (DWP) through the UK Data Archive. Material from the FRS is Crown Copyright and is used with permission. Neither the DWP nor the Data Archive bears any responsibility for the analysis or interpretation of the data reported here. An equivalent disclaimer applies to all other data sources and their respective providers cited in this acknowledgment.

NOTES

1. EUROMOD is currently subject to a major updating process. The aim is to include all EU-27 countries in EUROMOD, using EU-SILC as underlying data, by 2012.

2. In case of Italy the national version of the EU-SILC has been used because it includes more variables at the necessary level of detail.

3. This process is documented in EUROMOD Country Reports.

4. It can also result in the under-estimation of poverty rates, although this depends on the relationship between the level of income provided by benefits and the poverty line (potential claimants may be poor whether or not they receive the benefits to which they are entitled). For a comparison of poverty rates estimated using simulated incomes from EUROMOD with those calculated directly from EU-SILC see Ward, Lelkes, Sutherland, and Toth (2009) and Figari, Iacovou, Skew, and Sutherland (2011).

5. The absolute number of new unemployed selected in each country depends on the availability of potential new unemployed within each cell corresponding to the combination of demographic characteristics. In order to maximise the sample size, first we selected the new unemployed from the cell with the lowest number of observations and then we sampled the remaining new unemployed from other cells, maintaining the right proportions.

6. In any case, we are unable to simulate these schemes because they depend on the nature of the employer and the contract for which we do not have the necessary information in the EU-SILC.

7. EUROMOD simulations take into account the interactions of all tax–benefit instruments given the market incomes after becoming unemployed. When some benefits (e.g. family allowance in Italy) are assessed on the basis of income in previous year (i.e. before becoming unemployed), the changes in their amounts,

occurring one year after the unemployment shock, are not captured in the calculations.

8. This indicator is identical to the Net Replacement Rate (Immervoll & O'Donoghue, 2004).

9. In principle the RWRI can also be negative (in presence of negative disposable income due, for example, to losses related to self-employment) or greater than 1 (if the support offered by the tax–benefit system to the unemployed is larger than the earnings in the baseline scenario).

10. However, this analysis at the household level ignores the within-household role of JSA in maintaining individual incomes for the unemployed living with employed partners.

REFERENCES

Aaberge, R., Bjorklund, A., & Jäntti, M. (2000). Unemployment shocks and income distribution: How did the Nordic countries fare during their crisis? *Scandinavian Journal of Economics, 102*(1), 77–90.

Atkinson, A. B. (2009). Stress-testing the welfare state. In: B. Ofstad, O. Bjerkholt, K. Skrede & A. Hylland (Eds), *Rettferd og politik Festskrift til Hilde Bojer* (pp. 31–39). Oslo: Emiliar Forlag.

Atkinson, A. B., & Micklewright, J. (1991). Unemployment compensation and labor market transitions: A critical review. *Journal of Economic Literature, 29*, 1679–1727.

Bargain, O. (Ed.). (2006). Microsimulation in action: Policy analysis in Europe using EUROMOD. *Research in Labor Economics, 25*. North-Holland: Elsevier.

Bertola, G., Jimeno, J. F., Marimon, R., & Pissarides, C. (2000). Welfare systems and labour markets in Europe: What convergence before and after EMU? In: G. Bertola, T. Boeri & G. Nicoletti (Eds), *Welfare and employment in a United Europe*. Cambridge, MA: MIT Press.

Bonoli, G. (1997). Classifying welfare states: A two-dimension approach. *Journal of Social Policy, 26*(3), 351–372.

Bourguignon, F., & Spadaro, A. (2006). Microsimulation as a tool for evaluating redistribution policies. *Journal of Economic Inequality, 4*(1), 77–106.

Dolls, M., Fuest, C., & Peichl, A. (2009). Automatic stabilizers and economic crisis: US vs. Europe. IZA DP no. 4310. Institute for the Study of Labor, Bonn.

Eurostat. (2010). *European Labour Force Survey*. Eurostat New Cronos, delivered by ESDS International. University of Manchester.

Figari, F., Iacovou, M., Skew, A., & Sutherland, H. (2011). Approximations to the truth: Comparing survey and microsimulation approaches to measuring income for social indicators. *Social Research Indicators*, forthcoming.

Fiorio, C. V., & D'Amuri, F. (2006). Tax evasion in Italy: An analysis using a tax-benefit microsimulation model. *The ICFAI Journal of Public Finance, IV*(2), 19–37.

Immervoll, H., Levy, H., Lietz, C., Mantovani, D., & Sutherland, H. (2006). The sensitivity of poverty rates to macro-level changes in the European Union. *Cambridge Journal of Economics, 30*, 181–199.

Immervoll, H., & O'Donoghue, C. (2004). What difference does a job make? The income consequences of joblessness in Europe. In: D. Gallie (Ed.), *Resisting marginalisation: Unemployment experience and social policy in the European Union* (pp. 105–139). Oxford: Oxford University Press.

Jenkins, S. P. (2000). Modelling household income dynamics. *Journal of Population Economics*, *13*, 529–567.

Jones, M. T., Hilbers, P., & Slack, G. (2004). *Stress testing financial systems: What to do when the Governor calls*. IMF Working Paper WP/04/127. International Monetary Fund, Washington, DC.

MISSOC. (2008). *Social protection in the member states of the European Union*. European Commission, Directorate-General for Employment Industrial Relations and Social Affairs.

Nolan, B. (2009). *Background note for roundtable discussion on monitoring the effects of the financial crisis on vulnerable groups*. Paris: OECD.

OECD. (2009). *Economic outlook*. Paris: OECD.

Schubert, K., Hegelich, S., & Bazant, U. (2009). *The handbook of European welfare systems*. London: Routledge.

Sorge, M., & Virolainen, K. (2006). A comparative analysis of macro stress-testing methodologies with application to Finland. *Journal of Financial Stability*, *2*, 113–151.

Sutherland, H. (2007). EUROMOD: The tax-benefit microsimulation model for the European Union. In: A. Gupta & A. Harding (Eds), *Modelling our future: Population ageing, health and aged care. International symposia in economic theory and econometrics* (Vol. 16, pp. 483–488). USA: Elsevier.

Tatsiramos, K. (2009). Unemployment insurance in Europe: Unemployment duration and subsequent employment stability. *Journal of the European Economic Association*, *7*(6), 1225–1260.

Ward, T., Lelkes, O., Sutherland, H., & Toth, I. (2009). *European inequalities – Social inclusion and income distribution in the European Union*. Budapest: TARKI.